The Labour College Movement

by

J. P. M. MILLAR

(Formerly General Secretary of the National Council of Labour Colleges, Editor of Plebs *and Editor of N.C.L.C. Text Books)*

N.C.L.C. Publishing Society Ltd.
11 Dartmouth Street, London, SW1H 9BN

[1980]

A

To

CHRISTINE MILLAR

Table of Contents

ABBREVIATIONS

AEU	Amalgamated Engineering Union
ASLEF	Associated Society of Locomotive Engineers and Firemen
ASRS	Amalgamated Society of Railway Servants (afterwards the NUR)
ASSET	Association of Supervisory Staffs, Executives and Technicians
AUBTW	Amalgamated Union of Building Trade Workers
BSP	British Socialist Party
CLC	Central Labour College
ETU	Electrical Trades Union
ILP	Independent Labour Party
IFTU	International Federation of Trade Unions
IFWEA	International Federation of Workers Educational Associations
ITF	International Transport Workers Federation
IWCE	Independent Working Class Education
G & MW	General & Municipal Workers Union
NCLC	National Council of Labour Colleges
NUDAW	National Union of Distributive and Allied Workers
NUM	National Union of Mineworkers
NUR	National Union of Railwaymen
SDF	Social Democratic Federation
SLP	Socialist Labour Party
SPCK	Society for Promoting Christian Knowledge
STUC	Scottish Trades Union Congress
SWMF	South Wales Miners' Federation
T&GW	Transport & General Workers Union
TUC	Trades Union Congress
USDAW	Union of Shop, Distributive and Allied Workers
WEA	Worker's Educational Association
WETUC	Workers' Educational Trade Union Committee
SLC	Scottish Labour College

PREFACE

In 1964 the National Council of Labour Colleges (NCLC) came to an end when the Trades Union Congress (TUC) took over its work. Its closure also marked the end of the Labour College Movement, which had begun in 1908 with the formation of the Plebs League at Ruskin College, Oxford. The years between 1908 and 1964 were filled with varied and vigorous activities and numerous controversies.

At one of the last meetings of the executive Committee of the NCLC, George Cornes asked whether any steps were being taken to record the NCLC's history. J. P. M. Millar, the General Secretary, said that for many years he had been gathering material for such a history. It was then agreed that he himself should write the history and that he, Arthur Woodburn and George Cornes should be appointed Plebs Trustees in order to see the work through to publication. When however the TUC Office started to break up the NCLC's educational work and its educational machinery Millar, like two of the organisers,* became so depressed that he was temporarily threatened with a complete nervous breakdown. He therefore told his fellow Trustees that he had no heart in consequence for writing the history and recommended that the task of writing the book should be passed on to John Lowe. His two fellow Trustees insisted that Millar's unparallelled knowledge of the NCLC's affairs should not be wasted. They therefore decided on joint authorship.

To tell the story of the Labour College movement while still so close to it in time is to run the risk of seeing its operations and achievements out of focus. But the risk seemed justified, for when the authors began their work only a few of those who had contributed to it in the early days and who could throw light on the story were still alive. Even while the book was being prepared death removed one well-known NCLC personality after another.

In order to account for the genesis of the Labour College movement we originally thought that it might be necessary to trace back its antecedents to the earliest attempts to organise independent working class education at the end of the eighteenth century. However, on examining the scanty source material we were able to identify no discernible thread of continuity. The founders of the Plebs League were fully

* These organisers eventually left for other posts.

I

conscious of the ancestry of their political ideas but they did not look back to any historical precedents for organising working class education. Nor were they apparently influenced by nine-teenth century experiments in working class education inspired by middle class reformers and religious sects. If they knew much about the charity schools, the Adult School movement and the London Working Men's College they did not acknowledge the fact in their publications.

Our account starts, therefore, with the founding of Ruskin College in 1899 and the events immediately leading up to the establishment of the Central Labour College in 1909. In view of the publication of W. W. Craik's account of the Central Labour College we were faced with the problem of how comprehensive-ly to deal with the famous strike at Ruskin College and the subsequent history of the Central Labour College. On the face of it Craik had said the last word. Why retrace the same ground? We decided that it was necessary to cover some of the same issues for three reasons. First, Craik was only incidentally concerned to describe the growth of the NCLC. Secondly, he had access to virtually no primary sources apart from *Plebs*. He hadn't even the Minutes of the Central Labour College which seemed to have vanished. Thirdly, his justifiable preoccupation with the College's affairs led him to relegate other working class educational activities to the shadows. Accordingly, we have considered events also treated by Craik whenever his account seemed to be *ex parte* or could be filled out from additional sources or where they were an essential part of the history of the Labour College Movement. At the same time we have not gone into detail about episodes which he has treated exhaustively. The availability of his account of the Central Labour College left us free to concentrate mainly upon the history of the National Council of Labour Colleges as such.

The history of the Labour Colleges is one strand in the general evolution of the Labour Movement. That movement arose in Britain largely as a result of the industrial revolution. The rise of manufacturing industry and its development into machinofacture eventually sucked millions of peasants and their descendants all over Western and Central Europe into towns to man the new factories that were set up and made them relatively easy to organise in trade unions. Unlike the peasants they had no plots of land to cultivate, were housed in slum conditions

II

without gardens in the vast majority of cases and had no tools of production of their own. Their only means of livelihood therefore was to sell their labour power for wages. Thus a new social class, the wage labourers, appeared on the historical stage. It was their struggle to survive and improve their conditions that brought the Labour Movement into existence with its industrial, political, co-operative and educational organisations. In writing this story of the Labour College Movement we have no space to describe in detail the material conditions in which the Labour Movement found itself at the end of the last century and the beginning of this century and to explain why the Labour Colleges arose except to say that the economic conditions of the wage workers at the end of the 19th century produced the first British Socialist parties and later stimulated the rise of the Labour Party in 1906 and the Labour College Movement in 1909. This was a period, too, when the unskilled workers found their way into the Trade Union movement and when in 1911, 1912 and 1913 there were, to quote Raymond Postgate, 'furious industrial conflicts' and when the 1914 war itself produced a powerful shop steward movement in the munitions shops and shipyards 'whose leaders were drawn chiefly from the small Socialist Labour Party, the British Socialist Party, the Independant Labour Party and the Plebs League'.

In compiling this book we were faced with the problem of how to strike a reasonable balance between, on the one hand, the domestic problems and external relations of the NCLC and, on the other hand, the aims, nature and scope of its educational programmes and methods. Our solution was to divide the account into two parts. This enabled us to give a detailed description and assessment of the educational work in the second part without disrupting the flow of the chronological narrative in Part I.

In preparing our account we had access to a good many primary sources, as may be seen from the bibliography and the references. In addition we drew upon the personal recollections and records of Millar and his wife Christine, and of Arthur Woodburn. The final version was further enriched by suggestions from George Cornes, Stan Rees and Joe Crispin, the two latter being long-service former NCLC Organisers.

Our thanks are due to Christine Millar, George Cornes, Joe Crispin, Stan Rees and Arthur Woodburn for going over the

CHAPTER 1

THE BURNING QUESTION OF EDUCATION

In 1908 a group of students attending Ruskin College, Oxford, founded the Plebs League in order to promote what they termed 'independent working class education'. Shortly afterwards, incensed by the orthodox educational policies of the college authorities, they took the unusual step of going on strike. The authorities refused to meet their demands for curricular and constitutional reform, whereupon they established a college of their own. So began the Labour College movement, which was to lead in 1921 to the foundation of the National Council of Labour Colleges (N C L C). How did all this come about?

Three American postgraduate students, Walter Vrooman, his wife, Ann, and Charles Beard, later to become a renowned historian, had founded Ruskin Hall (afterwards called Ruskin College) in 1899. Their object had been to give socially conscious working men access to education in a residential environment so that they might

> increase their usefulness to the Labour Movement in general, and to the societies who sent them to the College in particular (through) a training in subjects which are essential for working class leadership, but which are not a direct avenue to anything beyond. (1)

The instruction was to be neither political nor sectarian. No Latin, Greek, Hebrew, metaphysics or geology was to be taught and no academic honours were to be awarded. The three founders hoped that this novel institution would be the pioneer of a nationwide movement.

The governing council had included three trade union representatives as well as Oxford University teachers known to be sympathetic to working class interests. Dennis Hird, who was appointed Principal, had been ordained as an Anglican minister and employed temporarily as an Oxford don before taking up a series of appointments, each of which he had lost because of his socialist views and insistence upon popularising Darwin's theory of evolution. His publications bore such titles as *A Picture Book*

1. Ministry of Reconstruction, Adult Education Committee, *Final Report* (Cmd, 321, 1919) Appdx. pt. 1, p.221; see also Bd. of Education, Inspectors' Report, April 1913 (N.L.S.); see also *The Story of Ruskin* (Oxford, 1968), p.5.

of Evolution, An Easy Outline of Evolution, and *Jesus the Socialist.* H. B. Lees Smith, whose subsequent career would suggest that he was an adroit trimmer, was appointed General Secretary and later Vice-Principal. Two tutors who sympathised with Hird's views were also appointed. The curriculum initially consisted of history, economics and political science, trade unionism, evolution, logic and English literature together with a new subject, sociology, taught by Hird himself.

Ruskin and the rich

In 1902 Vrooman, who had provided the bulk of the money required to found the college, returned to America and the college was immediately obliged to scratch around for funds. This soon led to a paradoxical situation. On the one hand, it was necessary to appeal to patrons, including members of the aristocracy, who frowned on political and industrial militancy. On the other hand, trade unions didn't even help much by paying for an adequate number of scholarships for students, many of whom, as soon as they arrived at the college, displayed their socialist convictions. The governing council, apart from Hird, thus found itself having to appease its benefactors at the risk of antagonising the students. For example, when appealing for funds the college claimed that one of its aims was to give 'working men *a sound, practical knowledge* of subjects which concerned them as citizens, *thus enabling them to view social questions sanely and without unworthy class bias.'*

The militancy of the students who were to form the Plebs League was largely explained by two factors. First, a significant proportion of them came from the South Wales coal-fields where industrial conflicts were endemic. Secondly, many of them had imbibed socialist ideas through membership of the Social Democratic Federation (SDF), the Socialist Labour Party (SLP) or the Independent Labour Party (ILP). The SLP had been particularly influential in shaping their ideas by publishing in cheap paper-covered form such works as *The Communist Manifesto, Historical Materialism* and *Wage, Labour and Capital,* and by organising classes on Marxist theories. The Marxist materialist interpretation of history had made a deep impression on them, for not only did it foretell an early resolution of the class struggle in favour of the working classes, it did so by appealing to what seemed to be empirically derived knowledge. The Rationalist Press Association had also a great influence by publishing books on evolution such as Darwin's *Origin of Species* and Hird's *Easy Outline of Evolution* in paper covers at 6d.

As to the interaction between education and society, the students were captivated by a line of reasoning that may be summarised as follows. By the early years of the twentieth century the more power-conscious wage workers had formed their own collective bargaining association — the trade unions, their own distributive agency — the co-operative societies, and their own political organisation — the Labour Party. Did it not logically follow that they should also control their own educational structure? They refused, so they declared, to be the dupes of the false idea that orthodox education, which Oxford University above all epitomised, was impartial. Nearly all forms of education claimed impartiality but were in fact more or less biased. Orthodox education was one of the main sources of power of the governing class in Britain. Labour's struggle was not to be confined to the political and industrial arenas but must also be extended to the educational arena. To achieve victory in its struggle for political and economic power the Labour Movement must create and vigorously control its own educational machinery, and above all provide a content reflecting the interests of the working class movement.

Some of the Ruskin students organised classes among themselves in order to study the socialist theories of Marx and his disciples. They also planned propaganda activities on behalf of socialism, launched a magazine *Young Oxford* and founded the Ruskin College Educational League with the object of arousing public awareness of their ideals. Of the students he had known, Sanderson Furniss, a tutor appointed in 1908, many years later recalled that 'they were practically all socialists of one brand or another, and there were amongst them some of the wildest and most revolutionary young men in the country'.

During the very years when the militant students at Ruskin were advocating autonomous working class education, other people were seeking to foster inter-class educational co-operation. At national level this orientation had found its most significant expression in the foundation in 1903 of the National Association for Promoting the Higher Education of Working Men, soon to be renamed the Workers' Educational Association (WEA). In Oxford, proposals for an association between Oxford University and Ruskin College led to a major confrontation between a majority of the college students and the College

3

authorities, except for the Principal, Dennis Hird and one other member of the staff — A. J. Hacking.

Oxford Dons Act

Following the formation of the Labour Representation Committee in 1900 and, in 1906, the quite unexpected election of 29 Labour Members of Parliament, it appeared to a few Oxford University lecturers that the Labour Movement was bound soon to become a serious political force and that something must therefore be done to ensure that its potential leaders were suitably educated. Since the university extension movement had obviously failed to attract working class support, a new approach was required. The suggestion was accordingly made to Ruskin College that university teachers should help in the planning and conduct of classes. First, A. L. Smith (the future distinguished master of Balliol College, then a lecturer in history) and shortly afterwards Lord Curzon, Chancellor of the University, visited the college and recommended a closer association with the University. Curzon's visit was described in a pamphlet *(The Burning Question of Education,* published at Oxford in 1908) in vivid language which polarised the fundamental division between Hird and the students on one side and the spokesman of 'orthodox' higher education on the other:

> The students were all standing and had formed a ring, in the centre of which Lord Curzon spoke. Mr. Hird also advanced to the centre and stood facing Lord Curzon while he replied. The contrast between the two men was very striking. The circumstances in which they met invested the event with a distinctly dramatic colour. Lord Curzon wearing his Doctor of Laws gown — not the glittering robes of office — but robes of dark coloured cloth devoid of ornamentation as if they represented the university in mourning for the condescension implied in his visit. Not so Lord Curzon himself, however. He stood in a position of ease supporting himself by a stick, which he held behind him as a prop to the dignity of the upper part of his body. A trifling superiority in height, increased by the use of his stick, allowed him to somewhat look down on Mr. Hird. It was easy to see that this man had been Viceroy of India. Autocratic disdain and the suggestion of a power feudal in character, seemed stamped on his countenance. As the purport of Mr. Hird's reply reached his comprehension he seemed to freeze into a statuesque embodiment

4

of wounded dignity. For Mr. Hird was not uttering the usual compliments, but was actually rebuking the University for having neglected Ruskin College until this, the day of its assured prosperity. As Mr. Hird spoke, the students instinctively moved towards him, as though mutually offering him support. Mr. Hird, who had begun with flushed cheeks and a slight tremor in his voice now seemed inspired with an enthusiasm and dignity which only comes to a man who voices the aspirations of a great Movement.

In substance, he said: My Lord, when you speak of Ruskin College you are not referring merely to this institution in Oxford, for this is only the branch of a great democratic movement that has its roots all over the country. To ask Ruskin College to come into closer contact with the University is to ask the great democracy whose foundation is the Labour Movement, a democracy that in the near future will come into its own, and when it does will bring great changes in its wake. As he concluded the burst of applause that emanated from the students seemed to herald the dawn of the day to which Mr. Hird had referred. Without another word Lord Curzon turned on his heel and walked out, followed by the remainder of the lecturing staff, who looked very far from pleased.

The overtures from Oxford University were welcomed by the governing board of the College and most of the staff. The students rejected them and begged to be excused from attending all lectures except those given by Hird. Another move that had already caused great feeling among the students was an attempt by some of the college governors to change Hird's subjects from sociology and logic to literature and temperance. As Hird's life had been bound up with the subjects he was teaching, this was an intimation to 'clear out'. The students had managed to scotch this plan. During the academic year 1907/8 they were aggrieved by the *de facto* introduction of twelve visiting university lecturers which they saw as a device to water down the syllabus, and by the setting of written examinations. They accused Sanderson Furniss of political bias in the marking of essays. What most disturbed the students, however, was the publication in 1908 of a report on the contribution which Oxford University ought to

5

make to workers' education (2), prepared by a joint committee of university and WEA representatives. This report partially reflected the desire of some Oxford dons to extend the university's public service role, especially in the industrial sector (3), but the Ruskin students saw it as a bare-faced attempt to seize control of the education of working men in the interests of the governing class. Thus, one section of the report read:

> ... it has become incumbent upon Universities to watch carefully every sign that a new class is to receive their guidance, in order that the seed of University culture may be deposited wherever it has suitable material on which to work. (4)

Another section read:

> It seems to us that it would involve a great loss both to Oxford and to English political life were the close association which has existed between the University and the world of affairs to be broken off or impaired on the accession of new classes to power. No doubt other Universities have done something in the past, and will do more in the future to provide higher education for the working classes and we are far from suggesting that the burden and privilege of making such provision should rest solely or even mainly upon Oxford. But we are strongly of opinion that recent political developments make it imperative that in her own interests, as much as in the interests of work people, it should be made possible for a far larger number to turn to her for teaching than have done so in the past. (5)

Two of the Report's specific recommendations had struck the students as particularly obnoxious. The first was that university tutorial classes should be offered throughout the country in collaboration with the WEA. To the socialist students it was intolerable enough that orthodox economic theories were being

2. *Oxford and Working-class Education: Being the Report of a Joint Committee of University and Working-class Representatives on the Relation of the University to the Higher Education of Work People* (Oxford, 1908).

3. Cf. [a teacher] must not only be able to guide and stimulate his students; he should also have sufficient knowledge of working-class life and habits of thought to be able to understand the lines along which students have reached their conclusions, and see the unstated assumptions from which their assumptions start.' (*ibid.*, p.65.)

4. *ibid.*, p.53.

5. *ibid.*, p.48.

taught at Ruskin; the consequence of their being disseminated far and wide by means of tutorial classes would be even more detrimental to working class interests. The second recommendation was that Ruskin students should become eligible for scholarships at Oxford University. The students construed that would-be egalirarian gesture as a plot to convert the College into 'a gloomy archway to the reactionary university.'

The controversy between the Board and most of the College staff on one side and the disaffected students on the other proved too fierce to allow compromise. A two-man delegation presented a list of grievances to the College Executive Committee, which rejected out of hand a proposal that the College should be directly controlled by organised Labour and appointed a sub-committee to inquire into the dispute. The sub-committee, consisting of three trade unionists and two academics, reported that many of the students considered the teaching to be pro-capitalist and hostile to socialism and that Furniss's presentation of economics did indeed appear to be partisan. In general, however, the sub-committee was critical of the students' behaviour, pointing out that the object of the Plebs League, which they had just formed, 'would be to force the executive to move in a direction in which it would not be desirable to go.' The sub-committee accused Hird of encouraging atheism and extremist political ideas and recommended that he be asked to resign. The executive committee thereupon formally dismissed Hird on the ground that he had failed 'to maintain discipline.' Seeing Hird's dismissal 'as only an attack on the students, which in this case were represented by him,' the great majority of the students retaliated by going on strike on 31 March, 1908.

Plebs League founded

Meanwhile, the students had founded the Plebs League with the avowed aim of providing a platform for pleading the cause of independent working-class education and appealing to the rank and file in the Labour movement. Its initial goal was to transform Ruskin College into a genuine *Labour* college run by workers for workers. Most of the students had recently read and admired *Two Pages of Roman History*, a well-known American socialist pamphlet that drew a parallel between the struggle of the plebeians in ancient Rome to overcome the patricians and the contemporary struggle between the workers and the propertied class. It seemed apt to apply the term *plebs* to those who, in 1908, upheld the principle of education for workers by workers. Membership of the Plebs League was to be open to former

7

students of Ruskin as well as to sympathisers for an annual subscription of one shilling. Local branches were to be set up wherever possible and annual general meetings were envisaged.

To disseminate ideas, news and information and to link the branches together, the League launched a magazine, which they called *The Plebs Magazine* and which was first published in Oxford in February 1909. The governing body of the college refused permission for Hird to serve as editor and so an editorial board was elected consisting of four students in their second year, W. W. Craik, George Sims, W. H. Seed and Stan Rees. George Sims was eventually appointed General Secretary and the task of editing* devolved largely upon him but it was Craik who wrote most of the leading articles with some assistance from Sims. In the first issue the students summed up their aspirations for Ruskin:

> . . . to point out its present weakness, to outline its possibilities, to demonstrate its value to the Labour Movement if definitely founded therein, to stimulate active interest in working class education and to open out propaganda of an educational character from the working class point of view . . . (6)

In the second issue they announced their basic strategy:

> To the organised Labour Movement we appeal for support on a question that lies at the very bottom of working class organisation. We cannot trust our economic safety to the good intentions of the possessing class. We do not rely upon the politics of our employers for measures of progessive legislation. We established our own economic fortifications — we have our own political weapons — we control our own literary despatches. Why then should we not as independently manage our educational affairs? Even as we have a platform of our own, let us have educational institutions of our own. (7)

The emphasis laid by academics on objectivity, they maintained, was a curtain behind which ruling class ideas could pass unchallenged. They enquired: 'Can a Labour College be neutral?', and answered: 'Who but a class enemy could advocate neutrality on the educational front?' Throughout history every

6. *Plebs*, 1909, p.1.

7. *ibid.*, 1909, p.27.

* The first editor was E. Brand, George Sims being the treasurer during that short period.

8

George Sims, Secretary of the Central Labour College

ruling class had manipulated education to reinforce its power.

Move against Hird

In view of their own experience at Ruskin the striking students had reasonable grounds for complaint about the irrelevance of the teaching they received. With the exception of Hird and one other tutor, Hacking, the staff repudiated socialist theories. Lees-Smith appears to have managed the campaign to get rid of Hird. Sanderson Furniss (Lord Sanderson 1930), after becoming Principal of the College, was to record among many revealing statements in his autobiography:

> I had never given a lecture in my life, I had no experience whatever of teaching beyond the very small amount I had had with Molly Pope at Clifton years before, and I knew nothing of working-class problems apart from some very abstract theories I had derived from books and my C.O.S. experiences at Clifton. I was completely ignorant of Trade Unionism or of the Co-operative Movement. I had read Economics entirely from what is rather absurdly, though conveniently, called the 'orthodox' point of view, I had never read a line of Marx, I knew very little of the Socialist writers, and those I had read had made no impression on my mind. I had hardly ever spoken to a working man except gardeners, coachmen, and gamekeepers. (8)

Charles S. Buxton, who was appointed Vice-Principal in 1908, published an article (9) in which he emphasized the important part played by Oxford University in the affairs of Ruskin College and described the College as an 'idealist experiment in *faeces Romuli'* (10) The Latin phrase gave offence to the students who translated it as 'the dregs of the People.' To cap it all, the students had to put up with the hostility of Oxford undergraduates.

The strike at Ruskin lasted for a fortnight and attracted comment in the national press, some of it critical of the governing board. During the strike the students themselves kept the College functioning even to the extent of organising their own lectures. They called off the strike only when the Board agreed to reconsider Hird's dismissal and to send the students home on a fortnight's vacation at the College's expense. When

8. H. S. Furniss, *Memories of Sixty Years* (London, 1930), pp. 83-4.

9. 'Ruskin College: an Educational Experiment in Faecie Romuli' in *The Cornhill Magazine*, Vol. XXV., Aug. 1908, pp.192-200.

10. *ibid.,* p.200.

the College re-opened on April 20, ten out of the fifty-four students did not return and a sizeable group of those who did return remained at odds with the Board. Hird was not reinstated.

The dissension at Ruskin was difficult to avoid. The College authorities refused to alter its teaching on economics whereas the students wished to identify the College with socialist theories. The students yearned to understand the causes of the social changes that were taking place around them and could obtain no satisfaction from their tutors who were ignorant of socialist theory and unfamiliar with the industrial environment. (11) The exclusion of any teaching about Marxist theories confirmed that they were being brainwashed. On their side, the Board sought to reduce Hird's influence to nought, viewing him as an obstinate man who didn't accept their views and who symphathised with the socialist views of the students. As for the tutors, they no doubt tried conscientiously to present their subjects as impartially as possible but failed to appreciate that their assumptions and often the theories they taught made them sound like mouthpieces of the governing class.

The Central Labour College

The students who did not return to Ruskin, in collaboration with a number of those who did, decided to establish an independent college of their own:

> They had now realised that Ruskin College was no longer worthy of their activities. Practically pledged to the University; governed mainly by Dons who did not possess an elementary fitness for aiding the democracy; incompetently staffed; and openly hostile to the working class idea; they decided that Ruskin College as an aid to the workers was worthless. They took a referendum vote of the members, and almost unanimously the 'plebs' decided to ask the Trade Unionists to go in for a college of their own. (12)

11. Cf. 'As a matter of fact there was something to be said for the point of view held by many of the students. Some of them were not getting the kind of education they thought they ought to have; they wanted to study nothing but Marx and to be trained as Socialist propagandists. There were, no doubt, certain modifications and extensions of the curriculum which might have been made with advantage. At that time we did not give them nearly enough information about the Socialist and Labour Movement, and insufficient attention was paid to trade union problems and co-operation. We hardly touched the history of Socialism.' (Furniss, *op.cit.*, p.100.)

12. *The Burning Question of Education* (Oxford, 1909), p. 17.

In the pages of *The Plebs Magazine* they sustained their attacks upon Ruskin. In their pamphlet *The Burning Question of Education* they recounted the causes of the strike and stated their case. The tone of the pamphet was messianic.

> We neither want your crumbs nor your condescension, your guidance nor your glamour, your tuition nor your tradition. We have our own historic way to follow, our own Salvation to achieve, *and by this sign we shall conquer* (13)

But it contained not one reference to Marx or Marxism.

The future facing the pioneers of independent working-class education was bleak. They had no financial resources and faced hostility even from within some sections of the Trade Union and Labour movement. But they were convinced that the tide of history was flowing powerfully in their favour. Their strategy was not only to establish a central residential college but to set up citadels of influence throughout the country by means of the Plebs League. They were much encouraged by the fact that within the space of a few months a large number of workers' classes for the study of economics and history had been formed in many localities in every big industrial area. The first priority of the Plebs League, however, was to open the new college without delay.

The committee responsible for founding the League had been disbanded temporarily because its members had feared they would lose their scholarships. In March 1909 they empowered Sims, whose part in the strike had cost him his scholarship, to manage the magazine and the League business on their behalf. Sims had played a dominant part in the strike and now devoted his formidable energy and organising ability to winning support for a new college. Forced to work at the age of eight, Sims had become a skilled carpenter. In his teens he was attracted to Marxism:

> I had tried for years to get a feeling of reality in religion, to feel that God and the Christ were of me, with me, but the reality never came . . . but with the first reading of the *Communist Manifesto*, how the pamphlet appealed to something in me, some revolt against things as they are, purely due to feeling — the appeal was an answer to my yearnings. (14)

13. *ibid.*, p.22.
14. Letter to Winifred Horrabin from '. . . out here in Lombardy with the world in flux.' Quoted in W. Horrabin, 'In Memoriam: G. F. Sims' in *Plebs*, 1943, p.126.

The simple directness of that account of his conversion was reflected in all his actions. His ebullience sometimes offended even his friends but he had a rare capacity for getting things done no matter how great the obstacles.

A provisional committee was formed for the purpose of establishing a college and obtaining financial support from the trade unions. It included two Labour MPs and one. Will Thorne, was the treasurer. Thanks to a financial guarantee it became possible to rent two houses belonging to St. John's College. Dennis Hird was appointed Warden, the title of 'Principal' being discarded, and agreed to lecture for one year on Sociology, Evolution, Logic and Rhetoric in return for no more than his out-of-pocket expenses. Sims was appointed secretary.

The College was formally inaugurated at a conference held in Oxford on 2 August 1909 and attended by some two hundred trade union representatives and former Ruskin students. The conference coincided with the Plebs League's first annual meeting, which attracted delegates from no fewer than seventy Labour organisations.

CLC opens

By the time the Central Labour College (CLC), as it was called, opened its doors for the first time on 8 September 1909, it was sure of assistance from the Amalgamated Society of Railway Servants (A S R S) and several Districts of the South Wales Miners' Federation (S W M F) all having terminated their scholarships to Ruskin College; the Amalgamated Society of Engineers (A S E) also offered some assistance. Twenty students took up residence, most of them having transferred from Ruskin. In November· 1909, when summarily expelled from Ruskin College, W. W. Craik and three other students were also granted admission to the new College. No fewer than two hundred Welsh miners applied for the six scholarships awarded by S W M F Districts.

Surprisingly the College committee almost immediately entered into discussions with Ruskin College about the possibility of a merger. Not that it could have expected the discussions to lead anywhere in view of the stiff terms it presented:

1. Will the authorities of Ruskin College agree to the appointment of a representative from all the trade unions who contributed scholarships in the years 1907-8 to form a committee to investigate the causes which led to the

dismissal of Mr. Hird with power to decide whether he shall be reinstated or not?

2. Will the Ruskin College authorities agree to cancel all the present staff appointments so that the trade union representatives can appoint or re-appoint all members of staff?

3. Will Ruskin College retire and hand over the whole control of that institution to the representatives of the contributing Labour organisations? (15)

Subsequently Ruskin was further requested to sever all connections with Oxford University and the WEA. No wonder that, when a joint meeting finally took place on 10 March 1910, agreement was not reached and the negotiations ceased.

Neither the Labour Party nor the majority of trade union leaders showed any real interest in the new institution. This was disappointing. As Craik has explained, the very choice of the College's official name had been dictated by the desire to occupy a strategic position within the general Labour movement:

> It was the political character of the education given at the new educational institution, its content and aim, which entitled it to the name of a *Labour* College . . . Because of a common historical origin and purpose the new educational institution had the right to share with the new Party the common title of Labour. (16)

Yet, as early as November 1910, J. T. Macpherson, M.P., chairman of the provisional committee, resigned, 'his reason being the decision of the executive committee of his union to have nothing to do with either Ruskin or the Central Labour College.' Nearly all senior trade union officials at that time held traditionalist views about the nature of education and most of them disapproved of what they regarded as the young upstarts who had unsettled Ruskin College. Some of them, according to Craik, went so far as to allege that the men behind the College were out to smash the trade unions. He might have added in fairness that they were also gravely overworked during the period of industrial unrest immediately preceding the First World War. For the College one comfort was the support it received from the *Daily Herald.*

CLC forced to move

Keeping accommodation in Oxford turned out to be difficult because of the hostility of the university landlords. The problem

15. CLC Minutes
16. W. W. Craik, *Central Labour College* (London, 1964), p. 14.

13

was solved in 1911 by transferring the College to the Earls Court district of London. It was less easy to overcome the College's appalling poverty. For lack of full-time help, two students had to do the cooking. The staff were poorly and irregularly paid. On one occasion as Craik was on the point of leaving to address a union branch meeting in the hope of obtaining a small grant, a student noticed that he had a hole in the seat of his trousers. For the rest of the day they exchanged trousers. Funds were raised by a variety of devices including musical and theatrical evenings organised by J. F. Horrabin and a women's committee which included Winifred Blatchford (daughter of Robert Blatchford), Winifred Horrabin and Rebecca West. Salvation did not come until 1915 when the National Union of Railwaymen (NUR — formerly the A S R S) and the S W M F assumed ownership of the College, a momentous step in the recognition by trade unions that they had a direct responsibility for providing education for their members.

During the early years in London, student enrolments remained small. In 1914 fourteen men were in residence and two women students were living out. Of these fourteen students, six were supported by the S W M F , two by the NUR, one by the Nottinghamshire Miners' Association, the two women by the Women's League of the Labour College, two by personal scholarships and one student supported himself. As a rule the period of residence was two years. Life was hard, the students having to study a great variety of subjects and to share the domestic chores.

A good deal of the teaching at the College was based upon socialist theories. As sub-warden, Craik testified in 1917 to the Adult Education Committee appointed by the Ministry of Reconstruction:

> It teaches the workmen to look for the causes of social evils and the problems arising therefrom in the material foundation of society — that these causes are in the last resort economic; that their elimination involves in the first place economic changes of such a character as to lead to the eradication of capital economy . . . For this reason the Labour College lays no claim to being non-partisan or non-political. As it exists for a partisan movement it must be opposed to all those in opposition to that movement. But its participation is a consequence of the actual facts which it scientifically unfolds. (17)

17. Ministry of Reconstruction, Adult Ed. Cttee., *Final Report*, pp.222-3.

The main courses were political economy, industrial history, general history, the history of social movements, English, formal logic, theory of knowledge, dialectical materialism, literature, elocution and sociology. A small correspondence course service was begun.

The work of the College was hampered by a long illness suffered by Hird, which threw a heavy burden on Craik. Hird was forced to take leave of absence early in 1917 and Craik took over as Acting Warden. Shortly afterwards, Craik and Sims were conscripted and the College suspended the full-time residential course until October 1919, although the local class work and postal tuition continued.

CHAPTER II

THE PLEBS LEAGUE
AND THE FORMATION OF LOCAL COLLEGES

Between them the Plebs League and the Central Labour College spread the idea of independent working-class education throughout many areas of the British Isles. One of the League's main objects was to establish branches wherever possible so as to start classes in economics and industrial history. From as early as 1909 members of the League who had been at Ruskin took the lead in founding branches in their local communities and conducting classes.

As soon as the Central Labour College had been re-established in London both staff and students reinforced and extended the classwork already under way in the metropolitan area. Evening classes were held on College premises but mainly in halls in different parts of London. Second year students were required to take classes as part of their general training. The missionary function of the College was made abundantly clear to all students and several of them were encouraged to teach outside London. Charles Gibbons has recorded:

> After finishing my first year at the Central Labour College in London I was sent by the College authorities to take seven classes in various parts of South and East Lancashire with my centre at Rochdale. These classes had been organised the previous year by Harold Kershaw, an ex-Ruskin College student who had participated in the students' strike there. (1)

1. C. L. Gibbons, Recollections of the Movement for Independent Working Class Education 1909-1914 (unpublished) NCLC MS. p. 18.

15

On the outbreak of war in 1914 it was claimed that approximately 1,000 students were attending classes under the supervision of the Plebs League and the College.

The First World War and Socialism

During the war the Plebs' concept of education won many adherents, and new colleges or class groups sprang up in considerable numbers. The belief that the war had ultimately been caused by a clash between the old imperialist power, Britain, and the new imperialist power, Germany, both in competition for overseas markets and political spheres of influence, led many people to become socialists, especially among the younger generation. The publicity of the Central Labour College and the Plebs League was deliberately aimed at the more radical elements in the Trade Union and Labour movement. Some of the anti-militarists who eventually became conscientious objectors had been attracted first by socialism and then to the idea of working-class education as a necessary means to the socialist end. When put in detention centres after being imprisoned for refusing military service, they turned the centres into schools of political education. While an inmate of Wakefield Prison, one of three prisons temporarily used as Home Office detention centres, J. P. M. Millar received each month a bundle of *The Plebs Magazine* which he sold to other detainees, many of whom were penniless except for the 8d a week paid for their enforced labour. Labour College classes were started in all three centres — Dartmoor, Knutsford and Wakefield — and there was no lack of tutors or students.

The Growth of Local Classes

Many of the Plebs groups and classes were started from scratch. A good number, however, had evolved from previous activities such as the classes arranged by the S D F , the S L P and the I L P and later the British Socialist Party. Up and down industrial Britain, especially in South Wales, Lancashire, the North East, the West Riding and in Scotland, self-financing classes and colleges were formed. At first, as the Horrabins[*] have pointed out: 'Every class was a practically autonomous unit, the only link between them being the Plebs League, in which the active spirits enrolled themselves as members, and *The Plebs Magazine* . . .(2)'. Very soon, however, some local Labour organisations, including trade union branches, would give their support and appoint representatives to augment the class

2. J. F. and W. Horrabin, *Working Class Education* (London, 1914) pp. 48-49.

committees and turn them into college committees. Teaching would be conducted by unpaid tutors except for a few who, like Craik and Gibbons, lectured in a circuit of towns and received small sums of money raised by class members or local committees. The last issue of *The Plebs Magazine* for 1917 listed classes held in South Wales and Northern England as well as classes organised by the Central Labour College, the Socialist Labour Party, the Scottish Labour College and the British Socialist Party. Details were given of classes in Birmingham, Fleetwood, Halifax, Huddersfield, Leeds, Leigh, London, Manchester, Salford, Sheffield, Rochdale, Warrington and Wigan.

The two regions in which independent working-class education aroused most enthusiasm were the South Wales coalfield and the industrial belt of Scotland. The reasons why the South Wales coalfield proved a forcing ground for radical educational ideas were identifield by a Committee of Enquiry into Industrial Unrest appointed by the government in 1917. In the first place, the Report said, there was a serious paucity of educational facilities: 'not a single municipally-maintained public library is to be found in the central Glamorgan block of the coalfield . . .'. 'Evidence has been brought before us to show that the workers view with alarm the shortage of teachers and the consequent failure of the local authorities to provide proper education for the children.' Secondly, the trade union movement did not suggest itself as a potentially political instrument or as a homogeneous social structure but rather operated largely as a mutual benefits club. Thirdly, the spread of elementary schools engendered a desire for more learning and a better understanding of the social environment. In the trade union lodges:

> The younger generation, fed upon the writings of the Fabian Society, the Independent Labour Party and the works of Continental and American writers, has tended more and more to formulate a theory of reform and of political action which is almost entirely opposed to that of the old.

And the lodges had become centres not only of educational programmes but of political activity and the organisation of libraries. The 'advanced men' had expressed the doctrine of industrial unionism.

Noah Ablett, a student at Ruskin College in 1907 and a member of the Plebs League wielded great influence in South Wales. On leaving Ruskin, Ablett returned to work at Cymner Colliery North in the Rhondda Valley with the express intention of persuading the SWMF to adopt the ideas of the Plebs League and support the Central Labour College. He was vigorously challenged by T. I. Mardy Jones, another Ruskin graduate employed as a checkweighman at Mardy Collieries. The pair of them engaged in a series of debates, mainly held in the lodges of the SWMF. At the first debate attended by Charles Gibbons the motion was 'Should the education of the workers in Social Science and particularly in Local History and Economics be purveyed by the Capitalist University or by an Educational Institution not subsidised by the Capitalist class or in any way controlled by it?' Mardy Jones was no match for Ablett. Inspired by Ablett, hundreds of miners, particularly among the younger generation, were converted to the cause of independent working-class education and put pressure on their lodges and district committees to support the newly-formed Central Labour College. According to the report of the Committee of Inquiry into Industrial Unrest, nineteen of the Central Labour College's forty-one classes were in South Wales, eight being held in the Rhondda.

> The number of students at that time in South Wales would not be less than 500. Since March 1917, however, the number of classes has largely increased, and steps have been taken to organise classes in almost every district of the South Wales Federation. (3)

Ness Edwards has also recalled: 'there was hardly a miners' lodge which was not responsible for an evening class tutored by the ex-students.' Many who attended these classes became students at the Central Labour College*and household names in the Labour Movement. They included Arthur J. Cook, W. H. Mainwaring, Ness Edwards, George Daggar, Ted Williams and Will Coldrick. It was the advocacy of former CLC students which caused the SWMF to become joint owner of the Central Labour College. Later, Cook became General Secretary of the Miners' Federation of Great Britain; Mainwaring and Daggar became Labour M.Ps.; Edwards became an M.P. and Postmaster-General; Williams became an M.P., Minister for Information and later still High Commissioner for Australia; Coldrick became an M.P. and Chairman of the Co-operative Party.

IWCE in South Wales

Organising classes was not the only activity engaged in by

3. *Commission of Enquiry into Industrial Unrest, No. 7 Division, Report of the Commission for Wales including Monmouthshire* (HMSO, 1917) p. 112.

* For convenience consistently called the Central Labour College in the text except in one or two instances.

Ablett and his associates. Ablett himself contributed frequent articles to *The Plebs Magazine* and wrote *An Easy Outline of Economics* for the League. But their most important activity was the establishment, in various parts of the Rhondda and other areas of the South Wales coalfields, of study groups which met in miners' halls or in cafés and private houses. The subject normally discussed was Marxist economic theory because it held out an intelligible explanation of the class stratification of contemporary society and the prospect of a socialist system. The group also participated in the establishment of the *South Wales Worker*, a weekly paper intended to popularise their educational and industrial views, and played an important role in writing and publishing two widely discussed pamphlets: *A Plan for the Democratic Control of the Mining Industry* and *The Miners' Next Step* described jestingly as 'not a step but a bloody ladder.' Charles Gibbons recalled attending weekly meetings at which the main topic of conversation was 'how to organise on a coalfield scale.' Ablett and other Plebs members played the major part in turning the South Wales district miners' organisations into a centralised industrial union. The forceful impact upon South Wales of Ablett and his associates was summed up in the Report of the Commission of Inquiry in 1917:

> The sense of antagonism between Capital and Labour has been considerably deepened during recent years by the propaganda of a small but earnest group of men whose teachings are rapidly permeating the entire trade union movement. Advance causes feed on discontent, and the indisposition of employers to concede the claims of the workers to a higher standard of life had provided fuel for the propaganda of the Independent Labour Party and, more recently, of the enthusiasts of the Central Labour College movement.

> The influence of the 'advanced' men is growing very rapidly, and there is ground for belief that under their leadership attempts of a drastic character will be made by the working-classes as a whole to secure direct control by themselves of their particular industries. Nearly all movements initiated by the SWMF during recent years, consciously or unconsciously, are directed towards the overthrow of the present capitalist system and the establishment of a new industrial order under which the workers will have a greater measure of

19

control over their industry and a larger measure of the produce of their labour. (4)

Scotland's Part

The industrial belt of Scotland also provided fertile soil for the idea of independent working-class education. In that area foundations for the new educational movement had already been laid by the SDF and the SLP and other socialist bodies. These bodies popularised the teachings of Marx and Engels by means of lectures and pamphlets. In 1912 John S. Clarke delivered a series of winter course lectures in Edinburgh, on behalf of the Central Labour College, to a class run by the Edinburgh No. 1 branch of the ASRS. Thereafter John Maclean, a Glasgow school teacher, played the leading role in establishing the Scottish Labour College. Maclean gave public lectures all over Scotland, expounding the ideas first of the SDF and later of the BSP. During the war, when Maclean was not in gaol for his anti-war activities, his class lectures in Bath Street in the centre of Glasgow were attended by audiences of between one hundred and two hundred.

In 1916 a proposal to establish a Labour College in Scotland was considered at a national conference in Glasgow attended by 471 delegates representing 271 trade union branches and local class groups. Bob Smillie, Scottish President of the Miners' Federation, should have presided but was prevented from attending by a cold. His place was taken by G. S. Shanks, chairman of the Glasgow Trades Council. The keynote speaker should have been Maclean but he had just been arrested for his political activities and his partly-composed speech was completed and presented by his friend and a fellow class tutor, J. D. Macdougall, and subsequently published as a pamphlet: *A Plea for a Labour College for Scotland.* The proposal to establish a college was carried unanimously. Millar represented the Plebs League at this conference. Measures were immediately taken to bring all the existing classes in Scotland under the wing of the new college. By 1918, 1500 students were attending classes. Although Maclean himself had shown unflagging energy in arranging classes, his main ambition was to found a residential college. For the best part of one year, with the assistance of W. McLaine, a Lancashire engineer and shop steward (later an Assistant General Secretary of the AEU) and W. Leonard, a furnishing trade worker and future M.P., he ran classes for

4. *op.cit.,* pp.23-4.

twelve full-time students, mostly miners, while still running a number of evening and Sunday classes. His dream of founding a permanent Scottish college on the London model was never realised and prison sentences played havoc with his educational work.

When the war ended, the number of Labour College classes everywhere increased rapidly. In London there were soon so many that it became necessary in 1920 both to create a London Council for Independent Working Class Education which could co-ordinate the various activities, and to appoint Robert Holder, a former CLC student, as full-time tutor organiser. By 1920 there were 2,854 students attending fifty-one classes in Scotland, of which thirty were in the Glasgow district.

Need for Co-ordination

As the number of classes proliferated all over Britain, so the problem of how to co-ordinate them increasingly concerned the Plebs League. In 1918 there was already talk of organising seven national divisions. At the League's annual meeting on 8 November, 1919, shortly after the post-war re-opening of the Central Labour College on September 25, plans were discussed for integrating more closely the activities of the League and the College. On behalf of the executive committee Mark Starr urged the formation of autonomous branches upon which the sole constraint should be an obligation to adhere to the objects of the League and the methods it advocated. These branches should arrange classes, encourage the distribution of *The Plebs Magazine* and generally stimulate interest in independent working-class education. There should be an annual general assembly, which should have only a consultative function, and any constitutional amendments required should be effected by means of a postal vote. Starr's proposal was considered further at a meeting of the executive committee held on 17th and 18th January, 1920, when a resolution was formally approved that the Plebs League should be organised into branches, each of which should promote classes and distribute suitable pamphlets and books. There was also a recommendation that full-time lecturers should be appointed on salaries at least as high as those of the average skilled worker and allowed necessary expenses. In the course of a long discussion it was agreed that, whereas classes tended to be ephemeral, branches of the League could be self-perpetuating. According to *The Plebs Magazine:*

The general feeling was that *decentralisation with co-*

21

ordination was the ideal policy; and in this connection it was made quite clear that neither the Labour College nor the Plebs League regarded a centralised authority as either practicable or desirable. (5)

The CLC re-opened in September, or earlier, 1919, with twenty-nine students in residence. Its name had been changed by the two unions to The Labour College, London. Hird was unable to return and Craik was confirmed as Principal. Although extensive improvements were made to the College during the five months preceding the re-opening, places could not be found for all the applicants. The two controlling unions later agreed to buy a large house with three and a half acres of ground at Kew, adjacent to the botanical gardens. This was set aside for the use of first-year students.

The CLC's Development Plans

The College wished to encourage the development of provincial local classes. At its meeting on 17 September 1919 the governing board minuted:

> . . . that Messrs Craik and Sims be asked to prepare a scheme for tutorial classes, lectures, and part-time lecturers and submit same to the next board meeting. (6)

Even before its doors re-opened the College also considered the possibility of arranging affiliation schemes with the local colleges on the following terms:

1. Acceptance of the principles of the Central Labour College by tutorial classes as a condition of affiliation.
2. The College to assist classes in framing curriculum, assisting teachers, and ensuring the efficiency of such teachers.
3. The terms of affiliation to be 3d per student per year.

In the June 1920 issue of *Plebs*, George Sims pointed out that regular reports were required so that the College might know best how to assist local work. But in the event no affiliation schemes were arranged and many of the local colleges soon reached the conclusion that the College was interested only in strengthening its own position.

The truth of the matter was that the College authorities were preoccupied with the problem of achieving financial stability. The NUR and the S W M F felt the strain of supporting the

5. CLC Minutes 1919., p.18.

6. *Plebs*, p.3.

22

College by themselves and reasoned that other unions must share their burden. The governors negotiated fitfully for wider support. At their meeting on 17 September 1919 they instructed the Secretary:

> . . . to place on the agenda for next board meeting the question of calling a delegate trade union conference for the purpose of ascertaining what unions are desirous of sharing in the ownership and managment of the College. (7)

Subsequently, at their meeting in February 1920, they considered a draft plan for wider control. They were also seeking a capital sum in order to build a new and larger college on the site of the property which had been acquired at Kew and for which an imposing architect's plan was prepared. In January 1921 Craik was instructed: '. . . to prepare a statement suitable for circulation throughout the Labour Movement inviting subscriptions towards the Building Fund and to ascertain how far trade unions interested in the College are prepared to subscribe to the appeal and to sign the same together with the secretaries of the N U R and S W M F'

Whether solely for financial reasons or not, the College did not officially play a leading part in the rapid expansion of the Labour College Movement after the First World War. The governors agreed to let a basement room for office purposes to the Plebs League and to the organiser of the London Council for Independent Working Class Education, which had appealed for aid.

In September 1920 they met the Plebs League executive committee in order to discuss closer collaboration but the meeting yielded few concrete results. They indicated that they were prepared to let the College be used as a central clearing house and to help train class tutors but in view of their straitened finances they did not see how to provide further support. As the strength of the local colleges increased the governors and the Principal may have become fearful that they would divert potential funds away from the College. George Sims, the secretary of the College thought otherwise and played a dominant role in forging the local classes into a close-knit organisation. When admonished by Craik for devoting so much of his time to promoting the creation of a national organisation embracing all the colleges, he replied that he was negotiating for

7. *ibid.*

the support of two unions which, if they joined the national organisation, would be well disposed towards the College.

A Manifesto Brings Unity

By the middle of 1921 several of the stronger local colleges decided that they could no longer tolerate the failure of the College to provide adequate leadership. The Manchester and Sheffield Colleges prepared a provocative manifesto which appeared as an article in the July 1921 issue of *Plebs* with the title 'The Co-ordination of Colleges and Classes.' After complaining that the College was giving scant support to the provincial classes and none to the local colleges, the authors urged the local colleges to form their own national association and to make one of its chief objects to solicit grants from trade unions and other bodies. They alleged that a number of colleges had applied for affiliation to the Central Labour College only to be informed that, whereas classes might affiliate, 'no definite reply is tendered to the affiliation of a college.'

At this stage the governors agreed to meet the executive committee of the Plebs League in order to discuss a memorandum from the latter simultaneously designed to obtain publicity for the work of the College and to foster co-ordination of the local classes. The memorandum contained four specific proposals;

1. That the Governors should print a supply of one or more *propaganda leaflets,* outlining the aims of Independent Working Class Education, and supply these gratis, or at least cost price, to the various classes. Each leaflet would carry an advert and appeal for the Labour College.

2. That the Governors should launch a *National Appeal Fund* for Independent Working Class Education, part of which would go to the classes (in proportions to be afterwards decided on). Such a National Fund would go far towards solving the problem of tutors' salaries, particularly during the summer months when most classes cease work.

3. That the Governors should permit the use of the College buildings and garden at Kew for a month or six weeks *Summer School* for intending class tutors next year. The Plebs executive would, if necessary, undertake the organisation and management of such a school, but would point out to the Governors that it might well be

possible, by appealing to unions, to grant short period scholarships, . . . to make the school a financial success.

4.   Finally, the Plebs executive committee urges the Governors to take an early opportunity of meeting representatives of the provincial classes, and discussing the whole situation and possibilities. To facilitate this, the Plebs executive committee would be glad to alter the agenda of its conference on teaching methods, arranged to take place at Birmingham on Saturday and Sunday, 8th and 9th October, so that the whole of Saturday be allotted to such discussion. (8)

Following the meeting with the Plebs executive committee the governors agreed to print propaganda leaflets, to issue short syllabuses for the use of classes and to lend the Kew premises for a month's summer school. They also decided to send three representatives to the meeting planned for October. As it was to turn out, this meeting would mark the foundation of the National Council of Labour Colleges.

The WETUC

By this time, the Plebs League was feeling its strength. Individual membership had risen to eight hundred, classes were being run in thirty centres and the sale of *Plebs* had reached a monthly total of 6,350. The volume of work had increased so much that Kathleen Horrabin had been taken on as a full-time paid assistant. The League was now convinced that it was essential to create a national organisation for providing educational programmes, and decided to convene a conference of representatives not only of the League but of the SLC, the residential Labour College, and the English and Welsh local colleges. Apart from being concerned about the need for nationwide co-ordination, it was also afraid that the WEA might make headway at the expense of the movement for independent working-class education. In 1919 the WEA had founded the Workers' Educational Trade Union Committee with the special object of getting unions to have education schemes under the sponsorship of the WEA. Without consulting the Labour colleges, the WEA offered through the WETUC to provide unions, as part of the WETUC's facilities, with access to local Labour college classes for members who wished to attend them. It was obviously hoped that by offering to provide Labour college courses in addition to WEA courses, unions would be

8. CLC Minutes.

25

tempted into the WETUC fold. The Labour colleges quickly made it clear that unions adopting WETUC schemes would be wrong to think that their members could, by means of such schemes, attend Labour college classes throughout the country.

Labour's Confusion over Education

During the period between the troubles at Ruskin College and the decision of the Plebs League and the local colleges to form a national Labour College organisation, the Labour Movement had become a power in the land but it spoke with a confused voice. The lack of clarity was notably evident in its attitude towards education. At one extreme there were those who admired the educational system as it was and simply wanted to ensure that their own children should have a reasonable opportunity to take advantage of it. At the other extreme were those who regarded the educational system as a major obstacle to social and political reform. The great majority of Labour party supporters believed that satisfactory progress could be achieved through a combination of liberal middle-class and working-class leadership. To bring about class reconciliation through education was one of the aims of the Fabian Society. Mary Stocks has also pointed out: 'It must be remembered that the early activities of the WEA were carried on within the framework of the class structure'(9). As the most respected spokesman of the WEA, R. H. Tawney argued that the great contribution of the working-classes to their country was their determination to seek reconciliation rather than conflict:

> The idea of solidarity which is the contribution of the working classes to the social conscience of our age has its educational as well as its economic applications. What it implies is not merely *la carrière ouverte aux talents*, indispensable though that is, but *egalité de fait* (real equality), not simply equality of opportunity but universality of provision. (10)

But Tawney had little time for the existing educational system: 'The aim of education is to reflect, to defend and to perpetuate the division of mankind into masters and servants.' Again and again in his writings and speeches he showed how the educational system helped to underpin the existing social system, a point which the Plebs League had taken as its first premise.

The Plebs League differed from Tawney over the question of

9. R. H. Tawney 'An Experiment in Democratic Education' in *The Democratic Tradition* (London, 1963), p.74.

10. R. H. Tawney 'Keep the Workers' Children in their place' in *ibid.*, p.51.

26

reform. Whereas he thought it possible to achieve reform by means of conciliation, the League believed that it could be achieved only if the working-class acted independently in both the industrial and political spheres and controlled their own educational arrangements and so achieve political power. For practical purposes, therefore, a battle was about to be joined between the Labour colleges and those who wished to work with and through the state educational system. The Labour colleges felt compelled to form a national organisation not only because it was the only way to negotiate nationwide schemes with the large trade unions, but also in order to counteract the influence of the WETUC which threatened to monopolize trade union education. The effective merger of the Labour colleges was to mark the beginning of a protracted campaign among trade unions and other working-class bodies to win support for the ideal of independent working-class education.

CHAPTER III

BIRTH OF THE NCLC

The first national convention of the Labour Colleges was held on 8/9 October 1921 at Yardley, Birmingham, in the old Clarion Club House. Delegates represented respectively the provincial Labour Colleges, the Scottish Labour College, the residential Labour College and the Plebs League. The meeting was chaired by Will Lawther, a CLC student from 1911-12, an active member of the Plebs League and a leading member of the Durham Miners' Union. Lawther was already a past master at jollying along audiences, and to Millar, at the time an intensely earnest young man, he seemed to spend too much time on repartee and on generally inducing an atmosphere of bonhomie instead of getting through the agenda.

The convention had originally been planned mainly in order to discuss teaching methods and only secondarily to discuss proposals for class co-ordination. But because of the interest sparked off by the Manchester and Sheffield colleges' manifesto, the executive committee placed the topic of co-ordination at the top of the agenda. J. F. (Frank) Horrabin (brother of Kathleen Horrabin), who in 1914 had taken over the editorship of *The Plebs Magazine* from George Sims, made an opening statement on behalf of the League. Born in 1884 and educated successively at Sheffield Grammar School and the Sheffield School of Art,

27

Horrabin had quickly established himself as a successful national journalist and illustrator and a pioneer of strip cartoons. He was an ardent and active supporter of the Labour College movement and its most sophisticated propagandist, abetted by his first wife, Winifred, also a graduate of the Sheffield School of Art who became honorary secretary of the Plebs League. Horrabin began by recapitulating the list of proposals already put forward to the governors of the CLC, which the Plebs League considered should be adopted without delay. He pointed out that 'a small group had been responsible for running *The Plebs Magazine* and for the propaganda which had resulted in the establishment of the Labour College.' Other groups besides the Plebs League had since founded non-residential colleges or class centres and to co-ordinate their activities had now become the prerequisite of further progress. To foster co-ordination the League had proposed to the governors that propaganda leaflets on behalf of the College should be distributed widely; syllabuses should be printed; a national appeal for funds should be launched; the governors should permit the use of the College buildings at Kew for an annual summer school to be attended by serving and potential class tutors. Horrabin observed that several unions which could not afford to finance two-year scholarships might well be willing to award summer school scholarships at Kew.

C. Charleton, who represented the NUR on the Board of the CLC, was at pains to stress that the governors and the Plebs League were not synonymous as some people seemed to think. Although initially in the hands of the Plebs movement, the Labour College was now run 'on business lines' by a Board representing the SWMF and the NUR, and was quite distinct from the Plebs League. In determining policy the governors had to take note that 'a large number on the railways were not sympathetic to the Labour College or the Plebs League. Up to a month previously the Labour College had cost the NUR £15,000. The SWMF had spent a similar amount.' The governors agreed with the first two proposals listed by Horrabin and to the use of the Kew premises for a summer school, provided attendance was to be on a non-residential basis. Before agreeing to the residential use of the buildings, however, they would have to consult their unions. The duty of the College was to train full-time students from the mines and the railways, not to train class tutors in general. Its main problem was a perpetual shortage of money. That morning at Unity House, headquarters of the NUR, there had been a meeting to discuss the need for economy. Charleton said that his union would be in a tight corner financially for the next year or two. It had tried to arrange meetings with other unions in order to obtain their financial support for the College, but only a few unions had accepted invitations, although several had expressed general support for the College. The Union of Postal Workers had turned to the WEA. As governors, he and his colleagues could not put their names to a national appeal for finance. The NUR executive had never studied the possibility of arranging classes on a nationwide scale and he did not think the NUR could give much financial support for such a venture during the following year. Doubtless the Plebs League had many suggestions to offer but they must be put in concrete form for the consideration of the governors. He could not give a firm pledge of help but would do his best to obtain one.

Speaking next, Craik said the College had been placed on a sound financial footing only since the two unions had taken it over. Although there was a 'theoretical identity between the College and the provincial classes there was a considerable diversity in the form of control; the London College was controlled by national bodies: the provincial classes were controlled by branches.' The governors were not empowered to issue appeals to trade unions on behalf of the various classes arranged throughout the country. The NUR and the SWMF intended the CLC to represent the whole Labour movement. The present was an inauspicious time to be issuing an appeal. A certain union (the Amalgamated Union of Building Trade Workers — AUBTW) had recently raised from its members a levy of 1/-d. per member for educational purposes amounting to between £1,400 and £1,500 and asked the College how it might be spent. He had recommended that the fund be split into two parts: one part should be used to send students to the College; the other should be devoted to educational activities 'in various divisions of the organisation.' The governors could assist the classes and the classes assist the College.

The delegate of the Sheffield Labour College, E. Bradshaw, concurred that the governors were not the right people to send out a national appeal. The residential Labour College was isolated from the rank and file of the working-class movement and the work of the local colleges was just as effective. The

29

business of the conference and of the bodies represented was to bring the College into close relationship with individuals and with branches throughout the country.

Intervening at this stage, Millar urged the governors to promote a publicity campaign in trade union journals. He advocated that the local colleges should launch a drive for local affiliations rather than a national appeal for funds, emphasised the necessity of trade unions taking responsibility for the education of their members and proposed that the Parliamentary Committee of the TUC be asked to finance locally-based classes. He pointed out that, because of the 'respectable' brand of education which it provided, the WEA appeared to have no difficulty in attracting press publicity.

Jack Hamilton representing the Liverpool Labour College also repudiated the proposal for a national appeal and suggested that leaflets should be circulated enjoining trade union branches to affiliate to local colleges and class groups. Many NUR branches might be expected to give more support to the local colleges. Turning to the problem of tutor training and supply, Hamilton said he did not agree with Bradshaw that the work of the provincial groups was of the same quality as that of the residential Labour College. The College employed staff exclusively as tutors whereas in the provinces the few full-time officials, of which he was one, carried out secretarial and organising duties in addition to their teaching commitments; in his own area they also had to compete with Liverpool University lecturers employed by the WEA. The College should be asked to set examinations for local college tutors in economics, industrial history and philosophy, but he did not agree that unless a candidate could pass written examinations he was incapable of teaching. Later on in the discussion Craik said his College was always ready to supply tutors if districts would pay their fees. That was an accurate statement so far as it went. Craik was well aware, however, that very few local colleges could afford to import tutors from London and he presumably made the statement as part of his attempt to prevent the influence of his college from being diminished.

One of the last speakers was George Sims, who firmly stated his conviction that the governors of the Central Labour College should support a comprehensive educational programme. 'The NUR and the SWMF must not be individualists in education.' More damage was done to Labour causes by apathetic sympathisers than by those who were openly hostile. The governors should take active steps to popularize independent working-class education, especially by appealing to the rank and file in the unions. During the prevailing economic recession they must enliven their educational work so as to ensure victory in Labour's future battles with its political opponents.

The NCLC is Founded

Finally, on a motion from the chair, it was unanimously agreed to set up a national association of Labour colleges and to invite the governors of the Central Labour College to join it. The formula was adopted with the twofold object of bringing into being a national organisation which would embrace the work of the non-residential colleges and of spurring the governors into pledging their support. The final business of the day was to appoint Bradshaw, Holder (London Council for IWCE) and Millar as a sub-committee 'to tabulate particulars of classes.'

On the following morning Millar reported back on behalf of the sub-committee that eighteen districts were represented at the convention, twelve by officially supported delegates and six by delegates who had paid their own fares and expenses. Only four districts had no affiliation scheme. The income from local affiliation schemes varied between 2d. per member in Scotland and *ad hoc*, usually nominal, grants elsewhere.

Discussion then centred on the name the new organisation should adopt. Several alternatives were considered before Millar's suggestion of 'The National Council of Labour Colleges' was eventually approved. The choice of this title was questioned by some delegates on the grounds that, properly speaking, only the Central Labour College was a true college. Yet it was a calculated choice, justified by the argument that a 'college' does not necessarily have to function in its own permanent premises or provide residential accommodation. In any case, the Edinburgh, Glasgow and Manchester colleges were occupying their own premises, although most of their classes took place in meeting-rooms scattered throughout their areas. It was agreed that each college should elect its own delegate to the Council's conferences and that in addition the Labour College governors and the Plebs League should be asked to nominate two delegates. As a first step J. Hamilton (Liverpool), J. P. M. Millar (Edinburgh) and T. D. Smith (Wolverhampton) were elected as a provisional committee, together with one representative each of the governors and the Plebs League executive committee. Subsequently George Sims was nominated to represent the residential Labour College and Mark Starr to represent the Plebs League.

In drafting the constitution an important concern was not to infringe the autonomy of the local colleges, which had no desire to lose their powers, and to differentiate between the functions of the Plebs League and those of the residential college. The new central organisation was, therefore, not to interfere with the work of the provincial colleges. It was agreed that the minimum affiliation fee payable to the NCLC by each college should be one guinea. For the time being no direct request for financial assistance would be submitted to the TUC since there was no prospect of obtaining any. Instead, requests would be made to individual unions at the local and national levels with a view to building up mass support within the trade union movement and then exerting pressure on the TUC from below. On the suggestion of Eden Paul it was decided to establish relations with foreign educational organisations sharing the same views as the NCLC. Finally, it was agreed that *The Plebs*[*] — the magazine's new name — should be the recognized organ of the NCLC, although it would remain under the control of the Plebs League. (1)

The first act of the provisional committee was to appoint Jack Hamilton as its chairman, and George Sims as secretary. In view of the importance of attracting widespread support for the new institution, Millar was specifically designated press secretary. In order to create a national organisation the first essential, as the committee saw it, was to ascertain what the independent local organisations were doing and how they were composed. And here it was necessary to tread cautiously. Practically all the local colleges had welcomed the formation of a national association, but some members of the groups felt that such an association was bound to fall under the control of the right-wing trade union leaders. In Derby the SDF minority took that view and walked

1. The formal record of the inaugural meeting at Yardley is contained in Volume I of NCLC executive committee minutes as well as in the report of the NCLC's annual meeting in 1922. There is no complete record of the minutes for the period immediately following the Conference up to the end of 1923. George Sims abruptly disappeared in that year and the minute book and the account book disappeared with him.

* Hereinafter called 'Plebs.'

Jack Hamilton (Liverpool Labour College)
the first President of the N.C.L.C.

out when their opposition was of no avail. When the NCLC National Executive Committee began its work it had to give some assurance that there was 'no intention of interfering with the local organisations.' The object of the NCLC was not to centralise the organisation but to bring together class groups, colleges and district committees 'with a view to extension and mutual assistance.' For the present the committee simply wanted to collect and disseminate information likely to be of value in the local areas. To this end it asked for copies of syllabuses and the names of full-time organisers and lecturers, and other details, to build up a national picture. Although renouncing interference with local autonomy, the committee was soon in practice encouraging its colleges and class groups to follow uniform methods. Its honorary Press Secretary, Millar, was providing the press publicity urgently required to make the new association widely known and its honorary Secretary, Sims, was busy negotiating for national union education schemes with George Hicks, General Secretary of the Amalgamated Union of Building Trades Workers (AUBTW) and with officials of the National Union of Distributive and Allied Workers (NUDAW).

Progress in the First Year

The NCLC held its first annual meeting at Manchester on 4/5 March 1922 in a mood of some satisfaction. The provisional committee was able to report that in 1921 the Scottish Labour College had headed the list for the number of classes and students with 65 classes and 2200 students. Edinburgh and District had the highest numbers with 27 classes and 917 students. Liverpool and South East Lancashire came next with 19 classes each; Darlington had 17 classes with 110 students. Sheffield had 9 classes with 155 students. A group of classes in the Midlands had 207 students in attendance. Mansfield had 8 classes with 170 students. Derby had 2 classes with 42 students. London and the Home Counties had 26 classes and 386 students. The appeal for affiliation to the National Council had drawn a favourable response from twenty-three bodies 'including the great majority of existing IWCE groups.' Since the inaugural meeting a national publicity campaign had been launched. Publicity was such a valuable weapon that the provisional committee recommended each college and district to appoint a press correspondent.

The two main tasks of the meeting were to approve the

constitution and to discuss relationships with the Plebs League. The aims of the NCLC were to be :

> The education of the workers from the working class point of view, through the medium of colleges, classes and public lectures.

> The co-ordination and extension of this independent working class educational work.

> The issuing of leaflets, syllabuses etc., for the assistance of tutors and students of classes.

Affiliation was open to:

> All Labour Colleges, district and national educational organisations or *bona fide* national bodies accepting the principle of independent working-class education. Isolated classes and branches of educational organisations may join, pending the formation of district groups on payment of 5/- affiliation fee per annum, but shall not have voting power on the National Council.

Supreme power was to be vested in the annual meeting of the Council. Executive power was entrusted to a committee of six: one representative each from the CLC, the Scottish Labour College and the Plebs League and three from affiliated organisations elected at the annual meeting.

The League's New Peak

At the 1922 annual meeting of the Plebs League, held in the same place and during the same weekend as the NCLC's second conference, it was reported that the total membership of the League had reached a new peak of 600. The League's role, it was agreed, was to recruit individual supporters of independent working-class education whereas the NCLC would seek support from affiliated and donor associations. Its aim was to convince workers that education could be a boon if it were of the right kind, but a liability if it were not. Given that the resources at the disposal of the Labour and Trade Union movement were severely limited, it was misguided to squander money on orthodox education, which in any case should be provided by the state. Rather, all Labour resources should be devoted to working-class education as interpreted by the NCLC, which the state as then constituted would not finance.

An offer from the Plebs League to nominate two representatives to a joint Publications Committee was accepted by the NCLC annual meeting. In addition, the meeting passed a

34

resolution formally recognising that the Plebs League should be the NCLC's source of 'Literature':

> That in view of the fact that all financial responsibilities for the issue of the *Plebs Magazine*, textbooks etc., are undertaken by the Plebs League; the National Council recommends Colleges, districts and classes to obtain all supplies of magazines and publications direct from the Plebs Office: also, that they should consider the desirability of obtaining other literature supplies from the same source. Further that every College, district and class should make arrangements for continuing the supply of the magazine to their members and others during the summer months, and that they should guarantee payment for at least two-thirds of their usual supply, at the same time making every effort to increase the sales of the magazine. (2)

The Per Capita Scheme

In its first year of activity the NCLC's total income was £30 in guinea affiliation fees. Clearly no national organisation could thrive on that basis. A sound educational programme would necessarily be expensive. The key to solvency lay in obtaining funds from the trade unions and the co-operative societies, the only two working-class organisations in command of relatively substantial resources.

It was crucial to devise an affiliation scheme which would bring in a regular income from trade unions. When the NCLC was formed the separate colleges drew most of their income in the form of grants from local organisations in the Labour Movement and a normal class fee of 2/6d. The Edinburgh District of the SLC had decided upon a 2d. per member affiliation fee, in return for which it offered representation on its executive committee and free admission to classes. This system was eventually adopted by all the colleges and applied to all locally affiliated organisations. Its virtue as a method for financing trade union education was that it shifted the burden of payment for educational facilities away from the individual member and deprived him of the excuse that he could not afford to take advantage of the opportunities offered, and produced a bigger income than donations. It was also easy to administer.

As a national organisation pledged to offer educational

2. NCLC Mss.

facilities to trade unionists all over the country, the NCLC could not expect to function with a fee as low as 2d. per member. For one thing its constituent colleges were mainly confined to industrial areas and a new way had to be found of serving other areas. In return for an affiliation fee of 3d. per member, the NCLC nationally offered to any union free access for all its members to classes and day schools and free branch lectures together with free postal courses and a seat on the NCLC executive committee as well as seats on divisional and college committees. Union cards were the tickets of admission to classes. Obtaining the affiliation of trade unions proved to be an arduous and protracted task. Since the NCLC adopted the strategy of gaining grass roots support, it had initially to rely mainly upon persuading local branches to affiliate to the local colleges. Accordingly, it was not just a question of approaching one central headquarters after another in London, Glasgow or Manchester but of soliciting local affiliation fees from a chain of local branches and persuading those branches to urge their unions to affiliate at the national level. As early as 1923 the NCLC executive committee sent out a general circular to all colleges and class groups exhorting them to ensure that friendly branches would send to the annual meetings of the unions a motion instructing their national executive committees to affiliate to the NCLC. Sometimes the executive committees of trade unions were put under pressure to resist it. C. T. Cramp of the NUR, for example, influenced no doubt, by the cost of maintaining the CLC forbade local branches to use their funds to pay local Labour College affiliation fees of 2d. per member but said that, if they could raise the required amount voluntarily, they could pay by that means.

The early Minutes of the NCLC confirm that, when Millar was not lecturing at weekend schools or conferences, he spent much of his time at union national annual meetings, lobbying delegates to support motions for national affiliation, discussing tactical ways and means of extending union support and obtaining information for new campaigns. Usually he had to operate in the background but occasionally he was invited to address the delegates. On one occasion, after he had addressed the Upholsterers' union's annual conference, his speech was published as a pamphlet entitled *Why Trade Union Education?*

On another occasion when he arrived at the annual meeting of the Trades Union Congress he found that the two elderly delegates of the small Plasterers' Union, which was affiliated to the NCLC, had agreed to drop their union's motion endorsing the NCLC's educational policy in order to give a clear run to a composite motion in favour of a WEA proposal. He persuaded them to return to the Standing Orders Committee and to withdraw their consent. They did so, but Millar himself was in consequence expelled from the Congress by the Standing Orders Committee for alleged interference with the Conference business. He was seen out of the conference hall by a senior official, Vincent Tewson, who was later to become General Secretary. Millar attended all subsequent Congresses without similar treatment.

The First National Union Scheme
The first trade union to affiliate on a nationwide basis was the Amalgamated Union of Building Trades Workers (AUBTW) which had 65,000 members. Before deciding to adopt the NCLC scheme the AUBTW invited Craik and Mactavish, the WEA General Secretary, to state the case for their respective associations, at its annual conference in 1922. The delegates then cast 59 votes in favour of the NCLC to 1 against. When the executive committee explored the practical implications of adopting the NCLC scheme they discovered that the members of the union were either lukewarm or hostile. A sub-committee looked into the matter and reported:

> In the first place we have attempted to gauge the opinions of our members generally towards education by going through the correspondence received from branches upon the matter. They can be summarised under the following heads:
>
> 1. Those who give unqualified support
> 2. Those who object to paying for education
> 3. Those who object to the amount of the levy (1/- per member was proposed)
> 4. Those who object to paying without a ballot
> 5. Those who object to any kind of education
>
> Nos. 2, 3, 4 and 5 may be regarded, we believe, as objections to education. In our opinion, or in the opinion of anyone who has an understanding of what independent working-class education means, and its absolute necessity at the present time, the objections

George Hicks, the General Secretary of the A.U.B.T.W.

arise from the fact of its not being understood by the mass of its members. (3)

The union thereupon decided that its first task was to help its members to understand why they should set about educating themselves. Accordingly the union circulated a special pamphlet entitled *Our Next Step — Education*, written and illustrated by Horrabin.

Under the scheme a shilling per member was to be earmarked for educational expenditure. 9d. was to be allocated to the NCLC and 3d. for the support of scholarships at the CLC. In 1923 9d. per member was a substantial amount designed to give the NCLC an effective start. Those concerned with the negotiations hoped that, as other unions followed suit, it would be possible to reduce the AUBTW's affiliation fees. The union was to be represented on the NCLC executive and its divisional councils, while its branches would have seats on the College committees. Every division of the union was to be catered for, the remote areas by the formation of study circles and the introduction of postal courses. For the editor of *The Plebs* the scheme was an expression in concrete form of 'a real Labour educational policy and scheme such as we have been advocating "since our day began — educationally".' To launch the scheme the AUBTW issued a green pamphlet entitled *Education Fund Manifesto*, for which Horrabin furnished in large hand-drawn type the slogan: 'What's the use of having a trade union ticket in your pocket if your boss has your head in his?'

NUDAW Joins Next

The second national union to affiliate, in May 1923, was the National Union of Distributive and Allied Workers (later called USDAW), which then had a membership of 86,000. The official primarily responsible for obtaining this union's affiliation was John Jagger, the full-time President and a Plebs League supporter. He was backed by Ellen Wilkinson, another full-time official, and other Plebs League supporters. In return for an affiliation fee of 3d. per member, which would provide an aggregate income of roughly £1,000 per annum, the NCLC contracted to provide similar facilities to those available to the AUBTW. The union would also fund six scholarships to the residential Labour College in 1923/24 and five scholarships in 1924/25. The whole scheme was estimated to cost £3,000 per annum.

3. *Plebs*, 1922, p.382.

In the event, NUDAW found it difficult to face all the agreed cost and the total number of union members taking advantage of the scheme turned out at first to be relatively small. Within a year the union was seriously considering whether or not to abandon the scheme. It decided to persevere only after Millar had intervened to say that it would be wrong to judge the scheme's viability on such a short term of trial. Nevertheless, NUDAW decided to jettison the plan to finance residential scholarships.

One of the NCLC's most important early achievements was to obtain the affiliation of the Amalgamated Engineering Union (AEU). At its National Committee meeting in 1923, under the influence of Labour College supporters, the AEU made provision in its rules for independent working-class education. No action was taken, however, mainly because the General Secretary was favourably disposed to the WEA. A letter from Millar protesting at the lack of action was ignored. Branch pressure resulted in a proposal to affiliate to the NCLC appearing on the agenda for its annual meeting in 1924. At that meeting the counter-arguments of the General Secretary and other speakers were decisively overcome by a group of delegates led by a blunt Clydesider, Tommy Clark, who subsequently became a full-time member of the AEU executive committee and a member of the NCLC executive committee. Millar waiting on tenterhooks outside the conference room heard the rumble of battle go on for what seemed hours.

When the NCLC executive committee met the AEU executive to discuss administrative and financial arrangements they were offered a composite sum of £1,000 per annum but not the affiliation fee of 3d. per member. The AEU executive justified this limited offer on the grounds that they were hard up. Later, when the first payment was made, a member of the AEU executive committee informed Millar that the prestige of his union was alone worth a great deal of money to the NCLC. That was true, but it was fortunate for the finances of the NCLC that George Hicks, a member of the deputation to the AEU, pledged that his union would continue paying 6d. per member, the amount to which his affiliation fee had been reduced. In addition to the AEU, the Electricians' Union, the Sheet Metal Workers' Union and the Tailors' and Garment Workers' Union adopted NCLC schemes in 1924.

Within the NCLC movement the account of how it gained the

allegiance of one trade union became a legend. In the 1920's the full-time organising tutor for the Liverpool College and President of the NCLC, Jack Hamilton, persuaded a member of the Liverpool Carters' Union to raise the question of affiliation. Hamilton's version of what then happened indicates the kind of workmen often attracted by the NCLC. Whereas the carters were rough and ready and poorly paid, their General Secretary had social pretensions. He opposed affiliation to the NCLC in favour of the WEA. A meeting of the members was summoned to hear the views of representatives of the two rival organisations. Hamilton, capable but then unimposing in appearance, was to speak for the NCLC. The case for the WEA was to be put by Mactavish. Lots were drawn to determine the first speaker, and Hamilton lost. Mactavish then rose to speak and drew from his waistcoat pocket a gold watch attached to what also appeared to be a gold chain. He laid the watch on the table where he could easily see the time. Hamilton at once sensed a hostile reaction among the impecunious carters and felt that no matter how he might present his case, the gold watch had already undermined Mactavish's advocacy. He may well have been right since the carters voted to affiliate to the NCLC.

Progress in the Unions

The NCLC's printed report for 1924/25 records that in 1923/24 five unions, apart from hundreds of branches with local scheme, had NCLC educational schemes — the AUBTW, the NUDAW, the Mid-and-East Lothian Miners, the West Lothian Miners and the National Union of Shale Miners and Oil Workers. It went on record that in 1924/25 the following additional unions had affiliated, a few of them having previously supported the WEA:

        Amalgamated Engineering Union
        Derbyshire Miners
        Sheet Metal Workers and Braziers
        Plasterers, Granolithic and Cement Workers
        Managers and Overlookers
        Tailors and Garment Workers
        Liverpool and District Carters and Motormen
        Fife Reform Miners
        Lanarkshire Miners
        Stirlingshire Miners

By the following year the NCLC report showed that the unions with Labour college schemes had further increased to 28. The list of unions, as before, included those with NCLC limited schemes as well as those paying affiliation fees for full educational schemes direct to the SLC or the NCLC. The Labour College movement had by 1925 obtained further support from what were described as associated bodies which made grants to the NCLC insufficient to provide educational facilities. These union bodies numbered thirteen and included the TUC, the STUC and the National Federation of Building Trades Operatives. The NCLC reports now also showed that many unions not affiliated to the NCLC nationally had branches which were affiliated to the local Labour Colleges.

The overriding problem for the NCLC was that few union executives considered providing education for their members as a necessary function. Even some of those who were well disposed continued to equate education with academic studies in schools and universities. At annual conferences the TUC often debated resolutions demanding equality of educational opportunity for the young. Then, as still in 1976, there was little enthusiasm for devising an integrated, nationwide educational programme for working men and women that would reflect the specific interest of the Labour movement as a whole. No British union went to the length of the Amalgamated Clothing Workers' Union in the United States by introducing a regulation that:

> all members admitted to the union shall be considered
> on probation for the period from one to two months and
> because of this not entitled to vote at local meetings
> unless they pass before the combined local education
> and membership committee an examination on a
> number of standard questions relating to the industry,
> the immediate tasks, the final goal and organisational
> structure of the union. (4)

The Scottish TUC

Two of the exceptions to the general lack of enthusiasm for workers' education among many trade union leaders were to be found among the South Wales Miners and in Scotland. Andrew Clark, General Secretary of the Mid and East Lothian Miners, was mainly responsible for his union becoming the first to pay a per capita grant to the Labour College Movement. In 1921 the STUC requested its parliamentary committee to explore the

4. Workers' Educational Bureau (U.S.A.), *Annual Report (1921)*, p.59.

possibility of acquiring the SLC or, alternatively, of creating an education department 'to foster and develop education along the lines adopted by the aforesaid college.' The 1922 Congress of the STUC passed the following motion:

> That this Congress considers that the present period of reaction and apathy through which the organised workers are passing, and which is due primarily to the economic depression of the time, could, in our opinion, be greatly obviated if the working class were educated to the full knowledge of their position as the wealth producers of society. This Congress, therefore, earnestly appeals to all affiliated societies to assist in the further-ance of the movement for independent working-class education, and that they consider and decide on the question of giving financial support to the Scottish Labour College and Labour College, London. (5)

The 1924 Congress of the STUC recommended that, in ex-change for representation, an annual grant of £50 be paid to the SLC.

Limited Schemes

Grudgingly, during its formative years, the NCLC negotiated six limited schemes with unions which were about to enter into an agreement with the WETUC. For example, Britain's largest union, the Transport and General Workers' Union, offered £50 each to the WETUC and the NCLC for educational facilities. The NCLC accepted, simply to avoid leaving that field entirely clear to the WETUC and in the hope of increasing the shabby payment later. This union's national officials, until Jack Jones' time, were WEA in outlook.

Whereas, after their unions affiliated to the NCLC, some general secretaries keenly supported the scheme, a substantial minority failed to do so. Furthermore, whereas the AUBTW for a time raised a shilling per member for educational purposes, the executives or general secretaries of several unions besides the AEU tried to avoid paying the modest standard fee of 3d. per member. Indeed, it sometimes happened that the executive committee of the NCLC had to reject applications for affiliation because unions would not pay the standard fee. An interesting example of this attitude was that of the English printers organised in the Typographical Association. When pressed to

5. *STUC Annual Report,* (1922).

affiliate by some of its members, the executive committee declined to pay the standard affiliation fee even though aware that the Scottish Typographical Association was paying the full amount. Instead, it offered to pay the class or postal course fees only for those members who took postal courses or attended classes. These fees did not cover the real cost. Knowing from his experience with the Scottish Typographical Association, which had affiliated earlier, that printers were particularly keen on education, Millar took the risk of accepting the offer. He then made an exceptional effort to recruit students. When, at the end of the first year, the NCLC's bill was submitted to the union's executive it was for a sum considerably in excess of the standard affiliation fee. Thereupon the executive invited Millar to see them and two or three of the members, identified by Millar as WEA sympathisers, accused him of the rare fault of enrolling too many students. Nevertheless, the committee drew the correct moral from the episode and agreed henceforth to pay the standard fee. By no means all the NCLC's encounters with unsympathetic executives anxious to save money ended so favourably.

The Labour Party

Although the bulk of the NCLC's national income continued to come from the unions it also received grants from the Labour Party, the Co-operative Union, the General Federation of Trade Unions, overseas unions and from Co-operative societies both local and national. The NCLC was always anxious to provide a national educational scheme for the Labour party. Its National Executive, like the TUC General Council, usually contained a majority of 'orthodox educationists.' Another difficulty was that the Party was always hard up. Its fee for individual members was trifling. Even in 1955 the fee was only 6d. per member per month minimum. At its Annual Conference in 1921, when the Party's minimum membership fee was only 1/- per annum for male members and 6d. for female members, the Party Conference passed a resolution in favour of the Labour College, though Ramsay Macdonald — always opposed to independent working-class education because it was Marxist — detracted from its value by remarking that the executive did not wish 'to undertake the duty of being a universal Correspondence College.' Some members of the National Executive felt that the Party simply could not afford an educational programme except for the training of constituency agents. The NCLC therefore continued to direct its energies to securing affiliation at the local constituency level at the rate of 2d. per member in return for the free admission to classes and in this had a good deal of success. When the party executive eventually became an associated body it was given one seat on the NCLC executive in return for its annual grant of £100, but this provided no free education and the party had to pay the expenses of its own representative.

The CLC Crisis

Scarcely one year after its foundation the NCLC had to surmount a tragedy when one after the other the three senior officials associated with the Central Labour College, now known as the Labour College London, turned out to be guilty of misusing some of the College funds. The first sign of trouble came when Sims disappeared into the East End of London and was subsequently dismissed by the Governors on 23 August 1923. Later Craik left for the continent and was formally dismissed on 23 February 1925. Later still the Governors discovered that Foot of the NUR, who acted as their secretary and their agent in dealing with the consequences of the defalcation, had himself been involved and was charged with theft. The three men were close friends. Craik and Sims had virtually created the College and had made tremendous sacrifices for it. What had caused them to endanger its reputation and ruin themselves was never fully discovered. After Sims disappeared Millar went to his room to try to collect the NCLC's Minute Book and Account Book. Neither was there but he did find batches of Irish Sweepstake tickets. Later, Winifred Horrabin informed him that Craik had met Jimmie Thomas (General Secretary of the NUR and a household political name) at a race meeting. It looked therefore as if the three men had taken to gambling.

Craik and Nupe

When Craik returned from the Continent no action was taken against him. What did happen was that a former CLC student, Bryn Roberts, who had become the General Secretary of the small National Union of Corporation Workers (later the National Union of Public Employees) and was building it into a very large union, appointed Craik as Editor of the union journal.* Roberts had a gift for picking out able people to help him to build up his union. Thanks to his predecessor, Jack Wills, the union had earlier affiliated to the NCLC. When Roberts

*While nominally remaining Editor himself.

succeeded him Roberts didn't increase his payments to the NCLC although his membership rapidly increased. This annoyed the NCLC Executive. He rarely attended the meetings and when Strawbridge, the Chairman, found himself on the way to the NCLC's Annual Conference at Coberhill near Scarborough he was astonished to find Bryn Roberts on his way to the Conference too. When, however Strawbridge chaffed Roberts on putting in an appearance the latter at once made clear that his real object was to try to persuade some NCLC organisers to give up their jobs and join his organising staff. Some time later he also tried to persuade Millar to give up his NCLC post and take over control of the union's Central Office. He continued to grossly underpay the NCLC and, eventually, to avoid the continuous pressure of the NCLC Executive for adequate payment, he took his union out of the NCLC all together without a qualm. Thus the Labour College Movement was rewarded for his long residential college scholarship and for his being appointed as the General Secretary by an NCLC union. What he didn't achieve was to become a member of the General Council of the TUC — he had blotted his copybook in the eyes of too many NCLC Unions.

In total, while Bryn built up a big union, he recruited only one NCLC Organiser, Albert Knight. Recently, shortly before giving a lecture on the NCLC to the National Labour Museum in London, Albert told Millar that the Union had paid dearly for leaving the NCLC. The result had been that many of its officials, even years later, felt the lack of knowledge that the NCLC could have provided. When the Union was serviced by the NCLC it was clear that at that time lots of its members were more educationally handicapped than the members of the average NCLC Union.

Millar becomes General Secretary

After the departure of George Sims, Millar was appointed General Secretary of the NCLC and his work as press and publicity secretary was amalgamated with the general secretarial work. His salary was to be £250 per annum, £10 less than he was receiving as the staff tutor of the Edinburgh district of the SLC. Throughout the entire succeeding history of the NCLC Millar was destined to be its chief executive officer. Born in Edinburgh on 17 April 1893 of lower middle class parentage, he was educated at an old fee-paying school, Musselburgh Grammar School. Like his father before him, who was an accountant, he was attracted to an office career. He had learned from his father

J. P. M. Millar, General Secretary of the N.C.L.C.

that in most efficient offices which took in apprentices, the apprentices were paid in the first few years in accordance with a fixed scale. A boy who managed to enter at sixteen earned the same salary to start with as a boy who went in at seventeen or eighteen and his annual increments were of the same amount. Millar therefore decided that the sooner he started work the better, since he had every intention of carrying on his education in his spare time. He left school three months before he became sixteen, after passing an examination, educational, personal and medical, which gave him an apprenticeship in the head office in St. Andrew's Square, Edinburgh, of a Scottish insurance company. This office normally took on apprentices about seventeen years of age. At the time St. Andrew's Square was reputed in Edinburgh to be the richest square in the world because it contained so many head offices of banks and insurance companies. Millar's father had ascertained that the future anti-capitalist was more likely to carve out a comfortable bourgeois career in insurance than in the Civil Service, the railways or banking, because the salaries of the insurance general managers were the highest.

Millar continued his education on a part-time basis. In the evenings he attended classes in Musselburgh and at the Royal High School in Edinburgh. Being fired with ambition to become a writer, he enrolled for the first postal course* on literary training run by *T. P's Weekly* correspondence institution. Encouraged by the laudatory comments of his ghostly tutor he went on to complete the advanced course. He also set about providing his school with its first magazine *The Grammarian* — unlike *Plebs,* a considerable financial success thanks to the numerous advertisements. This early insatiable taste for writing gave Millar a facility with words which he never lost and put endlessly to use as a vigorous polemicist and editor of *Plebs* and various NCLC leaflets, pamphlets and textbooks. Along with Bertrand Russell, James Maxton, Sir Norman Angell and others he contributed a section of *We Did Not Fight,* 1914-18 experiences of war resisters.

Like most men of similar social status Millar's father, who became chief accountant in the office of Edinburgh's City Chamberlain, was, when Millar left school, a Conservative. Millar took a youthful interest in politics at that time and inherited his father's beliefs and prejudices. Then in 1910 the

*His earliest postal course was an American one on Hypnotism. Of that his younger brother was the main victim!

46

family went to spend their holiday at a small hamlet called Pomathorn near Penicuik. Here he met and fell under the influence of James Robertson, a railway signalman. Robertson was one of the early socialists and a keen member of the ASRS, one of the more militant trade unions. His favourite paper was *The Clarion.* Trains between Edinburgh and Peebles were infrequent and the signal box was quiet. Time and again, despite railway rules which obliged him to crouch down out of sight when trains passed in case there might be an inspector on board, Millar went to the signal box with Robertson and they argued interminably about politics. Eventually Millar concluded he was on the wrong political side and he became a member of the Edinburgh Central Branch of the ILP and of the Clarion Cycling Club which carried socialist pamphlets into the country villages.

One day Robertson told him that if the trade unions and the Labour Party were to usher in a new type of society they would first need a new type of education. In his own terms Robertson proceeded to state the Plebs case for independent working-class education. At first Millar, who thought of education as exclusively confined to the type provided by schools and universities, resisted Robertson's arguments. In the end Robertson convinced him. During their discussions Robertson told him about the CLC, the Plebs League and the *Plebs.* Millar then became a member of the Plebs League and a collector of 6d. subscriptions for the CLC. He also enrolled for a CLC postal course on industrial history. Though that course and the other CLC courses he took afterwards were brief and primitive as compared with the courses later produced by the NCLC, they inspired Millar with a desire to spend a year at the residential college.

The Classical Socialists

As a result of his contact with the CLC and the Plebs League, Millar was introduced to the works of the classical socialist writers. The materialist conception of history threw an entirely new light on the past and on the class-struggles which had played such an important role in the evolution of feudalism and capitalism. As important for him was Marx's account of the capitalist system, showing that it was based on the exploitation of wage-workers who had no means of production of their own — the typist's machine and even her eraser were the property of her employer. To live, workers had to sell not their labour but their *labour power* and the capitalist reaped his profit because the value produced by that labour power was much greater than the value of the labour power.

Millar's socialist studies also turned him into an anti-militarist. When the First World War broke out he took the view, like many young socialists, that the war was essentially a conflict between competing imperialist powers. He became one of the first members of the No Conscription Fellowship and organised a branch which covered Edinburgh and the surrounding counties and later gave considerable trouble to the headquarters of Scottish Command, to the police and the local and Sheriff courts. Eventually he was conscripted, court martialled, jailed and drafted to forced labour in Home Office detention centres where he was later hired out to farmers, timber fellers and other employers. His experience in organising conscientious objectors and in establishing the Edinburgh and District Anti-Conscription League, which set out to secure the support of Labour organisations as distinct from individuals, gave him experience as an organiser which was to be useful later to the Labour College movement. Arising out of his fight against conscription he won a High Court case, which led to amendments in the second Conscription Act but which, alas, also wiped out his own small savings.

His wartime experiences in a variety of manual jobs* prepared him for the educational work he was eventually to do. Even more valuable was the fact that the vast majority of conscientious objectors were manual workers and thus he was put in close touch with the kind of men to which Labour College education was likely to appeal. His original training in clerical work and his further training when he was transferred to the Management and Investment Department of the insurance company also turned out to be of great value to him, not only as general secretary of the NCLC but as a lecturer on economics and finance

When the war ended there seemed no possibility of finding the fee of £100 required to enter the CLC. Following a visit

*In Wormwood Scrubs he was a hand sewer of mail bags, in Wakefield Gaol, a boiler stoker, than a hand-loom weaver making cloth for prisoners under-clothes, on Sir Edward Fry's estate a labourer for the carpenter and the home farm bailiff, in Guildford a cattleman, in Dumfries a timber feller and in Edinburgh a worker in some tomato hot houses but in this case only for a few days because the other workers threatened to strike unless he was "kicked out."

to Edinburgh by W. W. Craik, Millar's father persuaded an aunt to pay the whole course fee of £100 on condition that the balance of the expense involved would be met by someone else. The college course lasted two years but, having had the advantage of a longer school education than most of the other students and having been a postal student and learned much through Plebs educational work studied in Wakefield prison, Millar was able to complete the essential curriculum in one year. Towards the end of the course Craik was most anxious that he should become the full-time tutor in the Labour College evening and Sunday class programme in Vernon Hartshorn's area of the SWMF. Millar declined the post. For one thing, he wished to return to Edinburgh where he had been offered a financially less secure post at a salary of £5 per week, if the money could be raised, as the first organising tutor. Another reason was that he had fallen in love with Christine Hastie, a young Edinburgh teacher who had attended the SLC classes which he had started before he went to London.

Christine Millar

Christine Davidson Hastie was born in Edinburgh and educated successively at James Gillespie's School, Boroughmuir School and Moray House Teachers' Training College. She became a school teacher, the usual occupational outlet at that time for girls of good family. While at Moray House she had devoted free periods to voluntary work in two play centres for under-fives living in slum areas. That experience stirred her social conscience and led her to abandon the Conservative traditions of her family. Not long after Christine started teaching her father died, leaving his widow with a young son and a schoolgirl to provide for. As the sole breadwinner, in addition to teaching through the day, Christine was soon teaching at night school — first on two, then on three and finally on four evenings a week. Two of her classes were held in the Royal High School, Edinburgh, where many of her students were unemployed young men, including discharged soldiers. Through her friendship with Arthur and Barbara Woodburn she met a number of socialists and was introduced to Jim Millar. Soon Millar had interested her in the SLC and to it she switched her allegiance from the WEA, of which she was a member. She was the sort of young woman who throws herself energetically into work for deserving causes.

Early in her professional career she had led a successful local

49

campaign for better pay for young teachers. Her supporters, appreciating her untiring energy, not only made her a presentation but were responsible for her election to the Executive Committee of the Leith branch of the Educational Institute of Scotland. Her fellow members of the Committee were considerably senior and included headmasters and deputy headmasters. In energy and organising ability she and Millar were well matched.

Millar and Christine were married in Edinburgh on 11 August 1923 by the Sheriff, with J. F. Horrabin, editor of *Plebs*, and Winifred Horrabin, Honorary Secretary of the Plebs League, as witnesses. Theirs was to be an enduring happy union and one which led to an astonishing output of work over a long period of time. Christine helped Millar to build up and run the NCLC and in one capacity or another laboured along with him to keep it alive and flourishing. In their own way the Millars were to play a husband and wife role in the Labour Movement which was less widely known to the general public but worthy of comparison with the careers of the Webbs and the Coles. During Millar's frequent absences from the office Christine acted as deputy general secretary.

Christine has wittily described the administrative confusion that she stepped into when, as an unpaid and — to put it mildly, an over-worked secretary, she started helping her husband with the task of making independent NCLC units into a coherent national organisation, and preparing the first complete national directory and report entitled: *The National Council of Labour Colleges: History, Report and Directory:*

> In the first week I seemed to be surrounded by hatters' boxes, biscuit tins, and shoe boxes. Tile hats had gone out of fashion, and a few secretaries of local study groups had somehow acquired discarded tile-hat boxes which they used for filing student lists, minutes, syllabuses, and other documents. This heterogeneous mass was now arriving at the Central Office so that we could weigh up the whole position and build up a directory. I was no time study expert and I had no equipment. All I had was the NCLC's regional outline for 12 divisions — and the boxes and tins; so as a novice, I laid out the records alphabetically according to town or county — all over a floor 22 feet square. And when stooping made my back ache I crawled on all

50

fours from Auchenshuggle to Ystradgynlais, so to speak. But in the afternoons as the Supervisor of the new postal courses department* I had, as equipment, one table and one box-file with 100 cards; and it took from the summer of 1923 to 1924 to get names on 99 cards, i.e. to secure 99 postal course enrolments. (6)

When Millar became General Secretary of the NCLC he was still very young and unfamiliar with the top circles of the trade union movement. Without explicitly assuming the role of a mentor, George Hicks took every opportunity of introducing him to the leading officials. For several years Hicks brought him on to the platform at the annual conference of the TUC. Hicks also gave him a printed card on which he was described as the AUBTW's Education Officer for Scotland and this afforded him access to all the union's Scottish branches. NCLC organisers were given similar cards in England, Wales and Northern Ireland.

NCLC Organised into Divisions

Following the formal inauguration of the NCLC, Labour Colleges including class groups increased in numbers from 37 to 91 within fifteen months. By the 1924/25 year** there were 139 colleges and class groups of which 37 were in the latter category. The difference between a labour college and a class group was that the former had machinery for accepting the affiliation of union branches and other Labour bodies and these each had a seat on the local College committee. The class groups had not yet reached that stage.

It was in 1923 that it was agreed to organise the Labour Colleges throughout the country into eleven divisions, Scotland being Division 10 and Northern Ireland Division 11. Later, a twelfth Division with its centre in Nottingham was organised. Some of the more populated divisions were divided into two areas with an organiser responsible for each area. Colleges usually met monthly; divisional councils met quarterly. Some

*A railway postal student in a country signal box who tried to enrol agricultural workers for postal courses said he had failed "because they distrust anything that doesn't come from seed." Fortunately, agricultural workers are different today but are sometimes still in some cases victimised for union activity.

6. Extract from a speech given on the occasion of her retirement (NCLC MSS.)

**The NCLC's year was later changed to the calendar year.

Map showing the DIVISIONS of the National Council of Labour Colleges

IRELAND
11

J.F.H.

divisions appointed an executive committee, to which the full-time organiser acted as secretary while also serving as secretary to the Council. The main function of the Council was to oversee and help to extend the educational provision of the colleges, this provision being in time broadly planned by the organiser under the supervision of the NCLC Central Office. A not unimportant function of the Council members was to take back to the colleges and the unions reports on the work in the divisions. As the number of affiliated unions increased it became important for the union representatives on the divisional councils to bring suggestions for improving the service to their branches and to interest their members in the NCLC's work. As early as 1923 it was also decided to keep standardised divisional accounts. Once a month each organiser had to send a copy of his accounts to Central office while retaining one for himself.

The NCLC Invades Ireland

At the beginning of 1924 the NCLC's only class group in Ireland was in Belfast, where a voluntary tutor, Hugh Gemmell, was the leading spirit. That situation was soon to change. The second international conference on workers' education, sponsored by the International Federation of Trade Unions, was held at Oxford in 1924 and Millar reported to his Executive Committee in September 1924 that he had seized the opportunity of discussing with the Irish delegates the prospects of developing independent working-class education in Ireland. He had talked to Duffy of the Irish Union of Distributive Workers, O'Brien of the Irish Transport Workers, Mansfield of the Irish Teachers Union and Johnstone, the secretary of the Irish Labour Party and TUC, who were all greatly interested. He had informed them that the NCLC executive might soon be considering the appointment of an organiser for Ireland in view of the fact that some of its unions had Irish members, particularly in Ulster. At that time these unions were few, but included the AUBTW, the NUDAW and the AEU. Millar had also been influenced by the fact that the ILP in Belfast was proposing to start an educational group.

On returning to his Edinburgh office Millar made arrangements to hold conferences of all Labour organisations in Belfast and Dublin districts respectively. Over 300 delegates attended the Belfast conference. A conference almost as large and quite as representative was held in Dublin on the following day with

William O'Brien, General Secretary of the Irish Transport Workers' Union, in the chair. Millar addressed both conferences.

At the next meeting of the NCLC executive Millar reported on the success of his visit. He recommended that an organiser be appointed for Belfast and Northern Ireland but that it would be inadvisable to appoint an organiser for Dublin and the South unless the purely Irish unions were willing to give their support. The strength of nationalist feeling in the Irish unions, as distinct from the British unions with branches in Ireland, was so strong that the suggestion they should co-operate with the NCLC in Southern Ireland fell on stony ground. Instead they decided, following the NCLC's conference in Dublin and visits of active members to an NCLC's summer school in Rothesay, Scotland, to start some educational work on their own.

Shortly afterwards the NCLC executive appointed Albert Ellis, a member of the AEU, as the first organiser for Northern Ireland. The bulk of the AEU Irish membership was in the Belfast area, as was the whole Irish membership of NUDAW. It was not, however, until years later that the Northern Ireland committee of the Irish TUC affiliated to the NCLC.

By 1925 the NCLC had become far more centralised than had seemed likely or even possible at the inaugural meeting four years earlier but centralisation was absolutely essential if the NCLC was to operate efficiently and to support the colleges where they were weak and bring colleges into existence where they did not previously exist. In 1925 the constitution of the NCLC was amended. Its objectives were summarised as follows:

> To provide independent working-class education in order to help the workers to develop their capacities and to equip them for their trade union, Labour and co-operative activities in the work of bringing an end to the system of capitalism and enabling the workers to achieve their social and industrial emancipation.

And its methods were:

> Colleges, classes, correspondence courses, summer schools, public lectures, trade union schemes, the issuing of pamphlets, outline lectures etc. (7)

Correspondence Courses

Very shortly after its foundation the NCLC recognised that it

7. A copy of the original consitution is among the NCLC MSS. The amended constitution is contained in Volume 1 of the NCLC Executive Committee Minutes.

could not provide a nationwide service to trade unions by relying solely upon a network of local colleges overwhelmingly located in industrial urban and mining areas. One solution was to introduce a scheme of correspondence courses, which would incidentally have a variety of other advantages. Mactavish, General Secretary of the WEA had appreciated this fact but had not acted upon it. (8) The CLC had provided a few rudimentary courses by means of postal tuition as well as some full lecture notes for the use of voluntary tutors. Its correspondence courses consisted of *(a)* small four-page leaflets containing a short list of recommended books and *(b)* the titles of essays which the students were required to write. The NCLC decided that in place of this very limited CLC scheme it should establish a vigorous postal tuition service with much improved courses. To that end, it set up in another empty bedroom in the Millar's flat in Edinburgh, a special department under the direction of Christine Millar. No extra funds whatsoever were at first available for advertising courses. The latent demand for postal courses, however, was revealed by the rapid rise in enrolments up to the General Strike.

Year	Union Scheme	Postal Courses	Postal Students
1923	2	3	39
1924	7	6	516
1925	13	9	1224
1926	25	12	2373

The above figures indicate that postal courses had immediately begun to play an important part in enabling the NCLC to cater for union members all over the country, and not only in the big towns. Even so, it was not realised how important the postal course service would become in future years.

CHAPTER IV

RELATIONS WITH THE WEA, THE TUC AND THE COMMUNIST PARTY

Studies of working-class education in the twentieth century usually treat the long and sometimes fierce controversy between the WEA and the Labour College Movement as a minor theme.

8. See A. J. Corfield, *An Epoch in Workers' Education* (London, 1969), p.13.

Some writers mention the Movement entirely, or almost entirely, in the context of its relations with the WEA, often portraying the NCLC as a vindictive little terrier snapping at the heels of its far more prestigious and tolerant rival.

Albert Mansbridge

Unlike the founders of the Plebs League the founder of the WEA, Albert Mansbridge, did not perceive any connection between the national education system and the social stratification of society. 'It does not matter in the least who educates', he once wrote, 'so long as the education is real'. (1) That last phrase reveals the essence of Mansbridge's thinking. He esteemed what seemed to him to be the highest middle-class values: in education, the disinterested search for truth; in social behaviour, humaneness and a firm moral purpose. Education was an end in itself, culturally enriching and spiritually ennobling. All that was wrong was that too few people enjoyed the advantages it conferred. But this was not simply because the privileged greedily monopolised it. Rather it was that no effective machinery had yet been devised for bringing together the responsible leaders of middle-class and working-class opinion. Mansbridge believed it entirely possible to harmonise the relations between social classes. In particular, he envisaged the universities, the trade unions and the co-operative societies working in unison to provide a classless educational service. Not interested in theorising about education and society, he simply wished to help energetic and aspiring workers who sought to advance themselves. That his main object was genuinely to serve workers cannot be doubted: '. . . at least three-quarters of its members should be actually labouring men and women.' There was equally no doubt in his view that what they required was not something specially tailored to their needs as workers but the best that was available in the country — for him the type of education provided by Oxford and Cambridge. Significantly, the WEA began as The Association for Promoting the Higher Education of Working Men. The key clause in its revised constitution of 1907 ran:

> . . . the Higher Education of Working People primarily by the extension of University teaching also *(a)* by the assistance of working-class efforts of a specially educa-

1. A. Mansbridge, 'Co-operation, Trade Unionism and University Extension' in *The Kingdom of the Mind* (London, 1944), p.6.

55

tional character, *(b)* by assistance in the development of a School Continuation system, *(c)* by the co-ordination of popular educational effort. (2)

Though recognising that the trade unions could not fail to have influence upon working-class education, Mansbridge did not expect too much of them. 'The educationist who would estimate the forces of the future,' he wrote, 'would be wrong if he omitted the trade unions, although in his estimate of the past he is unable to grant them, in this immediate connection, high place.' Certain other supporters of the WEA thought it could help to change the social class structure but never intelligibly worked out the implications of such a role. Mrs. Stocks correctly summed up Mansbridge's achievement by stating that by the end of the First World War the WEA had completed an important job.

> The job done was the mobilisation of the universities in the cause of working-class education, and Mansbridge did it — and having done it, passed from the immediate scene of his labours to other and allied activities. The job yet to be done was the mobilisation of the working-classes in the cause of their own education. (3)

J. M. Mactavish

Mansbridge resigned as General Secretary of the WEA in 1915 giving way to J. M. Mactavish, who, unlike Mansbridge, attached special significance to the education of trade unionists. When still a dock worker at Portsmouth he had attended the famous conference on working-class education held at Oxford in 1907 and delivered an impassioned attack on the exclusiveness of higher education: 'I am not here as a suppliant for my class. I decline to sit at the rich man's gate praying for crumbs. I claim for my class all the best of all that Oxford has to give. I claim it as a right — wrongfully withheld — wrong not only to us but to Oxford.' But although a trenchant critic of privilege, Mactavish believed that the existing education system could be modified, not least through the endeavours of the WEA. To his task as General Secretary he brought to bear energy if not finesse. In the eyes of the Plebs League his appointment was a cunning move on the part of the WEA to exploit his unorthodox

2. See T. W. Price *'The Story of the Workers' Educational Association,'* (London, 1924), p.16.

3. Stocks, *op.cit.*; p.51.

reputation as a way of penetrating into otherwise inaccessible working-class terrain.

The first scheme negotiated between the WEA and a trade union was introduced in 1919 when, following discussions led on the WEA side principally by Mactavish and G. D. H. Cole, the WEA agreed to provide for the Iron and Steel Trades Confederation regular classes and weekend schools. Members of the union would be enabled to attend classes free of charge, class fees being returnable. The scheme was to be supervised by a joint committee. Thus was inaugurated the Workers' Educational Trade Union Committee (WETUC), committed by its constitution 'to administer funds contributed by the trade unions for the purpose of providing through the agency of the Workers' Educational Association facilities for the liberal education of its members'. The Committee's operations were to be carried out by WEA staff. For the Iron and Steel Trade Confederation the scheme guaranteed an educational service at low cost.

The NCLC and WEA Conflict Grows

The foundation two years later of the NCLC served to intensify a conflict with WEA policy that dated back to the occasion of the Ruskin College strike. In receipt of public funds, the WEA was far from being dependent upon trade union finance. The NCLC by contrast could not manage to survive without ample financial support from the trade unions. Apart from reasons of educational principle, it had accordingly no alternative but to compete with the WEA in order to prevent the WEA from gathering the lion's share of the scarce money at the unions' disposal. When still tutor-organiser of the SLC, Millar declared that 'the SLC can no more go on with its work without attacking the WEA than the working-class (can) go on extending its power without "stultifying" that of the capitalists.' The Horrabins admitted that the Plebs League was aggressive:

> The long, persistent and very vigorous controversy carried on between the Plebs and the WEA (or perhaps it would be truer to say, *the persistent offensive carried on by the former against the latter**) made more and more workers aware of the principles at issue. (4)

And in a letter to Millar dated 6 January 1944 Will Coxon would later reminisce: 'Truly the pioneers had an open field. *War to the knife with the WEA* seeking debates wherever

4. J. F. and W. Horrabin, *op.cit.,* p.57.   * Our italics.

possible.' Coxon, a schoolmaster, had been Honorary Secretary of the North Eastern Labour College.

The NCLC's denunciation of university social science teaching through WEA classes acutely embarrassed some prominent people in the Labour and trade union movement, many of whom were actively engaged in WEA work, because they saw it as a valuable contribution to workers' education. Now they found the WEA being impugned as an agency for purveying, however unwittingly, capitalist economics. The NCLC suggested that those socialists who were associated with the WEA were allowing themselves to be trapped into accepting a false educational philosophy. The suggestion was resented and aroused opposition to the NCLC. For tactical reasons the opposition was publicly muted, except when university lecturers occasionally reacted strongly to what they regarded as misrepresentation of their motives and their teaching. The aggressiveness of the NCLC's campaign was bound to offend some potential allies but its leaders believed that the obstacles in its path could not be overcome in any other way in view of the clash in educational principle between the two bodies, any more than the Labour Party could advance socialist policies without attacking the Conservative Party.

The WEA's Ambivalent Attitude

What seemed to be the ambivalent attitude of the WEA towards its educational role particularly irritated the NCLC. Had the WEA been content to operate as a straightforward voluntary educational body there would have been small reason for conflict, but besides collaborating with the state system of education as well as with the universities, it also claimed to provide for the distinctive educational needs of trade union and Labour bodies. Furthermore, its leading officials were mostly avowed socialists though not 'educational socialists,' to use the NCLC's phrase.

Mactavish himself seemed to epitomise this ambivalence. He could make radical speeches that appealed to workers and ideologically he often seemed close to the NCLC. Thus, writing in the organ of the U.S.A.'s International Ladies Garment Workers' Union, he declared: 'the aim of working class education should be to stimulate class consciousness . . . equipping the workers to evolve their own social valuations, their own moral

58

standards, judgement, code of honour.' (5) Addressing the second international conference on workers' education he said that it was necessary to equip the workers 'for the class struggle' but whereas the NCLC and the Plebs League tried 'to develop the war mind, the British Labour Movement in general wished to carry on the struggle by constitutional means.' When Mactavish retired and Millar was engaged in one of his periodic forays against the WEA, he was astonished to receive from Mactavish a postcard referring to the controversy and 'wishing more power to your elbow.' (6) The appointment in 1924 of J. W. Muir as the national Organising Secretary for the WETUC (subsequently he succeeded Mactavish as General Secretary) caused Millar to write to. S. Walker, Honorary Secretary of the SLC:

> I must say I am very much surprised because of the ex-MPs, apart from Newbold, he was the last man I should have thought would accept the job. Of course, I don't know what tale the WEA people may have pitched him. They may have told him that as regards ourselves and themselves, the TUC had practically brought an end to the differences. (7)

Yet, whereas nearly all the tutors employed by the NCLC belonged to unions affiliated to the TUC, most of those employed by the WEA did not. The fact that the WEA welcomed grants from the state, with which the trade union movement was time and again locked in battle, seemed to confirm that from the socialist standpoint its alleged independence was a sham. The NCLC argued that the governing class knew what it was doing in denying the NCLC exemption from income tax on its trifling earnings from interest, while financing the WEA and allowing it like the public schools — the NCLC was very conscious of the analogy — that valuable privilege. The NCLC made several attempts to escape tax under the charity legislation but each request was turned down.

Differences of Principle

For its part, the WEA considered that the NCLC's interpretation of the function of workers' education was propagandist and one WEA'er even thought that its principles and policy antagonistic to those of trade unionism. Mary Stocks has remarked:

5. Quoted in *The Daily Herald*, 10 Feb. 1922.
6. NCLC Corr.
7. *ibid.*

'between the study of *what* to think and the study of *how* to think, a great gulf seemed to yawn, and the WEA was irrevocably committed to the latter process.' The NCLC denied the existence of this distinction in education — neither the WEA nor any other organisation could teach people how to think without teaching them what to think. The academic standards of NCLC classes were thought by the WEA to be shoddy because of its reliance upon a great number of 'unqualified' tutors, but the WEA's poor estimate of the work of the NCLC derived mainly from a refusal to take its ideological position seriously. In the pages of *Plebs* and in occasional pamphlets the ·case for independent working-class education may have been stated too polemically for the tastes of some people, but this did not justify ignoring the clarity with which the Horrabins, for example, distinguished between the two opposing interpretations of working-class education. They summarised the distinction as follows:

> One school means the *extension* of the benefits of culture, in the general sense of the term, to the class which, by reason of its lack of means and leisure, has been debarred from a full share of these benefits hitherto . . . this school regards culture as something altogether apart from, and unaffected by, the class division of society.
>
> The other school means by 'working-class education' a particular *kind* of education, aiming primarily at meeting the specific needs of the workers as a class, and undertaken by the workers themselves *independently* of, and even in opposition to, the ordinary existing channels. The second school takes the view that all human culture, past and present, has been coloured by the outlook and prejudices of successive ruling (*i.e.*, leisured) classes; and that the working-class — the great mass of humanity — will add to that culture, not merely a new 'note' of its own, but will eventually revalue all culture by the standards of its own ideals and purposes.
>
> The first group may be said, in brief, to regard Education (with a capital E) as a good in itself; the second to place the emphasis on the Working Class. (8)

Although its usual strategy was to behave as though the Labour Colleges did not exist, the WEA was nevertheless

8. *op.cit.*, pp.9-10.

concerned to remove or at least reduce their influence upon trade union education. When the First World War ended, some leading left-wing members of the WEA realised that it was essential to play an active part in the education of trade unionists for two reasons. First, education must be used as a means both of facilitating social and economic change and countering the risk of the change being violent. To ensure that use, it was imperative to become intimately connected with the trade union movement. Secondly, they realised that, if the WEA failed to act positively, then the field might well be left clear for the Labour Colleges and the Plebs League. In a recently published study A. J. Corfield has pointed out that the WETUC was not intended to be simply an adjunct of the WEA:

> At the outset it was meant to be very much more than this. It was designed to be the framework for a completely co-ordinated system of trade union educa- tion, no less. The WETUC began in 1919 before there was any nationwide rival on the field. There were, of course, the residential Central Labour College, the Plebs League and the increasingly extensive Scottish Labour College; but these were at this time only limited in their influence and very loosely and informally related.

Accordingly, Corfield continues, the WETUC was given a flexible constitution in the hope of drawing 'into the fold all the existing educational bodies.'

The Trade Union Education Enquiry Committee

Soon after the formation of the WETUC its chairman, Arthur Pugh of the Iron and Steel Trades Confederation, invited a number of trade unions to send representatives to a meeting in order to discuss the whole question of trade union education. From this meeting on 16 July 1920 there emerged a Trade Union Education Inquiry Committee, sponsored by the sixteen unions which had sent representatives. G. D. H. Cole and Arthur Greenwood, now honoured figures in the Labour Pantheon, were co-opted to the committee, which Mactavish and Arthur Pugh served as joint secretaries. Six months later the Committee submitted a report to the TUC parliamentary committee which, according to Corfield, '. . . contained a cogently argued case for extending trade-union education. The way forward was charted upon a closely surveyed map of what was being provided.' In fact, the residential Labour College, the Plebs League and the local Labour Colleges had declined a request to supply information; the SLC had done so, however, although it questioned the committee's objectives.

The report of the committee of inquiry was endorsed at the annual conference of the TUC in September 1921. Some trade union leaders hoped that the WETUC would be eligible for direct state support. A few thought this essential, including Pugh himself, who argued that to ask trade unions to undertake the total cost of providing educational facilities for their members was to impose an intolerable burden on them. The Report of the Ministry of Reconstruction's Committee on Adult Education had recommended that there be a substantial increase in public expenditure on adult education and the tenor of such reports as that of the committee in South Wales had been that the state should give due attention to the education of workers if it wished to forstall the spread of socialist ideas and industrial unrest. The TUC decided to co-operate with the Inquiry Committee:

> . . . the time has arrived when the Trade Union movement should consider the best means of providing for the educational needs of its members. It declares that the recommendations of the Trade Union Education Inquiry Committee offer the basis of a scheme whereby the varied educational needs and demands of Trade Unionists may be met.
>
> It, therefore, instructs the General Council to co-operate with the Trade Union Education Inquiry Committee as to the best means of giving effect to the aims and objects of the Inquiry, including the taking over and running of existing Trade Union Colleges, including the Central Labour College and Ruskin College. (9)

Representatives of Ruskin College, the residential Labour College and the WEA agreed to support 'any scheme eventually adopted provided it does not essentially interfere with the policy they have pursued in regard to the education of their students.' On the day of the meeting Hamilton and Millar met the governors who decided to take them along to the meeting and to present the TUC committee with a letter

> expressing surprise that no reference appears in the memorandum to the Provincial Class work carried on throughout the country by the National Council of

9. TUC, *Annual Report* (1921), p.227.

Labour Colleges and the Scottish Labour College, and that no proposals appear in the recommendations to be made to Congress as to the role which they would play in any educational scheme worked under the auspices of the Congress. Thereupon it was agreed that the Labour College governors should be accompanied by NCLC representatives at the Committee's meetings. (10)

In *The Communist* Raymond Postgate commented acidly on what he regarded as the WEA's ulterior motive for inventing the committee of inquiry;

> . . . they were in deep water and were after safety. They could no longer control a golden stream from the possessing classes; they might get hold of Trade Union funds. The long and short of it is that the General Council is now proposing to take over all working class educational organisations, Plebs League, the Labour Colleges and all and run them. And in the selection of the Committee do a deal with this the 'wets' have been too clever, much too clever. The list reads:— A. Pugh (wet), J. W. Bowden (wet), A. H. Findlay (probably a wet — he addressed the NCLC deputation with tears in his voice), C. W. Bowermen (Ruskin College), George Hicks, G. D. H. Cole (wet), J. Mactavish (wet), T. W. Burdon (wet), A. Creech-Jones (wet) and Mrs. Calthrop (wet).
>
> This is a queer story of intrigue, and the moral of it is that the revolutionary movement in education is, like the revolutionary movement elsewhere, up against some people who may not be knaves but are certainly not fools. They hoped to nobble the London Labour College for the Ruskin College type of education. They thought that if they could do so the Plebs Movement would collapse. And, a propos of that, though it may be giving a card to the enemy, I cannot refrain from telling them to look again. (11)

The NCLC's Attitude to the New Move

The NCLC formally considered the proposals for a co-operative trade union educational service at its annual meeting in March 1922. It was decided to accept them in principle

10. CLC Governing Board Minutes.
11. *The Communist*, 8 Apr. 1922, p.4.

provided that all trade union educational classes should be placed squarely under the control of the trade unions and working-class bodies and that 'the definite and avowed aim of all such classes be the education of the workers with a view to equipping them for the class struggle and aiding them in the fight for the abolition of capitalism.' Craik has aptly described this resolution as supporting the principle of 'competitive co-existence but not co-partnership.' The minutes of the residential Labour College for 30 March 1922 recorded that, at a meeting with representatives of the TUC, it had been agreed to answer two questions in the affirmative:

1. Are we prepared to join in the TUC proposal on the condition that the present educational policy of the College is maintained?
2. Are we prepared to accept government grants provided that this does not, in any way, interfere with the pursuance of the present educational policy of the College?

Not everyone in the Labour College camp was pleased at the prospect of a co-operative venture. Jack Hamilton expressed his fear to Millar that the curriculum 'would be watered down from the Marxist standard and probably a weeding-out process of Marxist tutors would follow . . . We must insist that our educational policy be unconditionally accepted before we are under TUC control.' Horrabin thought the Plebs League would countenance co-operation on condition that all the interested parties recognised what they were consenting to do:

> . . . and I don't want the controversy in public . . . We'll have the united front all right — but we'll make it clear, please, past *any* misunderstandings, that we're united on *principles.* We can make a good stunt for independent working-class education out of this if we discuss it all around fully. (12)

In its report to the TUC the Committee of Inquiry proposed that the General Council should assume responsibility for Ruskin College, the residential Labour College and the WETUC as soon as adequate funds became available. The Council should be represented on each of the governing bodies and enter into preliminary negotiations with them so as to eliminate duplication of effort. Congress did not feel financially strong enough to accept the proposal for a complete takeover but

12. Horrabin to Millar in NCLC Corr., 10 Apr. 1922.

decided to make annual grants of £250 each to Ruskin, the WEA and the residential Labour College.

Little practical progress towards co-operation was made during 1923. The TUC took a step forward by creating a special educational fund of up to £1,000 per annum and there was an abortive attempt to link Ruskin and the CLC. In *Plebs* towards the end of the year Millar wrote:

> But for the formation of the NCLC the current TUC report would almost certainly have chronicled the complete capture of the official trade union movement by the WEA, at least so far as evening class work was concerned — the most important of all our activites.

> Today the NCLC claims that it has more classes and students dealing with subjects of direct importance to the working-class movement than any other educational body, and that the Labour College Movement, bearing in mind not only the above-mentioned activities, but those of the SWMF and the NUR, has the most extensive and most notable of trade union schemes in the British trade union world. (13)

TUC Dissolves Joint Education Committee

From the NCLC's point of view 1924 was a good year. The General Council of the TUC dissolved the Joint Education Committee in March and established an Educational Advisory Committee consisting of representatives of the General Council, two representatives each of the Co-operative Union, the WEA and the NCLC and one representative each of Ruskin College and the Central Labour College. The committee's function was to hammer out a policy for educational work under the aegis of the TUC and to co-ordinate existing facilities. It invited evidence from all the providing bodies. In Millar's opinion this committee's appearance showed that 'the propaganda of the Labour College Movement is steadily driving the Trade Unions leftwards in their educational policy.' His optimism seemed to have been justified by the time the TUC annual conference took place at Hull in September. At that conference Creech Jones proposed that there should be closer co-operation in the field of workers' education, always provided that the General Council should 'exercise such measure of control over their organisations as is considered necessary in the interests of workers' education.'

13. J. P. M. Millar, 'The Second Milestone' in *Plebs*, 1923, pp.440-1.

George Hicks, General Secretary of the AUBTW, rose to move an amendment to the effect that any scheme for co-operation should adhere to the principles of the NCLC and the Labour College. He argued that there was 'no particular narrow doctrine in the education of the National Council of Labour Colleges . . . the range of subjects is quite large enough for the worker to embrace after capitalism has kept him at work during the best part of the day.' For the sake of solidarity A. J. Cook, an NCLC supporter, persuaded Hicks to drop his amendment. In the event, no specific resolution was approved. The General Council agreed to make non-recurrent grants of £100 each to the NCLC, the CLC, the WEA and Ruskin College and informed the NCLC that the award of further grants would depend on the outcome of further negotiations.

In the continuing discussions the NCLC objected to a suggestion that every trade unionist should be allowed, under the proposed TUC scheme, to choose whether he wished to attend either a WEA or a NCLC course. In its view each union had a duty to choose either the WEA or the NCLC scheme. Cole wrote to Millar: '. . . quite clearly the wildness of your constitution is going to make much more difficult than expected any attempts to strengthen ours in order to get our draft agreement through.' There was contention over the qualifications of tutors: the NCLC proposed that

> All regular full-time, part-time and voluntary tutors and all organisers should be Trade Unionists and members of a *bona fide* working-class political organisation. So far as future appointments are concerned, it is to be the educational policy of the National Joint Committee and of the organisations participating in its work to employ as Tutors or Tutor-Organisers only those
> (1) who have been trained in the Central Institutions mentioned below, and who must have had experience as Trade Unionists, or
> (2) who have taken advantage of the other educational facilities under this scheme, who have passed a satisfactory test, and have had experience as Trade Unionists. (14)

Education for Emancipation Accepted

The NCLC eventually agreed, with deep reluctance, to accept the formula that tutors should be trade unionists or members of
14. ECM, 1925.

a professional organisation and 'properly qualified both by knowledge of the subject to be taught, and by sympathy with, and understanding of, the working-class movement,' on condition that the WEA accepted as the object of the TUC scheme, and in its constitution inserted the object, 'education for social and industrial emancipation.' (15) Led by Mactavish the WEA representatives persistently objected to this object even to the extent of invoking the support of Greenwood and Cole. Hamilton and Millar insisted, however, that the key phrase should be maintained and incorporated in the constitutions of all educational bodies expecting to participate in the scheme. Millar also realised that serious damage would be done to the WEA in the working-class movement if its refusal to incorporate the phrase were to be widely publicised. In the end, the WEA representatives stated that they would not insert the phrase in their constitution but would insert it in their general statement of aims. The NCLC accepted this compromise; the WEA would still remain vulnerable to criticism.

The aims of the scheme as finally defined were: 'To provide working-class education in order to enable the workers to develop their capacities and to equip them for the Trade Union, Labour and Co-operative activities generally, in the work of securing social and industrial emancipation.' Jim Reynolds, secretary of the residential Labour College, thought this 'a bloodless, lifeless, emaciated pronouncement without any spark at all in it (which) does not indicate that our education is in any way different from orthodox education.' Millar concurred but pointed out how difficult it was to get a more satisfactory wording.

The draft scheme was discussed at the annual conference of the NCLC in May 1925. Some delegates wanted to turn it down out of hand but were admonished by Postgate, among others, that rejection would impair the chances of arranging new NCLC union schemes and indeed that some existing schemes might well be terminated. George Hicks thought that the relative flexibility of the wording gave 'a virile organisation like the NCLC the opportunity of determining the interpretation.' The scheme was finally adopted by a majority of 31 votes to 6.

The TUC Scheme
The main TUC proposal was to set up a National Education Committee with the right to representation on the governing

15. *Plebs*, 1925, pp.182-3.

bodies of the WEA, the NCLC, the residential Labour College and Ruskin College respectively so long as it gave each one of them financial support. Divisional councils would be formed to regulate and publicise educational facilities. All parties would retain the right to canvass for support on their own account 'provided that there shall be mutual abstention from criticism of the good faith of any educational organisation recognised by the TUC.'

The sincerity of the NCLC in entering into this agreement was called in question. Herbert Highton, a WEA official, wrote to Millar:

> I am writing to you in the hope that . . . attacks on the *bona fides* of the WEA shall cease. I quite understand that this does not deter you from passing any criticism you like on the educational methods of the WEA. It does, I think, mean that the insinuations about its alleged capitalist character should cease. (16)

Millar replied:

> . . . we do not attack the good faith or good intentions of the WEA. As a matter of fact we have never done so . . . but this does not for a moment get away from the belief that the WEA's education is capitalist in character. (17)

Unimpressed, Highton retorted that the NCLC's promise not to impugn the good faith of the WEA 'would astonish not only neutral folk but your own supporters.' On the left the agreement was seen as potentially suicidal. Millar rejected the charge that the NCLC had joined forces with the WEA: 'Those who say so are unconsciously playing into the hands of the WEA.' (18) Cole thought that only the first step had been taken towards co-operation. Despite the misgivings of many delegates the TUC formally approved the agreement at its annual meeting at Scarborough in September 1925.

The WEA in Difficulties

In practice, the terms were never implemented. The WEA was attacked from several quarters for compromising its impartiality. In the view of the Association of Education Committees it had abandoned its non-political status by concurring with the specific object of the TUC scheme 'to provide working-class

16. Highton to Millar, 17 Mar. 1925., NCLC Corr.
17. Millar to Highton in *ibid.*
18. Millar to the Editor of *The Worker, ibid.*, 18 July 1925.

education in order to enable the workers to develop their capacities and to equip them for their trade union, labour and co-operative activities generally in the work of securing social and industrial emancipation.' The Local Education Authorities were warned of 'dangerous possibilities.' It was suggested in *Education*, the journal of the Association of Education Committees, that the phrase 'social and industrial emancipation' was merely 'a rhetorical flourish' or 'a curly tail' at the end of a sentence. (19) In a letter to *Education* Millar pointed out, however, that as a condition of the proposed scheme the WEA would be required to insert the contentious phrase in its statement of aims. *Education* invited Mactavish to explain the significance of the phrase since it did not appear at all certain that the phrase represented a mere 'rhetorical flourish.' Though he wrote several letters on the subject, Mactavish did not attempt an elucidation. In a second letter to *Education*, Millar drew attention to Mactavish's failure to admit that the WEA had accepted 'education for emancipation' as its official policy. He also pointed out that Mactavish seemed to have forgotten the gist of an article which he had written for an American trade union journal containing the statement: 'the aim of working-class education should be to stimulate class-consciousness ... equipping the workers to evolve their own social valuations, their own moral standards, judgment, code of honour, etc.' Mactavish replied that the article in question was four years old. Finally, Mactavish wrote a letter in which he stated: 'I am not in the slightest degree interested in Mr. Millar's interpretation of the agreement, and do not intend to assist him in his efforts to win either publicity or notoriety . . .' At one stage, Arthur Pugh entered into the dispute by protesting in a letter to *Education* that the NCLC was attempting 'to break the good faith which must be observed by all the bodies concerned.'

Board of Education Enters the Fray

Soon after the announcement of the TUC scheme Lord Eustace Percy, Conservative President of the Board of Education, decided to consult with the Association of Education Committees, the County Councils' Association, the Association of Municipal Corporations and the London County Council 'with a view to consideration by the Board of an education scheme adopted by the Trade Union Congress at its recent meeting.' He expressed his own opinion in a speech quoted in a

19. *Education: Elementary, Secondary and Technical*, 23 Oct., 1925, pp.395-6.

leading article in *Education:* 'The enemies of education are not those who preach economy. Its real enemies are men like the General Secretary of the National Council of Labour Colleges.' In opposing the NCLC we are 'fighting no political battle . . . but in very truth a battle against spiritual wickedness.' On November 13 Lord Percy again attacked the NCLC, using the phrase 'poisonous education.' His attack was echoed in the educational press which now roundly condemned the TUC scheme. An editorial in *Education* (20) stated that it contained 'Marxian phrases which have been administered to working-class audiences by a type of worker who either does not understand the meaning of the words he uses, or if he does understand them, he does not believe in them.' The *Times Educational Supplement* commented: 'The formula must not be allowed to grip and mould the activities of the Workers' Educational Association into a form acceptable to Mr. Millar and those who think with him.' It was questioned whether the State should still continue to make funds available to the WEA.

TUC Education Committee Intervention

The Ministry of Education and the Education Authorities were disturbed — from their point of view — about the potentially damaging effects of the TUC scheme. They could not be expected to go on supporting the WEA if it were going to alter its policy and provide 'education for emancipation.' If some WEA officials thought they could explain away the phrase as 'a rhetorical flourish,' it was because they underestimated the importance that the State attached to the provision of what is regarded as the right brand of education. Its view on that subject were as strongly held as were the NCLC's views on what brand of education was required by the working-class movement. Seeing the threat to the WEA, Arthur Pugh raised the matter with the TUC Education Committee, whose secretary thereafter wrote to the NCLC Executive Committee enumerating a number of complaints, mostly directed at Millar's conduct as general secretary. A letter was also sent to Horrabin complaining about 'various printed statements, letters and articles appearing over the name of your Secretary, Mr. J. P. M. Millar.' One TUC complaint was that the NCLC had parodied a Ruskin College advertisement, which had depicted a horse and rider under the

20. The Journal *Education* devoted considerable space to the controversy over the joint scheme in a number of issues during the period 25 Sept. 1925 to 20 Nov. 1925.

caption 'education needs direction.' The NCLC advertisement, which appeared shortly afterwards, depicted a man sitting back to front on a donkey and holding its tail; the caption read: 'education needs direction — the right direction.' The idea was Millar's, the drawing Horrabin's. The NCLC executive committee repudiated any suggestion that Millar's conduct had been in breach of the clause in the TUC scheme stating that educational bodies were not to question one another's good intentions. It appointed three representatives, including Millar and Hamilton, to meet the TUC Education Committee in order to make its position clear.

The TUC committee were dissatisfied with the representations of the deputation and sent a detailed list of their complaints so that they might be examined by the whole of the NCLC executive. The NCLC executive repudiated the complaints *seriatim*, pointing out that the WEA had also criticised the NCLC and asking why the TUC Education Committee had not complained to the WEA. The NCLC's Minute Book contains a statement saying: 'We very much regret to say we have the feeling that some people associated with the WEA desire to wipe out the Congress education scheme but have been endeavouring to put the onus for the break up of the scheme on the NCLC.' It made this judgement in view of (1) the WEA's attitude in the controversy in *Education*, (2) the statement issued by the Scottish Council of the WEA on the secession of the WEA's large Edinburgh branch, and (3) the fact that the Board of Education and the Education Authorities had conducted a searching examination of the WEA in connection with the Congress education scheme.

The WEA Asked to Explain

In the report of the NCLC's annual conference held in July 1926 a special section dealing with the TUC's scheme said that during the previous twelve months 'the General Council made no attempt either to call together the old committee (Joint TUC Committee) on which the NCLC was represented or to form the new National Committee laid down under the TUC (adopted) scheme.' The NCLC report went on to say that the controversy in *Education* had put the WEA in an equivocal light and that what the WEA feared was that the TUC objectives would result in the withdrawal of state support and that that explained the extremely unsatisfactory attitude of the WEA. That this was no

71

idle fear was borne out when later on, as a result of the publicity given to the objectives of the TUC scheme in *Education*, the Association of Education Committees examined the whole question and called the WEA before it to explain its position. Eventually, a sub-committee of the Education Authorities drew up a series of conditions under which grants should be made to the WEA. In accepting these conditions the WEA could no longer claim that its assistance from the state was without strings. The NCLC had all along argued that the grants were given because the WEA provided orthodox education and not independent working-class education.

In truth the NCLC had exploited the dilemma facing the WEA. The WEA was trying to serve two masters — the trade union movement and the Board of Education — whose interests did not coincide. In accepting the phrase 'social and industrial emancipation' it had taken a risk that it had been trying to avoid but which NCLC pressure had forced it to accept. The acrimonious controversy had repercussions on the credibility of the WEA. The Edinburgh Branch considered that by accepting the agreement it had jeopardised its independence and voted to quit the association, as did the Hawick and Dunbar branches. *The Lancashire Daily Post* averred that the doubts about the scheme had been fully justified by the behaviour of Millar and the NCLC, 'ruthless purveyors of Marxist propaganda.' For his part, Millar maintained that the Edinburgh Branch had been singularly honest in recognising that the WEA was attached to the Local Education Authorities and the universities. *Plebs* commented: 'since it believes in "impartiality" and all the other old WEA slogans — and needs university grants — it has made it clear that it will have nothing whatever to do with the TUC scheme.' The withdrawal of the South East Scotland branches was the most extreme course of action taken but it undoubtedly reflected widespread discontent in WEA districts. The press throughout the country strongly censured the WEA. The conflict with the NCLC had absorbed a good deal of time and energy which the WEA would have preferred to spend on other matters. Partly to reduce the burden and partly to undo the damage being inflicted upon its national image the WEA took the step in 1925 of appointing a special propaganda committee under the chairmanship of Arthur Pugh.

At the Scarborough conference of the TUC in September 1925 the delegates had considered proposals that the TUC should assume responsibility for the residential Labour College. These proposals, which had been agreed upon by the General Council, the SWMF and the NUR, could be summarised as follows:

1. The two unions would hand over the properties at Earls Court and Kew, for two years continue to finance the same number of students and thereafter guarantee to make financial contribution similar to that of other unions.

2. The General Council pledged to safeguard the teaching of Marxist doctrines and scientific evolution, to appoint ideologically suitable tutors, to accord in perpetuity seats on the governing body to the two unions, and to go ahead with the erection of new buildings at Kew.

3. Ruskin College would be included in the merger. (21)

The TUC and the Easton Lodge Scheme

The Countess of Warwick, who had joined the SDF in 1895 and ever after remained a staunch patroness of socialist causes, offered to give her house and grounds at Easton Lodge for use as a residential college. The TUC Education Committee, accompanied by Ruskin College and CLC representatives, visited Easton Lodge and the General Council decided to accept the offer. It was intended that G. D. H. Cole should become the first Principal. Not invited, the NCLC was sceptical about the value of the scheme and thought that the success of an enlarged residential college would depend on its being associated with evening classes. In the May issue of *Plebs* Millar wrote:

> . . . NCLC schemes, providing, as they do, opportunities for the rank and file *throughout the country,* offer facilities that are much more important from a trade unionist's point of view than residential facilities (important as they are), of which only a very small percentage can ever avail themselves. A Union that arranges residential facilities before it has provided evening class opportunities is to a considerable degree failing to spend its educational funds to the best advantage. This was the point of view of the Shop Assistants Union Conference held last month, when by 92 votes to 43, it was decided to have an NCLC scheme and to turn down the Executive's recommendation that

21. TUC, *Annual Report,* p.192. ·

the Union should support Easton Lodge and not the NCLC or the WEA. (22)

The residential Labour College was also unenthusiastic about the Easton Lodge scheme. In its view the TUC should locate its residential college in the grounds of Kew and not far away in a Warwickshire village. A Labour College should be situated in a major industrial centre where the students would be in constant touch with industrial and political activity.

In August the NCLC executive committee was invited to meet the TUC Education Committee. When it arrived for the meeting it found representatives of the WEA also in attendance. Speaking as chairman of the TUC Committee, Arthur Pugh stated that the General Council hoped eventually to take over all working-class educational organisations. Meanwhile, proposals from the WEA and the NCLC as to what part each was prepared to play would be welcomed. After the meeting the NCLC executive committee decided that 'it appeared to be desirable to make the NCLC the main part of the TUC's educational scheme by handing the NCLC over to Congress' and informed the TUC Education Committee accordingly. Its two conditions were that the NCLC's educational policy be maintained and its entire staff absorbed. Millar feared that the new residentitial college would be

> run on such an expensive scale that every penny of Trade Union educational money would be utilised in keeping it going, which would result in the evening class work throughout the country — undoubtedly the more important — being at the mercy of the Board of Education subsidies and therefore from the working-class point of view unsatisfactory. (23)

In a letter to Millar dated 5 November 1925 Frank Horrabin wrote:

> Lady Warwick sent for Win and self last Saturday — to meet Pugh . . . Pugh opened by declaring that we — you particularly, O my militant friend — were trying to wreck the scheme — didn't want it and didn't seem to abide by it, etc., etc. (24)

Congress Turns Down £50,000 Easton Lodge Scheme

When the full initial cost of the Easton Lodge scheme was

22. J. P. M. Millar, 'Easton Lodge and the NCLC' in *Plebs,* p.180.
23. *ibid.,* 1926, p.277.
24. NCLC MSS.

revealed as £50,000 the NCLC concluded that its own classes were bound to suffer: '. . . the present proposals which lavish finance on residential work alone are likely to put the Congress in the undesirable position of having a too costly cart and no horse.' At the 1926 Bournemouth conference of the TUC the General Council reported that it had become necessary to introduce several modifications into the original scheme. In order to obtain the required capital of £50,000 it proposed that one penny per member should be levied on each union for a period of three years and that it should be empowered to borrow in the money market. In addition, Ruskin College should continue to be located in Oxford for the time being. The General Council asked Congress to approve these proposals. Speeches were made for and against the resolution, NCLC sympathisers being prominent among the opposition. Millar was at the Congress, organising opposition to the Easton proposal with the help of a number of NCLC supporters among the delegates. In the course of his speech Jack Jones M.P., not an NCLC man, complained: 'We have had experience of men who have gone to Ruskin College dressed up as workmen who have come back with haloes, dressed in plus-fours and immediately wanted to be general secretaries of their unions.' The last general secretary to whom Millar spoke before the debate was W. J. Brown — also not an NCLC supporter — General Secretary of the Civil Service Clerical Association. Brown made clear that he did not agree with the point Millar had advanced, namely, that so much money would be spent on Easton Lodge residential education that there would be little or nothing left over for the education of the great mass of trade unionists. To Millar's astonishment Brown intervened during the debate to make a powerful speech against the scheme using the very argument which he had disputed. Winding up the debate, Arthur Pugh insisted that Congress must decide once and for all whether it desired a unification scheme or not; discussions had been going on for five years; they could be prolonged no longer.

When the vote was taken the conference formally rejected the scheme by a majority of 2,441,000 to 1,481,000. The Countess of Warwick then withdrew her offer. In the opinion of the WEA, the NCLC had defeated the scheme as part of its 'general game of using the Trade Union Movement for its own ends.' Millar was delighted with the result: 'The thanks of the Trade Union movement are due to the many delegates who, at Bournemouth,

75

prevented the Congress scheme from starting on the wrong lines.' In August 1925 he had proposed to Citrine that the General Council should consider the whole question of grants for trade union education and specifically give £100 to the NCLC. By December no communication had been received from the Finance Committee and Millar complained to Citrine. Two months later Citrine replied saying that no grant would be made available. Millar considered this refusal 'contrary to the Congress Education Scheme' and feared that all available funds were to be given to Ruskin; the NCLC was being discriminated against and 'That hurts a very great deal more than the actual loss in cash.' He was not alone in his fears. Winifred Horrabin had previously suggested that she should inform the Countess of Warwick *sub rosa* that the TUC intended to use Easton Lodge as a greater Ruskin but Millar opposed the suggestion. In his book *The Central Labour College* W. W. Craik suggests that the failure of the Easton Lodge scheme led directly to the closure of the CLC. This suggestion does not seem to be borne out by the facts. Nevertheless, Craik records that the two sponsoring unions had already given notice to the residential Labour College staff.

NCLC and WEA Embitterment Grows

Relations between the NCLC and the WEA could scarcely have been worse. In February 1927 the TUC Education Committee enjoined the two associations to stop attacking each other. At its annual conference in September 1927, the TUC commented upon the failure to implement the Scarborough agreement and stated that 'a proper observance of that agreement as regards the relations between the two bodies must be a condition of further support.'

At no time during the five year old controversy had the NCLC pulled any punches in criticising the role of the WEA. At the very beginning, in a letter to the *Daily Herald* dated 28 February 1922, Millar accused the WEA of being 'an agency for giving gentlemanly dope to the working-classes.' Relations between the chief officials on both sides were acrimonious. In a letter written in 1925 Ernest Green refuted a charge that he had suggested that NCLC organisers in Yorkshire had sought WEA posts. Millar accused Green of making incorrect statements. Green replied, out of courtesy, as he said, 'but (your letter) does not seem to call for any reply in view of your pronounced views on my veracity. On the occasion of the twenty-first anniversary of the WEA Raymond Postgate, as Chairman of the Plebs

Executive Committee, wrote a caustic letter to *The Highway,* the WEA's journal:

> Ever since our organisation was founded there has been steady and necessary opposition between us. You exist to extend the benefits of University culture to the working men that you patronise. We show our readers that your education, and all education that is not based on the central fact of the class struggle, is false history and false economics . . . We note the formation of the 'WETUC' — a rabbit in a lion's skin — as a last effort of camouflage on your part and thank you for the flattery it implies . . . We note with pleasure, in recent years, your decline and our rise. We hope and anticipate that when our 'twenty-first birthday' comes — not so long now — we shall be able to celebrate also your complete disappearance. (25)

WEA Loses Supporters

The NCLC's struggle for the support of the unions at the expense of the WETUC was not confined to verbal polemics. At the local level every effort was made to win converts. Thus, in 1923 the Edinburgh District of the SLC, having already obtained the affiliation of a large proportion of the trade union branches in the Edinburgh area, decided to undermine the support given to the WEA by the Edinburgh and District Trades Council. The Council was prompted by NCLC supporters to investigate the policy of the SLC, which submitted a printed statement entitled *Organised Labour and its Educational Needs.* The Council then interviewed Millar and other representatives of the SLC committee and afterwards resolved to drop its support for the WEA and support the Edinburgh District of the SLC. There is no question that the WEA sometimes found the local competition of the NCLC very irksome. Dr. Willoughby, secretary of the Chesterfield WEA, said in 1927:

> There was, of course, another thing which the Chesterfield Branch was suffering from, in common with all other branches over the country. That was the propaganda of the Labour Colleges, and numbers of mem

25. 'Greetings from Plebs' in *Highway,* Vol. XVI, 1924, p.186.

bers had transferred their affections from the WEA to these Colleges. (26)

Tawney and Cole

The opposition between the NCLC and the WEA was to continue until 1963 though it never again reached the peak attained in the Twenties. Two of the outstanding personalities on the WEA side, Tawney and Cole, disliked the conflict but by no means condemned the NCLC. On 23 January 1961, years after the quarrels of the mid-Twenties, Tawney wrote to Millar:

> I often think of our happy breakfasts together at Evan Evan's hotel when I was living close by in the Colonnade and you, I suppose, were coming to London from time to time. In spite of the fact that we were supposed to be bitter antagonists, I think we found that we had more in common than might have been expected, remembering the official denunciations launched from both sides in which I, at any rate, usually refused to participate. (27)

Tawney also frequently asked the question about the WEA 'Was the proportion of manual workers falling? He suspected that it was.' (28)

Shortly after the end of the First World War, G. D. H. Cole and William Mellor, who later became editor of *The Daily Herald,* had called at the CLC to see W. W. Craik and George Sims. As left-wing socialists they were intrigued by the work of the College and wished to be of service. They were given a somewhat cold welcome, perhaps because Craik and Sims were suspicious of their motives and, as the leading personalities in the Labour College movement at that time, fearful of potential competition. Although a prominent spokesman for the WEA, Cole showed unfailing cordiality to the NCLC. In his view, 'the Plebs method reaches large bodies of workers whom the WEA, with its non-propagandist appeal, cannot and does not reach. I want them to be reached, and I want the *Plebs* to reach them. When I go to speak in a new centre where a class is prepared, I advise them, if they do not like the WEA, to form a Plebs class if that suits them better.' In an article in *Plebs,* which appeared in 1916, Cole wrote of the WEA's co-operation with the Board of Education and the universities:

26. *Derbyshire Times,* 26. Feb. 1927.
27. NCLC MSS.
28. M. Stocks, *op.cit., p.106.*

I am as ready as anyone can be to bid that connection goodbye. The sooner Labour can stand on its own educational legs, the better for itself and the worse for the capitalist system. I do not believe that Oxford and Cambridge or the newer Universities are going intentionally to help Labour to secure emancipation. I am only waiting until Labour is prepared to take over the WEA and to run it as a definitely Labour concern — and *to pay for it.* (29)

In a contribution to the WEA *Education Yearbook* of 1918 he had expressed the opinion that the WEA and the CLC each had a legitimate role to play:

Propaganda is an attempt to bring others to one's own point of view. Education is an attempt to equip others with the means of making up their own minds. Both are legitimate forms of activity; the point is that they are *different.* The difference between the WEA and the NCLC is not the difference between education and propaganda, but the difference between an educational institution and a school for propagandists. In short, both have their place, but their places are different. When, therefore, the WEA and the CLC made their claims for trade union support those who treat their claims as fundamentally irreconcilable are wrong. (30)

In an article in *Highway* published in 1923, he again justified both approaches to workers' education:

Some WEAers enjoy denouncing the wickedness of the Plebs League as a perverter of the mind, teaching the workers not to think freely for themselves but to imbide certain doctrinaire opinions supposed to be a guarantee of rectitude in the class struggle. Personally, like many other WEAers I share many of these opinions of the Plebs; but I do draw the distinction, which the Plebs denies, between education and propaganda. In political and industrial work I am a propagandist, seeking to persuade others to my opinion; in education I am a mid-wife, trying to help them to bring their own ideas to birth.

I do not, however, at all enjoy denouncing the Plebs and I do not see anything to denounce . . . It is just as

29. *Plebs,* 1916, p.219.
30. WEA, *Education Yearbook,* pt. VI. p.372.

legitimate for a trade union to adopt a scheme under the Labour Colleges as under the WEA; for a trade union has to provide for propaganda as well as for education in the stricter sense. "Live and let live is my motto." (31)

He deplored the extent of the split and thought the two extreme positions should be modified: 'We may not transcend our differences, but we can, if we try, at least learn to differ intelligently.' But within the WEA Cole won little support as an arbitrator. Many of the leading figures abhorred the ideas and polemical style of the NCLC. Nor was Cole much helped by the tone of some spokesmen on the NCLC side. His brother-in-law Postgate, once wrote to Millar: 'I have taken the line with Cole up to now that it is no good talking of co-operation unless he can induce a declamatory resolution of some kind from his people which will not be a sham fight, but will involve a genuine breach.'

There is evidence that some rank and file members of the WEA were also indifferent to the controversy. In a letter to *Highway* in 1924 one correspondent criticised Cole for suggesting that there was a crisis to become concerned about. During the next year another correspondent wrote: 'When the officials and high priests of both movements realise that the average worker-student does not care twopence about the WEA and the NCLC squabble, we shall see some real progress made in workers' education.' Evidently this correspondent did not appreciate that the 'officials and high priests' in the WEA camp, while regarding the NCLC as an intolerable scourge, were desperately trying to pretend that it did not exist. Sincerely they believed that the conflict was caused entirely by the belligerence of the NCLC.

The Plebs League and the Communists

At the beginning of the period which covered the foundation of the NCLC several members of the Plebs League Executive joined the Communist Party, including Horrabin, Postgate and Maurice Dobb. The party was founded in 1921, when Stalinism did not exist, and was made up of several brands of socialists. Some of them wished at first to use the League and if possible the Labour College Movement to further the interests of the new British Communist Party. Jack Hamilton and Millar were

31. 'Crisis in Workers' Education' in *The Highway*, Vol. XVI., no.1, 1923, p.20-21.

determined to stop such moves. The *Sunday Worker* (Communist) made a brief attempt to cultivate Millar and got him to write an article on the NCLC. Millar did so but was never again asked to contribute to a communist newspaper. Later in 1924 Raymond Postgate tried to prevent Walton Newbold from being elected to the executive committee of the Plebs League because of his known communist leanings. Newbold was the first British communist to enter the House of Commons.

Here and there throughout the country communists tried to gain control of local classes but they met with little success. One reason for this was that the full-time organisers had sufficient knowledge of Marxist theories to be able to counter communist propaganda. For example, when Arthur Woodburn as Labour Party Secretary for Scotland spoke in various parts of the country he found communists planting themselves in the audience in order to ask tendentious questions. Again, when Charles Gibbons was nominated by the Edinburgh District Executive Committee for the post of organiser the recommendation had to face an unprecedentedly large district committee. It soon appeared that Eva Harris, a vigorous activist, had helped to pack the meeting with communist supporters. The District Committee in consequence rejected the executive's nomination and decided to appoint another applicant, William Joss who was a communist. What followed then was that Millar, still the District Tutor-organiser, called the Executive Committee and asked them what they proposed to do. 'What can we do?' one of them asked. 'Declare the decision null and void,' replied Millar, who had ascertained by this time, with the help of two colleagues, that a number of those who had attended as union delegates lacked a representative credential. The executive, therefore, declared the decisions of the meeting invalid and at the subsequent meeting of the District Committee no-one was allowed to attend without producing a card displaying Millar's signature and no-one was given a card who was not a formally appointed delegate. Charles Gibbons was then appointed. Soon after, Gibbons married Eva Harries, who later left the Communist Party and joined the Labour Party. As organiser for the East of Scotland, Gibbons thereafter lectured for a time on the theme of 'What is a Revolutionary Situation?' — a lecture that did not please the communists who, at that period, thought there was a revolutionary situation.

So far as can be ascertained, only one organiser appointed by the NCLC was a member of the Communist Party. This was Charlie Stead, who became one of the first South Wales organisers. When he died unexpectedly, his papers were sent off to the NCLC central office. These revealed that the communists had made every effort to turn the District into an instrument of the communist machine but that Stead had steadfastly resisted the pressure.

In his endeavour to persuade union executives to adopt the NCLC's educational scheme, Millar frequently requested an interview. At these interviews he was sometimes faced with an executive made up of four groups: WEA supporters; those who opposed all expenditure on education schemes; communists; allies of the NCLC. Sometimes the first three groups voted together to outwit the NCLC supporters.

The fact that the NCLC was far from being a communist organisation did not prevent its critics from insinuating to officials that it was. From an early stage, the ill-informed Home Office regarded the Labour Colleges as subversive. Many lies contain a fragment of truth. Because the NCLC attached much importance to Marx's theories, it was easy to jump to the conclusion that it accepted the way in which Marxism had been implemented in Russia after the 1917 revolution. It was in this belief that West Calder Co-operative Society refused to affiliate to the SLC and that the local branch of the Miners' union at Loanhead opposed affiliation to the ILP on the grounds that it was closely associated with the NCLC, some of whose tutors were alleged to be communists. The Labour Colleges occasionally found themselves having to refute allegations and insinuations that the NCLC was a communist organisation. In, a *Plebs* editorial in 1922 Millar wrote: 'We are not, we never have been, and we do not intend to be allied to any one *section* of the working-class movement.'

For a number of years *Plebs* carried the slogan: 'I can promise to be candid but not impartial.' Soon after Millar became the editor in 1927, he decided to drop the slogan because opponents of the NCLC cited it as evidence of dogmatic beliefs and because many workers did not understand its significance.

CHAPTER V

YEARS OF CRISIS

1926 was the year of the General Strike. As an educational organisation built up, financed and largely controlled by trade unions, the NCLC, of course, threw its whole weight behind the miners' struggle to protect their wages from being cut. On the morning of 1 May 1926, when it appeared that a national strike to help the miners was inevitable, the NCLC officials hastily drew up a brief anticipatory manifesto:

> Education for Action.
>
> In the great crisis now affecting the Trade Union and Labour Movement, the NCLC calls upon all present and ex-students, tutors and officials to render every possible assistance.
>
> All local activities should be carried out under the direction of the Trades Councils and local officers of Trade Unions actually participating in the dispute.
>
> For the Executive
> A. A. Purcell, Hon. President.
> J. Hamilton, Chairman.
> J. P. M. Millar, General Secretary.

The General Strike Begins

On the following Monday all tutors and students were requested to put aside educational work for the time being in favour of giving their undivided support to the strike. That same evening the small staff of the NCLC's head office in Edinburgh placed themselves at the disposal of the Edinburgh District General Strike Committee, whose area extended from Bathgate in the West to Galashiels in the South. Throughout the country NCLC organisers, tutors and students were prominent in strike activities. Many of those engaged on picket duties were fined or imprisoned. Organiser Barr, who acted as assistant secretary of the Birmingham Strike Committee, was fined £10 and Vin Williams, a full-time lecturer in Derbyshire, was sentenced to three months' imprisonment.

Plebs applauded the great number of trade unionists who rallied to the miners' aid. NCLC organisers strove mightily to arrange an *ad hoc* lecture programme designed to inform the strikers about the trend of events and the cause of the strike and sustain their morale. During 1926, 1125 single lectures were delivered at union branches to over 80,000 trade unionists. No fewer than 2,000 special lectures were arranged for the miners who stayed on strike for months after the general stoppage had come to an end. The NCLC's unstinting adherence to the embattled unions at this critical juncture earned it a fund of good will.

The failure of the strike was a cruel reverse for the trade unions and damaged the Labour Party. Trade union membership slumped and union funds were sadly depleted. All the organisations which had not readily conformed with the government's position, fell under suspicion. This was even the temporary fate of the WEA. Lord Percy told the House of Commons that classes arranged by the WEA 'as well as those conducted by other organisations which contain members who have political views and on occasions express them, ought to be closely watched, and I have watched them and am closely watching them.' One Member of Parliament, strangely misinformed, accused the WEA of being associated with 'the extremist NCLC.'

Compared with the NCLC, however, the WEA did not suffer as a result of the Strike. Immediately afterwards, a new Trade Union Act was passed which, among other strictures, forbade Civil Service Unions to affiliate to bodies like the NCLC but left them free to affiliate to the WEA and the WETUC. More seriously, the general impoverishment of the Unions led to a steep decline in the NCLC's income.

Thus far, in the brief space of four years, largely thanks to the correspondence between its type of education and the militant mood of many trade unionists, the NCLC had surged ahead. After 1926, however, the disillusionment of the workers affected the rate of enrolments. In Scotland:

> The effect on the Scottish Labour College did not become apparent immediately but, apart from some temporary outbursts of enthusiasm, the years from 1926 onwards saw a slow and steady decline in the overall membership of and support for, the classes organised by the College. (1)

Looking back retrospectively, the Annual Report for 1935 said:

> It will be noticed that in 1927, NCLC educational work received a check in growth as a result of the apathy

1. J. H. Roberts, The National Council of Labour Colleges; an Experiment in Worker's Education (unpublished Mss thesis, Edinburgh 1970).

following the National Strike and the Miners' Lock-out. In the following year the figures show an actual drop. Undoubtedly this is largely accounted for by the increasing apathy which followed 1926. 'Workers' educational organisations that drew a large proportion of their students from the middle-class and the professions, and which act as part of the machinery of the Universities and the Education Authorities have, as we forecast, shown an increase in consequence of increasing financial support from governmental circles. The NCLC, as part and parcel of the Trade Union and Labour Movement, can naturally not escape the effects of the economic conditions and the resultant apathy, although it naturally strives to make headway against both.' (2)

During the period immediately after the General Strike, the NCLC sought to spread its views on education to a wider audience. On behalf of the NCLC, Millar submitted a number of suggestions on school education to the Bradford branch of the ILP:

> The reforms usually advocated are largely confined to reduction of the numbers in classes, opening the gateway to universities and secondary schools to poor children etc., etc., all desirable enough in their way, but all completely ignoring the fact that modern orthodox education has been moulded by history to suit the needs of capitalism and must therefore be drastically changed if it is to meet the needs of Socialism or of a class struggling for Socialism (3)

On the resignation in 1927 of R. H. Tawney as Vice-President of the Teachers' Labour League, Millar was elected in his place. At the London and Southern Counties Division First Winter Conference of the ILP Guild of Youth in March 1927 a resolution was passed:

> The Guild declares its belief in Independent Working Class Education . . . By means of evening classes and study circles based upon this policy, it should train its members to become class conscious workers and well equipped exponents of the Socialist message. (4)

First International Conference

From an early stage both Horrabin and Millar were anxious

2. *Education for Emancipation* (1935), p.6.
3. *Plebs*, 1927, p.226.   4. *The Flame*, Mar. 1927.

to give the NCLC an international outlook and reputation. For example, although the NCLC had no money to pay for a delegate to attend the first international conference on workers' education, held in Brussels and called by the International Federation of Trade Unions in 1922, Millar and his wife attended by paying their own fares and expenses. W. W. Craik represented the CLC.

At the second international conference, called by the IFTU in Oxford in 1924, the NCLC was again represented by Millar and Christine. There were 70 Delegates representing 26 nations. The only educational items on show were the NCLC's postal courses and a selection of its illustrated publicity leaflets and pamphlets and textbooks. Among the proposals considered was the establishing of an International Workers' College.

According the the NCLC executive minutes of 7 September 1924 the agenda for the conference made clear that the provisional committee did not want the aims of workers education to be discussed. This conclusion could be drawn from the fact that the only motions dealing with the subject and which had been sent in by the NCLC were put well at the end of the agenda. The provisional committee, however, were unsuccessful in preventing a discussion as one of the first motions dealt with the formation of an International which gave the NCLC an opportunity of submitting an amendment to make clear the kind of education with which the International should be concerned. This resulted in a five hour debate on the subject. The NCLC's amendment was defeated on the plea that it might exclude organisations that in the meantime it was desirable to have in the International. The WEA was represented and could hardly welcome the NCLC's proposal.

The League's Financial Difficulties

The year after the general strike brought new troubles to the NCLC. First, the Plebs League fell on hard times. Its problems stemmed, in a small degree, from internal disputes, but mainly from the shortage of funds. After the foundation of the NCLC, which had been the direct result of a conference called by the Plebs League, the two bodies had closely collaborated. However, very soon the NCLC Executive, particularly its two chief officials, Hamilton and Millar, wanted the NCLC to have a say in determining the contents of *Plebs* and the other League publications. This desire was intensified when, for a short time, an influential section of the Plebs League Executive joined the British Communist Party and started to point *Plebs* in a pro-communist direction. Hamilton and Millar strongly objected. The problem was not easy to deal with because many active socialists, enthused by the Bolshevik Revolution, had become members of the British Communist Party following its foundation in 1920, and others felt sympathetic towards it. Although welcoming the downfall of Czarism, Hamilton and Millar had not been prepared to join the Communist Party. They realised that, if the Labour College Movement were to fall, or even seem to fall, under communist influence, the prospects for gaining substantial union support would be reduced. Accordingly, by rigorously opposing the new pro-communist orientation, they found themselves temporarily unpopular with a majority of the League's executive. Fortunately, the orientation was short-lived since all but one of the Plebs executive committee members who had joined the Communist Party soon left it. Horrabin, for instance, refused to allow the independent working-class education movement to be crippled by the Communist Party's quest for power. In *Plebs* he wrote: 'As I can't work happily with little Machiavellians of this type, I decided I should feel better outside.' Postgate took a similar view and also resigned from the Party.

Raising money to meet the cost of running the Plebs League had become a difficult problem as early as 1921 when Horrabin referred to an outstanding debt of £200. An attempt to raise the wind by a 'pound fund' had failed, a pound gift being beyond the means of most Plebs subscribers. It had been decided, therefore, to open an additional penny stamp fund. This had had good results but the Plebs League continued to sail near the reefs of bankruptcy.

The penury of the miners following the agonisingly long lock-out of 1926 led to a reduction in the sale of *Plebs* and other League publications. The major part of the circulation of *Plebs* was due to the efforts of individual miners and other trade unionists who took parcels of *Plebs* for sale each month and also regularly sold books and pamphlets. Many *Plebs* agents were now unable to pay for the magazine and other publications they had previously received from the Plebs League —the money had had to be spent on food in this period of great privation for the miners. As a result the Plebs League was quickly weighed down by debt. The biggest creditor was the printer and there seemed no hope of the Plebs League ever meeting its liabilities.

NCLC Takes Over Plebs

The executive committee of the NCLC decided that they could not afford to stand by and see the work of the Plebs League collapse, if only because of the crucially important role played by *Plebs* in disseminating information and heartening supporters and by the Plebs League pamphlets and books in providing material for lectures and classes. However, there was sharp disagreement within the Plebs League executive committee about whether or not to hand over to the NCLC. The decisive turning point came when Postgate became so angry at the unconstructive attitude of Eden and Cedar Paul that he saw absorption by the NCLC as offering the only possible solution. Millar was instructed by his executive committee to arrange the take-over and had to act quickly because of a crisis in the Plebs office. Of the paid staff of three Kathleen Starr had to go to hospital for an operation, the book-keeper went off to another job and the junior clerk fell down the office stairs and broke a leg. Left alone was the cleaner, the redoubtable Mrs. Gibbs of Battersea, who rejoiced in eighty years.

The League's Publishing is Taken Over

As a result of Millar's intervention, the NCLC Publishing Society was brought into being with the task of continuing to publish *Plebs* and occasional pamphlets and text-books and acting as a wholesale distributor of other publications. From the beginning the chief concentration, for both publicity and financial reasons, was on short pamphlets and small books commanding wide circulations. Many of these stated the NCLC's educational philosophy; for example, *The War of Ideas* and *The Trained Mind — Trained for What?* both by Millar. More ambitious texts included *A Pocket History of the Working Class* by Raymond Postgate.

At the time of the take-over the Plebs League had few assets — one or two tables, a small desk, together with a supply of books and Plebs badges designed by Frank Horrabin. The badge showed a large white question mark on a blue ground, a unique emblem in the Trade Union and Labour Movement. It had its origin in the fact that WEA spokesmen sometimes alleged that Labour College education was dogmatic. In fact, the NCLCers saw themselves as questioning orthodox education, questioning orthodox history and orthodox economics and questioning the very social system. Horrabin therefore conceived the idea of emphasising the League's freedom of thought by adopting as its emblem a simple, bold question mark and nothing but a question mark. When the NCLC took over the League, George Hicks did not care for the NCLC emblem becoming nothing but a big white question mark. He pointed out that if he were to sport such a badge in his lapel, he was sure his fellow delegates at union conferences and at the TUC would ask him pawky questions. In consequence Horrabin designed a new emblem having a much smaller question mark in gold on a blue ground with the letters NCLC added.

Taking over a magazine and other publishing work put the NCLC in a vulnerable position. There were such contingencies as libel actions to guard against and the NCLC was neither in a position to meet the Plebs League's liabilities to the printer nor to face civil action for payment. The NCLC Executive therefore agreed that the publishing work should be assigned to a newly-constituted body to be called the NCLC Publishing Society. This formula had the advantage of freeing members of the Plebs League or the NCLC from the risk of being sued for any monies due. The ultimate object was to turn the society into a limited society under the Industrial and Provident Societies' Act, but the transition would take time. Consequently, as the NCLC Publishing Society was not a limited liability body, it had to include the name of the person or persons who were running it on all the letter-heads. The result was that Millar's name and his name alone appeared and he became liable for the accumulated debts.

Shortly after the takeover the printer, who had waited a long time for payment of his bills, demanded settlement from the new society. Millar explained that the society had no money to pay the debt and that he himself, who had become legally liable, would not be worth suing as he had no money either. But, he said, if the printer would be patient the NCLC Publishing Society would pay off the debt by instalments. This it eventually did.

Frank Horrabin's Contribution

The NCLC took over one invaluable asset, though it was not one which could be used to settle debts or pay for the hire of classrooms. This asset was the spare-time, unpaid services of Frank Horrabin, brilliant cartoonist, cartographer, writer, editor

J. F. Horrabin, *Plebs* Editor, author and cartoonist

and kindest of men. He had edited *Plebs* since 1914, apart from one or two war years, and later when he acted jointly with Maurice Dobb for a short period. J. F. H. it was who in 1927 initiated Millar into the art of editing *Plebs* by commissioning articles for no payment and making a magazine with serious intentions both readable and humorous. But he could not show Millar how to write, as he himself did, regular articles that could go to the printer without a single correction on the part of the editor. Right up to within a month of his death in 1962 Horrabin wrote geographical footnotes with maps for *Plebs*, some of which were collated and published by the Plebs League under the title of *The Plebs Atlas*. He also wrote one of the Plebs textbooks entitled *An Outline of Economic Geography*, later editions being entitled *An Outline of Political Geography*. He wrote other NCLC books including *A Short History of the British Empire*. Horrabin sat in the House of Commons from 1929 to 1931 as the Labour Member for Peterborough.

The Move to London

From 1922 until 1927 Millar had found it possible to operate efficiently from Edinburgh as General Secretary of the NCLC. Indeed, he had at first little choice in the matter, for his only paid employment was as the tutor-organiser for the Edinburgh District Labour College. For a time he was also honorary national organiser for the Scottish Labour College as a whole. In 1927 Millar still remained the national organiser for Scotland but received his salary as General Secretary. Taking over the functions of the Plebs League now enforced a change. He could have continued to cope with the NCLC's own affairs from Edinburgh but it appeared to be inconvenient to supervise the publishing activities away from London. Mark Starr wrote indicating that, since Millar had deep roots in Edinburgh, he would want to remain there while Starr himself could take care of the publishing work. Millar feared that Starr might be hoping to become the General Secretary. This resulted in the NCLC executive deciding to transfer the headquarters to London. The central office was quickly re-established in the new building of the Iron and Steel Trades Confederation in Gray's Inn Road, the union, as it happened, which had jointly, with the WEA founded the WETUC and was still its principal supporter.

The CLC's Financial Worries

Less than two years after the dissolution of the Plebs League a crisis threatened the future of the residential Labour College. Maintaining the College had continued to be a severe strain for the two sponsoring unions. Other unions had failed to help them erect a new building at Kew and they had been forced to rehouse all the students in the original residence. They had banked upon the TUC taking over the College and indeed had received a letter to that effect at the end of August 1926. Two months' later the TUC had sent a second letter saying that the takeover was ruled out 'owing to the decision of the Bournemouth Congress and subsequent developments.'

Towards the end of 1926 a group within the NUR Executive proposed that financial support be withdrawn from the Central Labour College; ominously, two of the group, Pocock and Banks, were College governors. Several of the NUR leaders had always opposed or only grudgingly supported the College. J. H. Thomas (Jimmy), who still remained a formidable power in the counsels of the union, was an intransigent enemy:

> As far as J. H. T. is concerned he at no time was in favour of the Labour College. At no time did he plead that it should have a chance. On the contrary — and unsuccessfully. He has never been anything else other than an opponent and therefore his defence of the present turn-about of former advocates must be judged from this standpoint. (5)

Now some former supporters had also become disenchanted. The main reasons for withdrawing support were that the Union was desperately short of money following the General Strike and that little benefit appeared to accrue directly to the union from the activities of former students — fourteen out of twenty-nine of them were no longer working on the railways. As early as 1925 some executive committee members had become tired of sharing the burden of financing the College with only one other union. After negotiations had begun with the General Council of the TUC with a view to a take-over they had assumed that their burden would soon be lifted. The collapse of the Easton College scheme had come to them, therefore, as a bitter disappointment.

The attitude of the SWMF leaders was different. Collectively, they had for years felt warmly attached to the College. Many

5. Extract from 'Papers on NUR decisions that College should be closed and argument against' (NCLC MSS.). These papers, which are unsigned and critical of the NUR leadership, give detailed reasons for the NUR opposition to the College.

were former students. Unlike the NUR, the union had clearly directly benefited from the activities of former students. Its examination paper for Central Labour College candidates stated that the candidate must 'place his services at the disposal of his own organisation or of the general Labour Movement on the termination of his residence at the College. The owners of the South Wales Coal pits were not anxious to employ graduates of the CLC but they could not keep them out. By law the miners in each pit had the right to elect a checkweighman whose job was to see that the colliery did not cheat the miners over the amount of coal they had produced. Checkweighmen were, therefore, elected by the men and not appointed by the mine owners. This provided a gateway for ex-Labour College students to obtain positions of importance in the coal field. The result was, there could be no doubt, that ex-College students were rendering great service. This became even clearer when all but one of the South Wales mining constituencies became represented in the House of Commons by ex-College students. Yet, when NUR students left the College they often found it impossible to get a job on the railways because the management did not want to have to deal with Labour College-trained spokesmen.

The Governors and staff of the College hoped for salvation through the intervention of other unions. On the 4th February 1927 the Board resolved:

> That owing to the unsatisfactory position as to the future of the College through the decision of the TUC General Council to take no further action to co-ordinate Independent Working Class Education, and the decision of the NUR to discontinue their part-ownership and control after July next; also the absence of a definite reply from the SWMF as to what action they are taking in the matter: we are of the opinion that the two controlling unions should at once communicate with those Unions who have sent students to the College in the past; also to other unions who are favourable to the continuance of the College, asking if they are prepared to assist by sending students and also sharing in the responsibility and control of the College, financial and otherwise. If so, to what extent? The secretary to forward this decision to the two controlling unions, expressing the hope that they will take action on the lines indicated. (6)

6. CLC Governing Board Minutes (NCLC MSS.).

For its part, the NCLC Executive believed that salvation was through close collaboration between the NCLC and the two unions. The moment when in November 1926 Jack Hamilton heard that the NUR had decided to discontinue its part-ownership of the College, he wrote to Millar: '(this) should give us the opportunity to immediately enter into negotiations with the SWMF to assume joint control with them.'

The NCLC Tries to Save the CLC

After the departure of George Sims relations between the CLC and the Plebs League had become a little distant. As early as 1924 Robert Holder had prepared a memorandum which he entitled 'The Conflict between the Plebs League and the Labour College, London' and in which he deplored 'this conflict and the personal enmities to which it has given rise.' Holder cited a number of anomalies that had arisen 'As a result of the historical development of the residential Labour College on the one hand and the NCLC with its Divisional Councils and classes on the other.' He concluded that '. . . no matter how able the tutors at the Labour College may be there will always be conflict, and their teaching and curriculum judged unsatisfactorily, *so long as the NCLC (and through it the Plebs League) has no direct control over the College and its teaching staff.*'

'For some time,' wrote Millar in the February 1927 issue of *Plebs,* 'the Executive of the NCLC have felt that the lack of a closer relationship between the residential college and the class work throughout the country was not satisfactory.' The NCLC had therefore arranged a meeting with the two unions not only to endeavour to keep the College in existence but to bring about a "Closer contact between residential work and class work." The NCLC offered to take over the College subject to the SWMF continuing its financial support, provided the NUR would contribute £2,500 per annum to the NCLC as compared with the previous figure of over £3,000, which had been the NUR's usual annual cost of maintaining the College. The NUR would get six free places for residential students each year and free access to the NCLC's classes for the whole of its membership throughout the country. It was suggested to the NCLC representatives at the meeting that, as an alternative, they should ask each of their principal affiliated unions to subsidise the Labour College to the extent of £500 per year each. The NCLC representatives pointed out that this was not a feasible proposition. The fact that most of the principal NCLC unions were already paying more per

93

member per annum for educational work than was the NUR made it obviously unfair to ask them to increase their contributions in order to decrease those of the NUR.

The NUR representatives' reply stated that their average expenditure on the Labour College was in fact £3,500 per annum. In that case, argued the NCLC representatives, their proposals would result in a saving of as much as £1,000 while at the same time providing educational facilities not merely for a dozen members as two year residential students, but for a half dozen residential students and thousands of evening class students. The proposed scheme would also enable the NUR and the SWMF to share in the control of the NCLC. Such a scheme would have brought about a much more satisfactory relationship between the residential work and the class work, as Horrabin later pointed out. But the NCLC scheme was in due course turned down by both executives.

In a further attempt to save the College the NCLC called a conference of unions interested in independent working-class education. As a result, it was agreed that the governors of the Labour College should in turn call a meeting of representatives of the executive committees of the NUR, SWMF and the NCLC with a view to considering jointly the possibility of preparing a scheme for the joint administration of residential and class work. When the NCLC representatives attended the governors' conference they found that the NUR executive had decided not to be represented, just as they had refused to be represented at the conference called earlier by the NCLC, and that the SWMF was also unrepresented, having made its attendance conditional upon the presence of the NUR. However, the SWMF governors were themselves present as were the NUR governors.

The discussion between the governors and the NCLC representatives was long but not fruitful. Eventually the governors proposed that the two controlling unions and the NCLC should endeavour to formulate and agree on a scheme to give equal representation to the three bodies, with equal responsibilities. financial and otherwise. Further, that an endeavour should be made to co-ordinate evening class and residential college work. The NCLC subsequently agreed to shoulder a third share of the financial responsibility for the College together with a third of the control, provided the NUR and the SWMF shared financially on an agreed scale in the cost of classwork and correspondence course work. Unfortunately, as Millar pointed out in the

June *Plebs*, the governors' resolution 'while designed to commit the NCLC to a definite expenditure on residential work does not commit the two unions to any expenditure for evening class and correspondence course work.'In truth the governors showed no enthusiasm for the NCLC's proposals. At a meeting in July 1927 they recorded:

> That having heard, and fully considered, the correspon-
> dence from the NCLC, we are of the opinion that there
> is no possibility of a satisfactory arrangement being
> agreed to for the continuance of the College in their
> proposals that would be acceptable to the two controll-
> ing unions and the NCLC. We, therefore, decide to send
> two copies of the correspondence to the two controlling
> unions to enable them to take action if they so desire,
> and that the Secretary advise Mr. Millar accordingly.
> (7)

NUR's General Meeting Stops Closure

For the NCLC the key to resolving the crisis lay with the Annual Meeting of the NUR, to which a number of branches had submitted resolutions condemning the executive commit-tee's decision to close the College. Millar declared in *Plebs* that the first announcement of this decision had been received 'with unconcealed satisfaction by the capitalist press throughout the length and breadth of the country.' After all, the NUR was paying nothing for class work and only £3,000 towards the College, not a large sum for a union with 360,000 members. The NCLC felt sure therefore that 'the NUR Annual General Meeting will look twice at proposals which are intended to wipe out entirely the national expenditure of the union on educa-tional work.' Nevertheless, as Frank Moxley has recorded in his appendix to *The Railwaymen*, a history of the NUR, the summer of 1927

> proceeded on the assumption that soon this unique
> educational institution (the Labour College) would be
> finally closing its doors at the end of the term. Once
> again, however, an NUR executive's decision was
> overturned by the Annual General Meeting. At Carlisle
> delegates stopped the closure of the College by 41 votes
> to rest of conference. An appeal by Warrington No. 2
> and six other branches and the Glasgow and West of

7. CLC Governing Board Minutes.

Scotland District Council, against the E.C's decision not to accept the NCLC's solution to the problem of the maintenance of the College was defeated, 29 voting in favour. (8)

According to *Plebs:*

> Mr. Cramp's arguments in favour of closing the College hardly deserve consideration here. He had a good deal to say about 'learning by rote' as compared with 'true education' which aimed at developing a 'free mind.' In fact, he repeated by rote all the stock arguments of the WEAer. We forbear making the obvious comment on the advantages of a 'free mind' to a certain sort of T.U. leader; only remarking that we still believe a working class mind to be of some value to the working class in the long run. (9)

Before he became Industrial General Secretary of the NUR, Cramp had given the impression of supporting the IWCE Movement which was very popular in the NUR. However, once he had become the Industrial General Secretary, after Thomas had entered Parliament and became Political General Secretary, Cramp showed hostility.

The TUC and the CLC

As for the TUC and the residential college, abortive negotiations took place between the TUC General Council and the two unions. A small delegation visited the College on 10 February 1927 and reported back favourably. Citrine wrote to the secretary of the governors on 25 March, stating that: '. . . the same measure of assistance as will be provided in the Ruskin College Scholarship scheme should be afforded to the Labour College; and in view of the fact that five scholarships have been taken up by members of affiliated unions at Ruskin College . . . I have pleasure in enclosing a cheque for £375 . . .'

At the September 1927 Edinburgh Congress it was formally announced that the General Council would endow three annual scholarships at the College. At the next Congress held in Swansea the General Council presented several heads of agreement reached with the NUR and the SWMF. Financially, there would be a short-fall of £2,000. The General Council

8. F. Moxley, 'Railwaymen and Working Class Education,' Appdx. A in P. S. Bagwell, *The Railwaymen* (London, 1963), p.688.

9. *Plebs*, 1927, p.251.

invited Congress to take or leave its proposal. In the course of a long debate Jimmy Thomas for the NUR and Will Mainwaring for the SWMF argued that their unions had borne the heat of the battle for many a year and must now ask other unions to share the burden. Their pleading was in vain for when the votes were cast an overwhelming majority voted against the proposal.

Last-Ditch Efforts,to Save CLC

William Rutherford, a student during the last two years of the Central Labour College, has described the circumstances in which the end came. About ten of the students, including eight who were members of the Communist Party or at least fellow travellers, were discovered to be bringing in agitators from the East End of London and organising communist cells in some of the unions. The other students resented this behaviour and complained to the Principal, Tom Ashcroft. He was a decent, kindly man but with an unsure touch in coping with disciplinary problems. Although he explained that such proceedings could not be tolerated in a College owned by the SWMF and the NUR, the ten malcontent students ignored him. Led by a Kilmarnock communist named Campbell, they did not easily yield to threats of sanctions and indeed there were frequent scuffles between them and other students. The impasse was eventually reported to Tom Pocock of the NUR, secretary to the College governors. His first reaction to the news was to exclaim 'this is, along with a lot of other things, about the bloody end,' presumably a reference to previous complaints about the activities of the group of communist students and the fact that there was an immediate danger of the College being closed because of the financial embarrassment of the two controlling unions.

In the first issue of *Plebs* in 1929 the editor expressed the hope:

> . . . that the Federation will think twice before it takes a step which is almost certain to close the only Trade Union residential college in this country — a college which it has done so much to create.' (10)

Its next issue declared:

> What we must work for is a closer co-ordination of the work of the College and that of the classes organised throughout the country in the NCLC. The lack of direct

10. *Plebs*, 1929, p.1.

contact during recent years has tended to render much of the work of the residential College sterile. On the other hand, the great need of the classes is for more — and more — trained tutors. We need a residential College. We need one which is an integral part of our whole educational work, and not simply a separate highly specialised 'side show.' (11)

And Jim Reynolds, secretary to the College, wrote in an article for *Plebs:*

'There is a great and growing need for the co-ordination and extension of the educational work of the residential College and the NCLC. A larger measure of unification of forces — financial and otherwise — than that which exists at the moment is needed.' (12)

On 18 May 1929 a conference of SWMF delegates considered a recommendation from its executive council:

that the responsibility of the South Wales Miners' Federation for the Labour College shall cease after July 1929, unless the Conference decide to provide additional funds for this purpose by special levies.

On a show of hands there appeared to be a majority in favour of providing additional funds but a card vote produced a majority in favour of the motion. The executive committee thereupon assumed that its inclination to withdraw from the College had been reinforced.

The NCLC made last-ditch efforts to keep the College in being. George Hicks and Millar went to see Ashcroft in the hope of planning a salvage operation. Present at the meeting was Jim Reynolds, a determined man who did most of the talking while Ashcroft sat smiling and largely silent. Reynolds argued that the existence of the College had been threatened several times before, yet it had survived; it would successfully overcome the present crisis; help from the NCLC was not needed. On leaving the College George Hicks turned to Millar in disgust, 'You know, Jim,' he exclaimed, 'if I wasn't married to Mrs. Hicks I'd marry Tom Ashcroft.' He was dismayed that the gentle Ashcroft should allow Reynolds to dominate him and fail to see that aid from the NCLC remained the College's only hope of survival. Reynolds himself could not apparently face the unpleasant truth that the first and best-known Labour College, which he had

11. *ibid.*, p.27.
12. *ibid.*, p.39.

attended as a student sponsored by the SWMF and with which he had been associated for many years, should have to turn for succour to the relatively upstart NCLC. Craik, in his book *The Central Labour College,* surprisingly makes no reference to the NCLC's offer of assistance which was made at a considerable risk in view of its own delicate financial position.

A meeting between the College Board and NCLC representatives was held at Unity House to discuss the NCLC's proposals. Will Mainwaring, who had been a student and afterwards a lecturer on Economics at the College, was the chief spokesman on the College side. Instead of backing the NCLC he raised several objections to its proposals. The reason for his opposition may have been his conviction that the College could still survive and the fact that his vanity, like that of Reynolds, was wounded at the very idea of the newer NCLC, with which he had not been associated, coming to the aid of the residential College with which he had been intimately connected. At any rate, his opposition helped the Board to reject the NCLC's offer. When shortly afterwards in 1929 the College had to close, the NCLC executive felt that the main individual responsibility on the SWMF side was his.

After the meeting at the College a group of Labour College supporters assembled at the House of Commons 'with a view to seeing what could be done to save the existing residential College,' but the meeting reached the conclusion 'that in view of its past history and difficulties, there would be a distinct advantage in not continuing at Penywern Rd, and if anything could be done it would have to be done by the NCLC.'

The governors did not offer the NCLC any part of the College equipment, which was sold up at public auction. Responsibility for that decision may have lain with the executive committees of the two unions. George Phippen, London organiser of the NCLC, went along to the sale, however, and managed to take possession of a bust of Dennis Hird together with the Central Labour College banner (which the students had carried in May Day processions to Hyde Park). These were many years later presented to the National Labour Museum by the NCLC Trustees. The NCLC also bought six hundred books from the College Library for the sum of £124.

The CLC's Contribution to Labour

In *Plebs* Millar lamented the demise of the College:

99

> . . . this year, which brings round the twenty-first
> anniversary of the residential Labour College, is appar-
> ently to celebrate, not the anniversary of its foundation,
> but the day of its dissolution, to the unconcealed joy of
> the capitalist press. (13)

From the point of view of the whole Labour movement the
passing of the Central Labour College was regrettable. It had
produced a steady flow of students of high quality who had
already made their contribution to the Labour Movement and
to the general improvement of social conditions. Many of them
were destined to make a still bigger contribution in the future.
The students during the session 1919/20 numbered no more
than twenty-nine. Of them, Tom Ashcroft became Principal of
the College and later editor of *The Railway Review* — the only
weekly trade union paper in Britain; Aneuran Bevan became a
Labour Cabinet Minister in the post-Second World War Labour
Government; Joe Crispin became an NCLC organiser; Ness
Edwards became an M.P. and Postmaster General and was to
write three short works on aspects of Labour history; D. J.
Davies became a member of the NCLC executive committee
and Chairman of the Welsh Council of Labour; James Griffiths
became a Cabinet Minister in the post-war Labour Government
and Deputy Leader of the Labour Party; Jack Jones became a
lecturer at the residential college; Dick Lewis became an NCLC
organiser and later the educational secretary for a large
co-operative society and a member of the Co-operative Union
education executive committee; George Phippen became the
NCLC's London organiser; Bryn Roberts became the General
Secretary of a small Union, the National Union of Corporation
Workers, which he subsequently transformed into one of the
biggest unions, the National Union of Public Employees; D. W.
Thomas became an NCLC organiser; Mark Starr became an
NCLC organiser, the author of two Plebs League books and
later the Educational Director of the International Ladies'
Garment Workers' Union of the U.S.A.; J. M. Williams became
the book-keeper in the Plebs office, a winter organising tutor for
the Scottish Labour College, a Glasgow City Councillor and
later an M.P; Will Owen became an NCLC organiser and later
an M.P.; Will Coldrick became an NCLC organiser, an M.P.
and Chairman of the Co-operative Party; and Millar became the

13. *Plebs,* 1928, p.170.

General Secretary of the NCLC and editor of *Plebs*. Others became M.P.s, Union and Labour Party officials.

Among Labour College students of other years were Will Lawther, who became the President of the National Union of Mineworkers and a member of the TUC General Council; Morgan Phillips, who became an NCLC organiser and later General Secretary of the Labour Party; A. L. Williams, who became successively an NCLC organiser, a Labour Party regional organiser, and General Secretary of the Labour party; Jack Bailey, who became General Secretary of the Co-operative Party; Hubert Beaumont became an M.P.† and a Deputy Speaker; Frank Hodges and Arthur Cook both became General Secretaries of the Miners' Federation. When the members of the post-war Labour Government entered the House of Commons in 1945, among them were fifteen who had been residential college students.

Craik's Error

In his history of the *Central Labour College* Craik fairly and squarely laid upon the NCLC the blame for the dissolution of the College:

> Willy-nilly, the separate existence and claims of the two institutions led to a competition between them for trade union support that was, in the end, to facilitate, first, the demise of the Labour College, and, very much later, lead to the disappearance of the NCLC itself as an independent entity. (14)

The NCLC was also largely responsible, he claimed, for the abandonment of the Easton Lodge scheme, which had offered the College a secure future. Craik can scarcely be blamed for making no reference to the disappearance of Labour College funds between 1922 and 1925. But that episode undoubtedly had some lasting ill effects by playing into the hands of one or two NUR leaders. Craik, in preparing his book, was also

†Beaumont during the first world war rose from Private to Captain-the only socialist Captain in the Regiment. At his first election meeting after the war who should be sitting in the very front of the hall with his arms aggressively folded across his chest but his Colonel! His was the first question "Were the Labour Party and the Candidate in favour of the Nationalisation of Women? Beaumont rose and beamed at the Colonel, saying "I'm sorry. I must lose my friend's vote, for neither the Labour Party nor I favour the Nationalisation of Women."

14. *op.cit.*, p.130.

101

W. W. Craik, former Principal of the C.L.C., and J.P.M. Millar
— August, 1961, when Craik. was up getting material for his
book on the Central Labour College

apparently unaware of the activities of the communist group which so offended Pocock of the NUR. The interrelated causes of the College's final decline were the continuing relative poverty of the NUR and the SWMF, greatly aggravated by the General Strike, their vain efforts to persuade other unions to share their financial burden and their failure to co-operate with the NCLC to keep the College alive.

Rutherford wrote to Millar in 1950:

> Concerning your letter of 3 May, though the cause of the closure of Labour College in 1929 was financial, I think it was assisted by the internal troubles to which you refer (though, naturally, this was not put forward officially as a factor). The financial position of the South Wales miners continued to get worse after 1926 and most miners' district offices were heavily mortgaged. You'll recall too that the depression began in 1929 and put the finishing touch to matters. (15)

Though conceding Craik's point that, after the General Strike the trade unions could not afford to support both the Central Labour College and the NCLC, Ness Edwards was far from blaming the NCLC for the College's final collapse:

> The organisation of the evening classes into the National Council of Labour Colleges, and its organisational separation from the College, gave rise to conflicting demands upon the voluntary financial resources of the Trade Union Movement. Craik's allocation of blame for the closing of the colleges to the NCLC appears to be exaggerated. There were other personal reasons. But the resources of the trade unions after the General Strike were inadequate to maintain both the residential college and all the evening class work of the NCLC. The depression and disillusion that followed the General Strike, the unemployment and the revenge of the coalowners took the guts out of the movement. The Central Labour College was to all intents and purposes a victim of the General Strike. The best memorial to it is the part its ex-students played in the founding of the welfare state. Craik should have remembered that the fall of an institution could only be explained in terms of

15. 6. May 1950, NCLC Corr.

the social conflicts behind it. The 'if's' of history are for the novelist and not for the historian. (16)

The closure of the CLC was discussed at the annual meeting of the NCLC in 1929. The President, George Hicks, seized the opportunity 'to correct a misapprehension widely current in the working-class movement that the NCLC had some responsibility for the closure of Penywern Road College. No such responsibility existed.' He also referred to a plan to establish a new residential college. But in the event the NCLC was unable seriously to pursue that plan and the need for a residential college did not again become an issue until almost ten years later.

The NCLC and the MacMillan Report

During the great slump which began in 1929 and caused unemployment on an enormous scale the Government realised that accurate information was needed about the mechanics of the country's financial system and therefore appointed a Committee to enquire into banking, finance and credit, under the chairmanship of Lord Macmillan. J. T. Walton Newbold, who had been a member of the Plebs League and had written a number of widely-circulated pamphlets bearing on financial questions, was one of the two Labour representatives appointed to the Committee. Macmillan asked each member of his Committee to give him some ideas as to how to proceed. Newbold learnt that Arthur Woodburn, who had recently written the NCLC's *Outline of Finance,* was preparing evidence for the NCLC to submit and travelled up to Edinburgh in order to consult him. However, Newbold felt he could not commit himself to an analysis which experts might later discredit and did no more. George Hicks then became worried. Was the NCLC not taking a risk in facing such a high-powered committee? Millar assured him that the NCLC knew something about the subject as Arthur Woodburn had made a special study of it. When Arthur Woodburn met the Committee, Macmillan, the chairman, asked him what was his position in the NCLC. Woodburn said that he was Secretary for Scotland. Macmillan, pretending this meant the Cabinet position with that title, smiled and congratulated him on his distinction. Neither Woodburn nor the Committee foresaw that Lord Macmillan's jest was

16. *South Wales Argus,* 20. Feb. 1965; see also G. Phippen to Millar in NCLC Corr. 27. Jun. 1955.

prophetic, and that he was eventually to become Secretary of State for Scotland and a member of the Attlee Labour Cabinet.

The Macmillan Report was published in 1931 and involved about two years' work. George Hicks agreed afterwards that his fears had been groundless. The Committee paid tribute to the NCLC evidence by indexing its original contributions to the understanding and solution of national financial problems. Mr. Curtin, Prime Minister of Australia, was later to tell a House of Commons meeting of Labour MP's that his Government's financial policy was based on the ideas in the *Outline of Finance* and discussions by correspondence with the author.

CHAPTER VI

THE THIRTIES

The ten years that began in 1929 were scarred not only by the long-term effects of the General Strike but also by the great economic slump that continued into the early thirties. The slump further reduced trade union membership. As the funds of the unions diminished, so the NCLC's income from affiliations fell. Some fees were slashed and others were suspended altogether.

The slump brought down the minority Labour government led by Ramsay Macdonald, whereupon, as nearly all Labour supporters saw it, their leader betrayed them by heading a so-called national government. The election that followed for the time being destroyed the morale of the Labour Party. Will Coxon, the North Eastern Labour College secretary, stood against Macdonald, who had always been an opponent of the Labour College movement, but to no one's surprise failed to unseat him.

The Slump Hits the NCLC's Income

The NCLC's annual report for 1930-1 shows that the AEU, already paying affiliation fees at a per capita rate well below 3d. per member, reduced its annual payment from £1,000 to £250. Millar was never to forget the sick feeling he experienced when the news was broken to him at a chance encounter with a union executive member at Hendon Underground station. The NCLC executive chose not to disaffiliate the AEU but to suspend only its postal courses entitlement, despite the fact that other services

THE PLEBS

Monthly, 4d.

OCTOBER, 19.

Special Financial Crisis Number.

which the AEU continued to receive cost much more than £250. The Scottish Painters' Union was forced not only to terminate payment of its affiliation fees to the NCLC but its dues to the Labour Party and the TUC. In 1932 the secretary of the Padiham Weavers wrote to Millar:

> I very much regret to have to inform you that the Padiham Weavers have decided not to continue their educational scheme for this year at least, owing to the financial position and a lack of interest in the educational facilities. (1)

Its payment to the NCLC was small, but similar retrenchment measures added up to a serious loss of income. Overall the slump led to a decline in affiliation fees from some of the Unions ranging from fifty per cent to a complete cancellation. All the unions which had to reduce their payments, except the AEU, continued to receive full education services because they had previously been paying the appropriate per capita affiliation fees.

Inevitably, the NCLC soon faced a financial crisis. Millar had no recourse but to present his executive committee with a plan for retrenchment, which included a proposal to cut his own modest salary by £26 per annum. Other economies included reducing the number of organisers in Division 8 from three to two and partially meeting the salaries of several organisers by employing them to correct some of the answer-papers of the postal course students.

In 1930 the NCLC launched a national appeal for donations to meet the cost of purchasing its new headquarters in Hampstead. It was signed by George Lansbury, the Countess of Warwick, George Hicks, William Elger, W. A. Strawbridge, Alfred Hodgetts, A. Honora Enfield, Secretary of the International Co-operative Women's Guild, J. F. Horrabin and Millar. The appeal attracted only modest support but provided some favourable publicity.

The NCLC Wins Over the NUR

One coup compensated for some of the trade union losses. At the annual general meeting of the NUR in 1930 a resolution was carried instructing 'the Executive Committee to negotiate forthwith with the representatives of the NCLC with a view to the

1. NCLC Corr.

adoption of a scheme for the education of members of the NUR, including education by correspondence courses.' In moving the resolution the proposer pointed out that the aggregate expenditure would be substantially less than that formerly incurred in subsidising the Central Labour College. The NCLC was soon invited to send a deputation to meet the NUR executive committee. The deputation was received with friendly handshakes but the moment the discussions began the deputation was appalled to discover that the committee apparently had no intention of carrying out what appeared to be a clear mandate from the general meeting. The committee insisted that local union branches must pay out of their own restricted funds for NCLC schemes. The NCLC deputation offered full educational facilities not in exchange for the standard fee of 3d. per member but for 2d. per member. As an alternative, since many NUR members worked shifts and could not regularly attend classes, it offered to provide postal courses for 1d. per member. The committee remained adamantly unhelpful and the deputation went away deeply annoyed.

The NCLC had no choice but to embark upon a second campaign for NUR support, a campaign brought to a successful conclusion at the union's next annual general meeting. The resolution recommending affiliation was moved by Jack Martin, a signalman and a postal student, who eventually became the delegate of Division 3 on the NCLC executive committee and later Vice-President of the Council. By its decision to affiliate the NUR agreed at first to pay the NCLC on the scale of 2d. per member. For many years the gross payment, which reached over £4,000 per annum, made to the NCLC by the NUR was far greater than that of any other union. Besides shoring up the NCLC's income at an opportune moment the NUR scheme had an electric effect on the extent of the NCLC's work and sharply raised central office costs. The railwaymen's response to the free educational facilities, especially their demand for postal courses, was enormous. In the first year of operations NUR postal course enrolments totalled 2951. The flood of work added greatly to the administrative costs of the central office and necessitated the acquisition of more staff and office space.

During 1932 there were no new union schemes. There was also a marked decrease in the number of resolutions submitted at union conferences asking for education schemes.

The Training of Organisers

At the beginning of 1931 the NCLC entered into a critical domestic phase which brought Millar's own future into question and caused deep pain to Christine Millar. The trouble stemmed largely from the personal hostility of several organisers towards Millar himself. They bitterly resented what they regarded as his high-handed behaviour and there was general chafing at his businesslike methods.

It was a struggle for the NCLC to recruit, train and hold efficient organising tutors, officially described as 'organisers.' The difficulty was caused partly by its inability to pay adequate salaries but mainly by a shortage of candidates not only with teaching ability but with the requisite knowledge of socialist theory plus a capacity for office work and administrative ability. The recruitment problem was aggravated after the closure of the Central Labour College in 1929, for the College had been the main source of suitable candidates.

In the years immediately following the foundation of the NCLC the executive committee had to grapple with the task of welding the organisers into an effective team. This was not easy since some of the organisers who had been appointed and paid locally resented the loss of their independence when they came under national direction. Since nearly all of them had been manual workers, they had not received any administrative training apart from what they had casually acquired in the Labour Movement. Some of the clerical work in the South Wales Miners' branches in the early days was here and there rudimentary, letters sometimes being written in pencil. Several organisers were puzzled and annoyed at being called upon to renounce local customs and conform to regulations emanating from a distant headquarters. The policies deemed desirable by the executive committee, viewing the total scene, and energetically implemented by Millar, did not always seem desirable or even make sense to organisers operating at the local level. Nor did they take kindly to being asked to reduce some of the activities they enjoyed, such as lecturing, in order to undertake others they found less rewarding, such as unromantic clerical tasks. They also resented the tight control that Millar exercised over their expenditure. A good number of organisers had political ambitions, the pursuit of which absorbed time demanded by their normal duties. When informed that they were neglecting their duties or performing tasks irrelevant to the work of the NCLC they tended to become rebellious.

Realising that trade unions could hardly be expected to hand over substantial sums of money to a seemingly makeshift administration and that bodies hostile to the NCLC were always ready to challenge the quality of the NCLC's work, and completely without justification to challenge the veracity of its enrolment figures, the executive committee was determined to insist on the orderly methods required to transform a collection of disparate local colleges and divisions into a national body. Millar's strong will sometimes ran up against the equally strong will of one or another of the organisers, of whom few were men of straw. Slackness was not tolerated by the NCLC executive committee, as its records clearly show. At its annual meeting in 1928, for example, it interviewed two organisers. One 'was interviewed with regard to his Summer Weekly Report Forms and the Committee decided that the reports on the summer work were not satisfactory.' Another organiser 'was interviewed regarding the small amount (£18) raised in local affiliation fees in the whole of his division during the year ending March, 1928, and the relatively small number of *Plebs* sold. The Committee decided that no satisfactory explanation regarding the small amounts of local affiliations and *Plebs* sales had been received by them.' There is no doubt that behind such control the organisers detected Millar's hand.

This was also a period when male workers were strongly prejudiced against married women — such as Christine Millar — holding jobs of considerable responsibility. Many Education Authorities, in fact dismissed women teachers when they married. The fact that Christine, after two years of arduous, unpaid labour occupying unlimited hours, became a salaried employee played into the hands of Millar's critics. As early as 1927 Woodburn had warned Millar:

> I have not had time yet to type out the Minutes of the National Committee but hope to do so within the next few days. When you get them, however, you will see that they have had a field day of personalities and salaries, and as you will anticipate the main bone of contention or non-contention is you and Christine and what you get, and from another side, Mark Starr and Kath and what they get. (2)

2. Woodburn to Millar, 13. Jun. 1927, NCLC. Corr.

108

Civil War Begins in the NCLC

At the NCLC's Annual Conference at Scarborough in 1930 the President W. A. Strawbridge learned from a former organiser, Morgan Phillips, some disconcerting information. Morgan Phillips had been taken into Central Office because it was no longer possible to finance his payment as an organiser. Younie, in the same position, had been planning trouble for the Central Office and had been taking papers out of the office without authority and unknown to Millar. Strawbridge at once insisted that Millar should dismiss this offending organiser. In consequence of that dismissal a number of absolutely false allegations against the Millars were soon being widely circulated. When the dismissal of this ex-organiser was reported to the executive committee a three-man Inquiry Committee, (anti-Millar) was set up. This Committee quickly produced a Report virtually condemning the Millars. Despite the executive decision that it should be treated as confidential and that all copies of the Report should be handed in at the end of the meeting, one or two copies were deliberately retained and the contents were afterwards widely disseminated.

Perhaps the most serious accusation in the Inquiry Committee's Report was that Christine Millar had recently been absent from the office for a period of three days without justification. The Inquiry Committee's Report alleged that some members of the staff had marked Christine's absence without explanation on a calendar in their office. The Inquiry Committee refused to specify the dates or produce the calendar. Some months later the Committee was required by the Executive Sub-Committee to give the dates of her alleged absences. It was then proved that the first day of absence was the day on which Christine Millar and other members of the staff, including members of the Inquiry Committee itself, had travelled from London up to the Annual Conference in Scarborough. The following days of Christine's alleged absence were the days of the Executive meetings in Scarborough and of Christine's obligatory attendance at the Scarborough Conference itself.

Millar had no intention of resigning or of accepting the suggestion made by some of his critics that he should cease to be General Secretary and be appointed National Organiser. Strawbridge afterwards told him that the man who was pushing that suggestion had a personal ambition to become the General

Secretary himself. This man was in fact the drafter of the Inquiry Committee's Report.

Having resolved to stand fast until the Annual Conference Millar rallied the support of his allies and, with the help of the Sub-Committee, extracted from the Inquiry Committee facts that would reveal how grossly and deliberately misleading it was. When the opening day of the conference arrived, feeling was still so high that he was still uncertain of being rehabilitated. He had arranged for a House of Commons reporter to attend and record a verbatim account of the proceedings. His intention was to take legal action should the conference be led into accepting the case against him.

Attendance at this NCLC Annual Conference was so unprecedently numerous that some participants had to sit on window sills. Millar noticed that for the first time several organisers' wives were present. He sardonically assumed that some of their husbands had scented a blood-letting. A merry delegate from Belfast assured Woodburn as the delegates were assembling that in the event of trouble he was 'READY FOR IT.' Supporting his word he opened his jacket and revealed the butt of a revolver.

The conference was initially chaired by the President, Strawbridge, a member of the AUBTW executive. However, the opposition carried a vote against the executive which reflected on his previous handling of the crisis and he at once left the chair. George Hicks was so angered by this slight upon his executive member that he walked out. Realising that he carried his union's voting card, Millar dashed after him crying: 'For God's sake, George, leave your voting card.' Millar then handed the card to Strawbridge.

In place of Strawbridge the conference elected William Elger, secretary of the Scottish TUC. Almost immediately Elger found himself reading out the lengthy document, written and circulated by Younie, the dismissed organiser, which cast reflections not only upon Millar but also upon several NCLC personalities including Elger himself. Surprised as he was, Elger did not so much as pause or raise an eyebrow. The hostile tone and content of the document had the unexpected effect of causing many delegates to begin discounting the allegations against the Millars. Thereafter the tide flowed powerfully against the opposition. Jack Wills, one of the first members of the Plebs League and then General Secretary of the National Union of Corporation Workers, spoke so passionately in Millar's defence that he damaged a bone in his hand through thumping the back of the seat in front of him. When all the votes were finally cast, the Millars were entirely vindicated.

Important Constitutional Changes

Painful for the Millars as had been the many anxious months preceding the 1931 conference, there were several valuable outcomes for the NCLC as a whole. To begin with, the executive committee now felt enabled to institute some important constitutional changes. It informed the organisers that the reputation of the NCLC was scarcely helped by so much time at the annual conference being devoted to their complaints about salaries and other matters and invited them to form a professional association which should elect one of their number to the executive committee. At the same time organisers would no longer be allowed to represent their respective divisions on the executive. Each year in the future, upon the occasion of the annual conference, the organisers should meet with the executive sub-committee in order to discuss their working conditions or any other points they wished to raise. Speaking at the annual conference in 1932 John Jagger, President of the NUDAW, laid the blame for the crisis of 1931 on the separatist tendencies of some of the divisions:

> . . . there has been a determination on behalf of the Executive to make this a national organisation with a national policy. There has been a determination on the part of the divisions that they were going to be a law unto themselves and that they were not going to take the discipline of national and central control. It is there that this matter starts. It is there that our trouble has been at the last delegate meeting and the one before that and the one before that and the one before that. I am glad that at last the Executive Council have taken the courage to deal with one of these people, the most gross offender of the lot, who have been defying the policy of the organisation, the decisions of the delegate meeting and the instructions of the Executive Council (3)

Another outcome of the conference was that Arthur Woodburn became the President of the NCLC and so chairman of the executive committee. His two predecessors, Strawbridge and

3. Annual Report 1932.

Hodgetts, had had little direct experience of the NCLC's divisional work and Hodgetts thought that this greatly handicapped him when dealing with organisers or divisional affairs. By contrast, Woodburn had long served the Scottish Labour College both as a lecturer and as the Secretary of the Edinburgh District. He was also thoroughly acquainted with the duties and problems of an organiser and had played a leading part in the Millars' defence. It rapidly became clear to the organisers and his colleagues on the executive that Woodburn knew what he was talking about. Woodburn was ably seconded by the new Vice-President, Jack Martin. From the time of Woodburn's election until the NCLC disbanded thirty-three years later, executive affairs went much more smoothly than in the past and the turbulence of the early thirties never recurred.

In general, the area of jurisdiction of the NCLC executive committee was also clarified in the early thirties. At its inception the NCLC had consisted of a large number of colleges loosely co-ordinated by a small executive committee. Within eight years the number of smaller colleges had declined, territorial divisions had been defined (see facing page), the divisional councils had become stronger and the executive committee had become a much larger and more representative body. Every division and every affiliated union now had a seat and the organisers were represented by one of their colleagues. Any three of the NCLC's constituent bodies and divisional councils could demand a ballot of the membership on constitutional or policy matters and the annual conference reserved the right to overturn decisions of the executive committee. The growing size of the executive might have caused great difficulties had not most of the business been dealt with in the first instance by a small sub-committee, which met more frequently. Thus, the executive committee itself received its agenda mainly in the form of minutes of the sub-committees, minutes of the publication committee, the General Secretary's report and statistical records.

At the time of the conference which debated the Inquiry Committee Report a college with two classes and an income of £10 enjoyed exactly the same voting power as an affiliated union with a membership of 100,000. The constitution was now altered so that a card vote could be demanded under which each organisation was allowed only one vote for every contribution of £50. Since the income of the local colleges was small compared with the affiliation fees coming from the unions, they were allowed voting strength on the basis of one vote for every two hundred class students enrolled during the previous year. Divisions were allowed one vote for every four hundred enrolments. This modified arrangement still left preponderant voting power in the hands of affiliated unions and other bodies.

The first few NCLC executive committee meetings were held in the CLC. Later meetings were held at the headquarters of the AUBTW when that union affiliated. The AUBTW had bought an old house in Clapham, aptly called 'The Builders.' When the executive committee had become large, meetings were held in the NUR board room or at TUC headquarters or in the board room of the Transport & General Workers' Union or in the Labour Party Committee rooms in Transport House.

Trouble in Birmingham

The events of 1931 had been wounding beyond measure for Millar but he had to endure still further calumnies. James Younie attacked him and published a pamphlet in which he claimed that the NCLC had betrayed its birthright. The decline in class enrolments, he lamented, was 'the funeral knell of the NCLC.' In place of revolutionary Marxism there was now a feeble policy of gradualism.

More seriously, Albert Ellis, who had been one of the leaders in the attempt to unseat Millar in 1931, attempted to seize control of the Birmingham Division when the executive committee dismissed him in 1936. He refused to hand over its records to the new organiser appointed. Ellis's attempt having failed he published privately in 1937 a venomous diatribe against Millar in which he incorporated a verbatim account of the report of the Inquiry Committee that had been repudiated at the 1931 annual general conference. The NCLC executive committee effectively countered Ellis' allegations by publishing a circular entitled *Dismissal of an Organiser* which dispassionately explained the reasons for his dismissal. So finally ended the 'NCLC's Dreyfus Affair,' to quote Archie Kidd, Assistant General Secretary of the Sheetmetal Workers' Union and a member of the executive committee.

But for practical purposes Millar's own position was reinforced after 1931. Previously, executive committee meetings had all too often been a battleground with himself the main target of attack; previously, his authority had been undermined persistently. Henceforward his position was strong and he faced his

113

daily tasks with confidence, Nevertheless, in 1932 yet another problem arose relating to the organisers. A few of them were still local appointees paid by custom out of local funds. Charles Gibbons, organiser for the Edinburgh and East of Scotland area, asked that such officials' jobs should be treated as national appointments and paid for accordingly. The executive committee readily agreed but Joe Payne, the locally appointed organiser for Glasgow, preferred to keep his independence and persuaded his district to secede from the NCLC. Several Scottish Colleges, including Aberdeen under the influence of James Younie, supported Glasgow's secession. However, when the executive committee boldly reformed the Glasgow College and Arthur Woodburn persuaded Bob Scouller to accept the office of Secretary of the Glasgow District, the secessionist movement began to weaken and quickly collapsed.

Training of Tutors

Besides dealing with the problems of organisers, the executive committee frequently discussed the problem of recruiting competent tutors. The closure of the Central Labour College had immediately aroused concern about the future recruitment and training of tutors. In his presidential address to the annual general meeting in 1929 Hicks said:

> The NCLC Executive realises the need for residential institutions, especially for the training of tutors, and is hoping to provide such residential facilities. Consequently, when the Executive heard that the Residential College was going out of existence, it decided to explore the possibilities of itself providing residential tuition and a committee was instructed to go into the matter.

The committee duly confirmed the need for regular training facilities but asked from where financial support was to come. The executive committee invited the divisions to make contributions. Some agreed to do so but the majority pleaded poverty. For years there were frequent complaints about the lack of suitable training facilities but no attempt was ever made to set up a permanent national centre and the small funds earmarked for the purpose had eventually to be used to compensate for some of the decline in general income.

Another proposal occasionally mooted in the NCLC was to undertake applied research studies on behalf of working-class

114

organisations. The minutes of the executive committee for 1930 record that:

> . . . a Research Department should be set up and that working-class organisations should be advised accordingly. The Department was to be set up on the understanding that it will pay for itself and consequently no liability will fall on the NCLC. (4)

The timing of this particular proposal was occasioned by the availability of W. T. Colyer, who was giving the Publishing Society valuable assistance and who, it was thought, would make an admirable research officer. A department was, in fact, nominally established but in the event it undertook no studies. The NCLC was indebted to Colyer, however, for writing one of its books, *An Outline History of Unemployment.*

The BBC and the NCLC

By no means all the time of the executive committee was devoted to internal problems. There were also such external matters to be considered as the role of broadcasting in adult education. Not surprisingly, the BBC paid no attention to the NCLC. However, upon hearing in 1929 that the BBC planned to set up a Central Council for Broadcast Adult Education, the NCLC enquired whether it was to have representation in view of its being the largest purely educational working-class body in the country. Unofficially, it was given to understand that its inquiry would receive sympathetic consideration but in the event the Council was set up without any further reference to the NCLC. The NCLC then wrote formally to the BBC asking if it was to be entitled to a seat and the BBC replied that, since the TUC General Council was to be represented, the NCLC would be adequately covered. In what way? inquired the NCLC. The reply was that, since the NCLC operated through a TUC scheme, it should be represented by the TUC. The NCLC pointed out that since the scheme was dead, the NCLC could not be represented by the TUC.

The NCLC Minutes read:

> In accordance with your decision I wrote the BBC asking them to receive a deputation from us on the question of representation on their education committee. I have to inform you that they decided not to accede

4. ECM, 1930.

to our request. A number of Labour MP's have written
them protesting against their attitude, but the fact is
that, while we are refused representation, representation
is given to such bodies as the Adult School Union,
YMCA, and such tiny organisations as the Tutors'
Association, which is an association largely, if not
entirely, made up of WEA tutors. The WEA, of course,
has a representative of its own. (5)

As a counter to the BBC's argument about the prior standing of
the TUC, the NCLC pointed out that the WEA was also
engaged in trade union schemes, The BBC replied that the
matter of NCLC representation would be referred to its advisory
committee. Meanwhile, delegates to the NCLC's annual general
meeting passed a resolution:

This annual meeting of the National Council of Labour
Colleges, representing working-class organisations with
over 2,500,000 members, strongly protests against the
action of the BBC in refusing to the NCLC (the largest
purely working-class educational organisation in the
country) representation on its Adult Education Committee and instructs the Executive to interview the
Board of Governors of the Corporation. (6)

All protestations were in vain and once again the NCLC felt that
'the establishment' had deliberately frozen it out of a national
body. They saw that, by contrast, in the Scandinavian democra-
cies, bodies like the NCLC received full recognition from the
broadcasting authorities.

The Co-operative Union Joins the NCLC

In 1933 the NCLC won support from the Co-operative Union.
The main objects of co-operative education, then as always,
were to train their staffs and to instruct society members in the
principles of co-operation and in general to encourage them to
become more socially aware and politically active. The Co-
operative Union, together with many individual societies, had
for long supported the WEA. A considerable number of societies
had also paid annual association fees to the NCLC: the SCWS
had provided a hall in 1916 for the foundation conference of the
Scottish Labour College and later made an annual association
grant. Many members of the Co-operative Movement, sharing

5. ECM, 1930.
6. *ibid.*

116

with the Plebs League the conviction that independent working-class education was indispensable, had accordingly welcomed the formation of the NCLC in 1921. In 1933 Millar, with the Assistance of J. Reeves, Education Secretary of the Royal Arsenal Co-operative Society and for a time a Labour MP, set about obtaining the support of the Co-operative Union. Thanks to Reeves' mediation and the fact that many local societies were already giving grants to the NCLC, Millar was invited to appear before the Committee. After a few polite words of greeting, the chairman, a retired schoolmaster named Rae, who was a fervent supporter of the WEA, essayed a deadly thrust: 'I believe, Mr. Millar,' he said, 'that the NCLC provides a biased education. Isn't that so?' Having anticipated such an allegation, Millar was able to reply promptly: 'Well, Mr. Chairman, I recently read a report in a co-operative journal of a speech on education by a well-known co-operative educationist. In that speech he said, and I quote his exact words, 'There's no such thing as an unbiased education.' I think you know who made that speech.' The speaker had been Rae himself.

After Millar had withdrawn, there was a lengthy argument, Although one group associated with the WEA stuck to the view that the NCLC was educationally unsatisfactory, the committee eventually decided to ask it to send copies of its postal courses for inspection. Christine Millar duly put together a selection of courses in attractively coloured bindings. After the Co-operative Union's next meeting Reeves reported that, when her parcel had been opened, the smart professional appearance of the course materials in their tasteful wrappings had surprised and disarmed the opposition. Affiliation followed.

The value of the co-operative connexion to the NCLC was above all financial. Association grants were paid by the English Co-operative Wholesale Society as well as by the Scottish Co-operative Wholesale Society. They thus became entitled to representation at the annual conference. In addition, large numbers of local societies also paid annual association fees. Classes were also occasionally arranged specifically for co-operative bodies, although normally co-operative society members attended the ordinary NCLC classes. Lecturers were provided for both the Women's and Men's Co-operative Guilds and Co-operative rooms were often used for classes.

Fiftieth Marx Anniversary

In 1933 the London Division of the NCLC arranged an exhibition to commemorate the fiftieth anniversary of the death of Karl Marx. The NCLC celebrated the event at national level by arranging a dinner in London on March 4th. Some one hundred guests took their seats in the restaurant, which was appropriately decorated with red flowers. George Hicks, seconded by Harold Laski, proposed a toast to Marx's memory, to which Marx's grandson, Jean Longuet (a French Socialist MP) responded. Ben Tillett offered a toast to the International Labour Movement. On March 14th an NCLC delegate laid a wreath on Marx's grave. The grave was so unkempt that the NCLC executive decided to undertake responsibility for looking after it. On two occasions in 1933 and 1934 the NCLC asked the LCC to put a plaque on the house where Marx had lived. Both requests were refused. However, when a Labour majority was returned to the LCC, the NCLC renewed its request and a plaque was provided reading:

Heinrich Karl Marx (1818 to 1883)
Socialist Philosopher
Lived here

In 1934 the NCLC, although uninvited, joined in the TUC celebrations of the centenary of the Tolpuddle Martyrs. As part of its celebrations the TUC arranged to hold its summer school in Dorchester, which is near the village of Tolpuddle, and arranged for the International Federation of Trade Unions to hold its summer school there too. Hearing of these arrangements, the NCLC decided to hold its own school in Dorchester. The Workers' Travel Association had been asked to find accommodation for all the delegates of the Trades Union Congress, which was to be held in the nearby big town of Weymouth. When the NCLC asked the WTA for help in finding suitable accommodation for its summer school, the WTA said there was only one such building close to Dorchester, but suggested Millar should see it before he booked it. He and Christine Millar therefore went down to inspect and sought the advice of the NCLC's local voluntary tutor, William Clark, an early member of the SDF who had become County Postmaster Clark met the Millars at the station and told them that the building suggested was an old, disused workhouse, with stone floors and tiny fixed windows. One glance at the place was enough and Millar and Christine returned to Dorchester. Clark then pointed to the roof of a large building which could be seen not far off through the trees. 'That,' said Clark, 'was Lady Mountbatten's house during the War. It stands in its own grounds and is now a preparatory school for girls. The TUC tried to get it for their Tolpuddle School but were turned down; Millar and Christine decided there was no reason why they should not call on the principal of the school, and try their luck. After all, the National Council of Labour Colleges sounded rather more middle class than the TUC; and the word 'Colleges' might count in their negotiations. To their astonishment they got the school. Since the TUC and IFTU students were accommodated in lodgings and the lectures were given in very uncomfortable school-rooms, the students were not slow to express their criticism of the TUC education department. Many of them on arrival in Dorchester had been deposited by taxis at the former Mountbatten home only to be directed to their proletarian lodgings booked by the TUC. The TUC Education Secretary, Wray, was a keen WEA man. It was only years later, failing to get the TUC to increase his pension to compensate for galloping inflation, he combined forces with Millar on this issue and they won a miserable 3% per annum increase to "Compensate" for an enormous loss in pension purchasing power.

The NCLC Exhibition

The year after Dorchester, the NCLC celebrated the twenty-fifth anniversary of the foundation of the Labour College Movement. The highlight was an exhibition, largely designed and arranged by Christine Millar, on the history and educational activities of the Plebs League, CLC, SLC and NCLC. The exhibition was laid out in the very extensive hall of the Quakers' headquarters in Euston Road, London. It was judged so successful as to be turned into a permanent display and shown in most of the large cities. In 1936 the exhibition was shown in London at the International Conference on Workers' Education in Transport House, London, and in the Usher Hall, Edinburgh, at the time of the Labour Party Annual Conference in that city.

Financial Recovery Begins

The number of NCLC national education schemes showed a marked increase in 1936. One highly welcome recruit was the South Wales Miners' Federation, which agreed to pay an annual affiliation fee of £1,000. Subsequently, nearly all the unaffiliated miners' unons had arranged schemes, with the result that collectively they came to provide a substantial part of the NCLC's total income and students.

At its annual meeting in 1936 the Scottish Trade Union Congress effectively disaffiliated from the WEA by passing the following resolution:

> That this Congress realising the effective work of the NCLC and the fact that it is solely maintained by working-class organisations hereby decides to adopt the NCLC as the only education organisation worthy of financial support. (7)

Unions which had been obliged to reduce their grants or even suspend payments because of the economic slump resumed their support. The Furnishing Trades' Association increased its payment from £5 to £100; the Scottish Painters' Society, which had been forced to suspend payment, paid £50; the Dyers' Union decided ro re-affiliate and paid £121. The National Union of Blastfurnacemen, unable to take advantage of the class facilities for its members because of the large amount of shift work in the industry, negotiated a scheme providing for free postal courses.

By 1937 the AEU was once again paying £1,000 per annum and the NUR had raised its affiliation fee from 2d. to the standard 3d. per member. The annual report for 1937 recorded that total receipts from union schemes had reached the unprecedented figure of £9,795, an increase of £2,010 over the previous year. The general recovery was confirmed by a rise in postal course enrolments of fifteen per cent.

In the year ending 31 March, 1938, the following unions arranged NCLC standard educational schemes: The Associated Society of Locomotive Engineers & Firemen, the Fife, Clackmannan & Kinross Miners' Union, the National Union of Pearl Agents, the Scottish Horse & Motormen's Association and the West Lothian Miners. By the end of that year the number of unions with standard educational schemes had increased to 27, while the total number of unions and other organisations with education schemes, including the limited schemes, was 48. The affiliated organisations included the Clarion Cycling Club and a section of the Labour League of Youth. The income from the educational schemes had risen from about £9,900 to £12,000 in the course of one year. In addition about 50 Co-operative Societies, including the CWS and SCWS, contributed £297.

7. STUC, *Annual Report*, 1936.

The NCLC, however, was still frustrated by the fact that some union executives continued to raise strong objections to paying for the education of their members. In 1936 the Railway Clerks' Association and the Boot & Shoe Operatives, which already had WETUC schemes, agreed to adopt a limited NCLC scheme. The NCLC recorded:

> It is against the policy of the NCLC to accept limited education schemes, because these schemes are very much less effective than the standard educational scheme, An exception had to be made in the case of these two Unions, however, as they had already an educational arrangement of a limited character with another educational body. (8)

The financial policy of the WETUC continued to exasperate the NCLC. Thus, in 1938 a meeting of the National Union of Printing, Bookbinding & Paper Workers agreed to affiliate to the NCLC. In the following year its executive reported back that it did not feel justified in acting upon this decision; first, because it must affiliate to the NCLC on its full membership and this would cost £1,000 per annum; secondly, because enquiries among branches had indicated that only 192 members seemed to be interested. Following further discussions at the annual general meeting in 1940 the executive committee reported in 1941 that the WEA had submitted a scheme which they found more satisfactory. For this scheme the union would pay an affiliation fee of five guineas and an additional sum of £50, any unexpended balance to be repaid. This union had a membership of 71,000.

In 1938 the Vehicle Builders, which had a membership of 24,000, offered the NCLC £25 for an education scheme. The union was advised that no satisfactory scheme could be arranged for that minute sum. It then decided, without consulting the NCLC, that it would meet the cost of the fees of any members attending NCLC classes. The union was informed that such an arrangement could not be accepted as it would mean, first, that only a few members would take advantage of the facilities and secondly that, under such an arrangement the union would be getting class facilities at much less than cost. The Vehicle Builders did not affiliate. The National Association of Theatrical Employees' Conference carried a motion recommending adoption of the standard education scheme and the prospects for

8. *Education for Emancipation* (1936), p.4.

121

affiliation seemed to be excellent. However, the executive committee asked its branches whether they wanted a scheme. In what terms the question was put the NCLC did not know, but it was aware that a similar method had been used before to stop a scheme being introduced. The method was to issue a circular asking how many members wanted to enrol for courses. Few replies would be received, some of them negative, and it would then be argued that there was no demand. The secret of the NCLC's education work was not based on the mistaken idea that trade unionists were dying to educate themselves for the good of their Movement, but on the realisation that the NCLC's direct publicity approach to branches stimulated a demand which did not previously exist. Needless to say, the Theatrical Employees did not affiliate.

Effect of Cinemas on Classes

Despite its improved financial situation, the NCLC was worried about the lack of adequate union support for its educational work and the fall in class enrolments. The Annual Report for 1936 referred to three sources of competition facing its classes: technical training courses; WEA and university classes; cinemas. The contrast between the comfort of the luxurious picture-house and the average Labour hall was striking:

> . . . it is obviously much more agreeable for the average person to sit in a luxuriously furnished picture-house than to sit on a hard seat in a Labour hall. That is doubly true if the Labour hall is, as happens in quite a number of cases, noisy, badly ventilated, badly heated and dirty. True. the Labour movement is a poor movement, but does it add to its members and, therefore, to its income, by tolerating halls of the kind mentioned above? . . . Ordinary people are not attracted by discomfort or by organisations that meet in dingy premises. There is no doubt that Labour meetings and NCLC classes could be made much more attractive if steps were taken to hold them in attractive premises in all cases. (9)

After the turmoil of the early Thirties, the main preoccupation of the NCLC was consolidation. Will Coxon later recalled the transitition:

9. *Education for Emancipation*, (1936), p.5.

How the Agendas changed. At first, they were crowded with particular grievances of local divisions. Then they gradually changed to motions of general policy. The Annual Meetings grew from almost family gatherings to terribly business-like conferences. Of course the inevitable consequence of development. (10)

Millar himself strove tirelessly to keep the local organisations up to scratch. Almost every issue of *Plebs* carried an injunction to greater effort:

There are several respects in which the NCLC's educational work could be improved. The state of college organisation, for instance, whilst satisfactory in some areas, is definitely capable of improvement in others. Every town of any size should have an NCLC committee officially representative of the local Trade Union and Labour and Co-operative movement and carrying on propaganda for independent working class education. (11)

Some effort was directed towards strengthening the NCLC's individual membership. At one annual conference a resolution had been passed to the effect that:

the Plebs League and Students' Associations should either be recognised so as to function effectively as a national body or their affairs should be wound up and affiliation to the NCLC cancelled. (12)

Women and the NCLC

From time to time the question was raised of strengthening the role played by women in NCLC affairs. About one in twenty of those who attended classes were women. In 1929 a local women's committee was set up in Newport. In his presidential address in 1931 George Hicks stated:

The women must be brought into the movement, and bound to the movement by the closest ties, and made active and articulate in the movement. There is an immense field of activity for the NCLC in training women to become propagandists, Trade Union organisers and active in politics and co-operatives. (13)

10. Coxon to Millar, NCLC Corr.

11. *Plebs,* 1937, p.201.

12. ECM, 1929.

13. *ibid.*

Occasionally day schools were held solely for women but normally they attended day schools at which the majority of students were men. The executive committee considered that female sub-committees of local Labour bodies and colleges should be formed. There was only one women's committee though the executive committee recognised that:

> . . . in larger districts such committees would be of tremendous assistance to the colleges and we are hoping that the Divisions and Colleges will take the matter up. (14)

When, on one occasion, a male union member sent in his final postal course lesson work, it was accompanied by a letter from his wife. She said she had seen the NCLC leaflet which her husband had received by post. It had listed the free postal courses to which he was entitled. He had not been prepared, however, to enrol for a course and she confessed she had enrolled in his name and all the work sent in had been hers. She understood that a certificate was sent to the student when he completed the course and saw no reason why her husband should get the certificate. Was it possible for the NCLC to give her the certificate? The postal course department sent her the certificate and the executive committee decided that in future the wives of members of unions with standard (not limited) education schemes should not only be able to attend classes free of charge on producing their husband's union cards, but they should also be entitled to take postal courses. The NCLC's financial resources made it impossible to run a campaign to enrol wives but those who did apply took the courses as surrogates for their less energetic or less interested husbands.

The Nazis

The NCLC had very early reacted to the advent in 1933 of the Nazi regime in Germany:

> Trade Unionists who regard as a luxury a solid grounding in working class theory and who feel assured that their organisations are able to withstand the rapid drift towards Fascism are surely entering into a dangerous gamble with the future. (15)

After Hitler had attained power a stream of German refugee socialists soon found their way to the NCLC office at Hampstead

14. *ibid.*, 1930.

15. *Education for Emancipation*, 1933. p.3.

and received a warm welcome. Those who spoke English well were encouraged to lecture at Trade Union branches and Labour Parties on the growth of Nazism. Others were invited to attend NCLC lectures so that they could improve their English and meet members of the British Labour Movement.

Of the refugees who came to the NCLC office the most valuable was Edward Conze. He was sent to Millar by Ellen Wilkinson. He was greatly interested in socialist education and particularly anxious that the British Labour Movement should have a real appreciation of the nature of Hitler's National Socialism. Communists and some other mistaken socialists were arguing that the Nazis were simply tools of German big business. Conze argued that they were much more dangerous than that and were using big business for their own purposes. He not only lectured on the subject at NCLC meetings — his English was good — but contributed some important articles on Nazism to *Plebs*. This resulted in the NCLC being able to play an important part in preventing sections of the Labour Movement being misled about the situation in Germany.

The last annual conference of the NCLC before the outbreak of war with Nazi Germany was a confident occasion. Readers of *Plebs* were informed:

> We had the satisfaction of learning at the Conference that the NCLC was in a stronger position today than ever before. Its support from Unions and working class organisations is greater, and the state of its own organisation is substantially better. (16)

Three months' later the title of the leader in *Plebs* was War Comes Home.

CHAPTER VII

THE SECOND WORLD WAR AND AFTER

The NCLC's reaction towards the outbreak of war was summed up by Millar in an article in *Plebs:*

> At the moment, the workers in Britain and the workers in Germany are powerless to stop the present struggle. They can, however, continue with that educational work which will eat away the mental chains that tie the

16. *Plebs,* 1939, p.176.

people to the economic system responsible for the present catastrophe. (1)

But continuing to provide an educational service in wartime turned out to be far from easy. When conscription was generally enforced Millar became alarmed that many of the divisional organisers would be called up. The Parliamentary Act allowed for the exemption of trade union officials, the category in which the NCLC included its organisers, but Millar anticipated that, if he were to submit an application for exemptions, they would be referred to the TUC where they might be disowned, since Vincent Tewson, the General Secretary, was unsympathetic to the NCLC. Millar discussed the problem with Luke Fawcett, General Secretary of the AUBTW and also a member of both the TUC General Council and the NCLC executive. At Fawcett's instigation they paid a joint visit to TUC headquarters and informed Tewson of their intention to apply for exemption on behalf of the organisers. Fawcett then made it plain that they expected Tewson to be helpful.

When eventually asked to give a ruling on the status of the organisers, the Ministry of Labour replied that they could not be classified as being in a reserved occupation and that the NCLC as such could not be treated as a trade union. Nevertheless, when a deputation called at the Ministry, they obtained a ruling that the organisers would be classed as social service secretaries. In practice, this meant that each organiser could independently apply for deferment to a national board rather than to his local Labour office.

Another threat to the educational work that could not be averted was the bombing of London in 1940. Though London at one time was being raided every night, *Plebs* had still to be made up and the proofs had to be checked by Millar and Christine underneath the floor of their house in Hendon. There was only about three feet between the cement base and the floor of the lounge above, through which an opening had been cut for access. Arthur Woodburn, at the time a member of the House of Commons, usually came out to Hendon and spent the night underneath the floor on a 'lilo' as did the Millar family — parents, children and grandmother.

1. J. P. M. Millar, 'War comes Home' in *Plebs*, 1939, p.252.

NCLC Moves to Tillicoultry

When the bombing had become persistent and land mines had twice damaged the NCLC's Hampstead Office, Arthur Woodburn advised Millar to follow the example of many of the trade unions and a variety of other organisations, and seek a safer haven for the central offices somewhere in the country; for one thing, he pointed out, if a bomb were to strike the building, all the postal course material and some thousands of postal students' reference cards might be destroyed. He had heard that in his constituency there was a small, recently vacated boarding school that might prove suitable. Having opportunely to attend a conference in Scotland, the Millars took the opportunity to inspect the property but quickly decided it would be too costly to run. However, during their visit they heard of another property for sale at a reasonable price in the nearby town of Tillicoultry. This building was a large three-storey manse originally built for a minister with twelve children. Having got the approval of his executive sub-committee and successfully quashed local rumours that he represented either a London syndicate or a firm of printers, Millar took over the property, which was known as St. Margaret's. This property — supplemented after the war by an office building erected in the paddock — was to serve as the headquarters of the NCLC until its dissolution, when it became the TUC postal course centre, which it still is. Because of the fall under the TUC in the volume of work done at Tillicoultry and in the staff one building was later sold.

St. Margaret's had seventeen rooms, together with a garage, and stood in its own grounds on a little private road facing the public park. It cost only £1,000 because the owners — two maiden ladies — were anxious to sell a house ridiculously large for them and most expensive to keep warm. It was a perfect retreat from war-torn London. In peace or war it had the inestimable advantage of being economical to run, labour being easier to find than in London, and much less costly. Eventually all the staff was accommodated in the new building in the paddock and St. Margaret's housed the library, records and stationery supplies as well as continuing to serve as a home for the Millars.

The NCLC and Refugee Socialists

The outbreak of the Second World War added to the flood of refugee socialists entering Britain, many of whom had found their way to the NCLC Office in Hampstead while the NCLC staff still worked there. Those who spoke some English were given free postal courses on request and the executive decided to provide a number of free places for them at the annual Summer Schools. Those who spoke good English were sent round to trade union branches and other bodies, to give lectures based partly on their experiences and partly on their knowledge of socialist theory and international problems. Some of the refugee socialists became NCLC voluntary tutors and wrote for *Plebs*. Among them was Hans Gottfurcht from Germany who later, on Millar's recommendation, was appointed the first Education Officer of the International Confederation of Free Trade Unions and rose to be assistant general secretary. Another lecturer was Julius Braunthal who had edited an Austrian socialist daily and later served as secretary of the Labour and Socialist International which collapsed during the War, and who afterwards became secretary of the new Socialist International and later the author of a three-volume history of the Socialist Internationals. Yet another refugee was Adam Ciolkosz, an escaped Polish socialist MP. A fourth was Peter Petroff, accompanied by his wife. Petroff had been associated for a short time with the Scottish Labour College during the First World War, returning to Russia after the Revolution. Under Lenin he was appointed Under-Commissar for Foreign Affairs and he told Millar he had signed the *first* Brest Litovsk treaty. When he found that the growth of Stalinism was driving democracy out of the Bolshevik Party, he and his wife took advantage of his diplomatic passport to go to Germany, never to return. Then the Nazis came to power in that country and the Petroffs feared they would be arrested and handed over to the Russian secret police with whom they knew the Nazis had close contacts. They fled to Britain, therefore, arranging for their children to escape by another route. The Petroffs became two of the gifted refugees who not only lectured for the NCLC at branches, classes, day schools and summer schools but wrote for *Plebs*.

The Council for Educational Advance

In February 1941 a joint delegation from the TUC, Co-operative Union and the WEA went to the Board of Education to request that a new Education Bill be prepared which should include raising the school leaving age by one year. On 18 September 1942, prompted by the WEA, the TUC and the

National Union of Teachers, the WEA and the Co-operative Union Education agreed to form the Council for Educational Advance with the object of exerting influence on the impending Education Bill. The NCLC was not invited to join. A delegate from the AEU protested at its omission at the TUC annual conference but was mistakenly informed by a member of the General Council that the reason for omitting the NCLC was that 'there was no evidence from the public pronouncements of that body that they were particularly interested in . . . the general education of the children of this country.' The NCLC had protested to the Education Committee of Congress but when its chairman 'had asked the chairman of the NCLC whether, in the event of an invitation being extended, there was any prospect of the NCLC accepting it, . . . he was told that they could not, or would not, answer the question.' This statement was seriously misleading.

In Scotland the STUC nominated four representatives to sit on the Scottish Branch of the Council of Educational Advance (SCEA) without any reference to the Scottish Labour College. The Executive Committee of the NCLC pointed out that the parent body of the Council was dominated by the WEA and asked that a conference to discuss the matter be called with representatives of the STUC, the Labour Party and the Labour Colleges in attendance. This conference duly met in March 1943 and the STUC delegates reported that the NCLC would be invited to join the SCEA. In June the invitation arrived and the NCLC asked the Council if any officials had been appointed. The Council did not reply until one week after its inaugural meeting and the NCLC decided, in view of the belatedness of the invitation, not to join the Council. The NCLC Executive noted that the Chairman and the Secretary of the Scottish Council for Educational Advance were respectively the Chairman and the Secretary of the WEA; that a memorandum issued by the WEA clearly stated that the WEA was responsible for the formation of the Scottish Council for Educational Advance had already been drawn up; that the Council had already held a national conference covering the whole of Scotland; that these councils would provide the WEA with an opportunity of getting in touch with Trades Councils and other working class bodies, an opportunity which the WEA was exploiting to the best of its ability. In all these circumstances the Executive agreed to take no action regarding the belated invitation extended to the NCLC to join the Scottish Council for Educational Advance. Its refusal was regretted by the STUC especially as 'the creation of the Scottish Council, and the association of the General Council with it, was unanimously approved by the 1943 Congress.' The attitude of the NCLC towards the SCAE was conditioned by the fear that the WEA would gain financially in trade union support. In *Plebs*, Millar commented that the NCLC's objections to money going to the WEA was 'based not on any element of jealousy or on a dog-in-the-manger policy, but on basic principle. The principle is a very simple one and is that the kind of work done by the WEA is already financed either by the State or by Education Authorities or University Extra-mural committees and in many areas by all three.'

In Scotland, cause for alarm about the future deepened when, at the annual conference of the STUC in 1944, a motion was moved and carried by a large majority that the STUC should affiliate to the WEA. The proposers argued successfully that a number of unions had education schemes with the WEA as well as with the Labour College and that the TUC collaborated with the WEA. An amendment in favour of retaining exclusive recognition of the NCLC on the ground that its only revenue came from working-class sources, was defeated. Millar was saddened by the decision. In an editorial in *Plebs* he wrote:

> It does seem a dreadful admission to make that the British Trade Union Movement should have to ask University people who have little or no first hand knowledge of the Trade Unions to undertake the training of trade union officers and other active workers.

The WEA had profited from establishing the Council for Educational advance and in appealing to wage workers' desires to provide their children with the educational possibilities that would enable them to climb the social ladder into middle-class jobs.

The War and After

In 1943, the NCLC wrote a formal letter to the Central Advisory Council for Education in the Forces requesting that it should play a part in Forces' education. The Council's reply was negative. *Reynolds News* (14 May 1943) reported that the NCLC interpreted this refusal as a deliberate attempt by orthodox educationists to monopolise education in the Services. But no one within the NCLC was really surprised or dismayed by what had happened.

During the war period the method of funding the NCLC became a matter of acute concern to the executive committee. The existing practice required that one-third of the income deriving from the affiliations of trade unions (excluding branches) with members confined to one division, should be transmitted to headquarters, the remaining two-thirds being retained for the payment of the expenses of the organiser and the part-time tutors, if any. Meanwhile, however, the costs of the headquarters' administration had risen sharply whereas local costs had remained relatively static. In 1943, therefore, the executive committee ruled that the divisions should not automatically retain two-thirds of affiliation fees but only that amount required to pay for work actually completed. Any surplus was to be put into a reserve fund which would be used to finance a proposed central training scheme. This was a rational reform but it irritated a number of the organisers, who objected to having to appeal to headquarters for funds to carry out new work. As an economy measure the executive committee also decided to employ some part-time tutors.

Throughout the war the postal course department did not cease to operate. A number of postal students worked on their own courses in Anderson shelters or while on fire-watch duties. One set of postal course lessons received came from a student seemingly at sea, whose ship had been torpedoed. The package of answer papers had travelled through several countries, as the cancelling stamps indicated.

The NCLC was jubilant when the Labour Party won its great election victory in 1945. Millar proudly reported to his executive committee:

> Scores of NCLCers are among the MPs elected to the House of Commons. They ranged from those who helped to found the NCLC to the younger generation of NCLC tutors. Among those elected are three who signed the Round Robin which was the declaration of the strike at Ruskin College in 1909. They are Arthur Jenkins, Hubert Beaumont and Meredith Titterington. Among NCLC MPs four are members of the Cabinet — Ellen Wilkinson (Minister of Education), Aneurin Bevan (Minister of Health), Jim Griffiths (Minister of

131

National Insurance), E. J. Williams (Minister of Information). The following are parliamentary secretaries: Arthur Jenkins, Ness Edwards, William Leonard, Arthur Woodburn and Ellis Smith. One small NCLC class taken in Glasgow a few years' ago by Arthur Woodburn has now four representatives in the House including himself. Four members of the NCLC executive have been elected, viz. A. Lyne, W. Coldrick, Arthur Woodburn and T. Williamson. W. N. Warbey, ex-NCLC organiser, has also been elected as have a number of ex-NCLC executive members as well as tutors and four postal course examiners — A. Gilzean, J. T. Robertson, A. M. Skeffington and A. Woodburn. The result of the General Election is likely to stimulate a considerable interest in the NCLC's work. (2)

In addition to the four postal course examiners some postal course students became MP's for the first time.

The executive committee decided that it would arrange a dinner in honour of the many ex-Labour College students who had been elected or re-elected. However, when the total number of people eligible to attend had been totted up, Woodburn pointed out that no restaurant was large enough to hold both them and the members of the Executive Committee.

Labour's Political Victory and Curriculum Changes

The advent of a Labour Government seemed to augur well for the NCLC, though it necessitated a change of emphasis:

> From being principally concerned with fostering an anti-capitalist viewpoint, independent working-class education had had to concern itself with the more difficult task of engendering a constructive socialist outlook and providing a training necessary to the intelligent grappling of the vast and complex problems confronting this country and the world . . . We must close our ranks in preparation for the coming struggle — a struggle which will determine the future of socialism in this country and perhaps the world. (3)

The appointment of Ellen Wilkinson, a long-time member of the Plebs League, as Minister of Education, encouraged some members of the NCLC executive to believe that the time was

2. ECM, 15 Sept. 1945.
3. Edinburgh and District Committee Minutes, 1947.

ripe to follow the example of the WEA and ask for a state subsidy. When the matter was raised on the executive committee Millar argued that it would be a mistake to submit an application as it would lead to grave difficulties. The Labour Government would be exposed to fierce attack from the Conservative Opposition if it did agree, for the Conservative Party never mistook its educational enemies for its friends. The first act of the next Tory Government would be to cancel the subsidy and the NCLC would find itself in financial trouble. The executive resolved not to make an application, and later on Ellen Wilkinson expressed her appreciation of their wise decision. At the same time her affection for the NCLC remained. When Dr. Kuppers, the educational secretary of the resuscitated German Trade Union Congress, visited her in order to learn something about the British arrangements for education in, and by, the trade unions, she referred him to Arthur Woodburn, then installed as Secretary of State for Scotland. Her allegiance was even more clearly shown in a private letter to Woodburn written in 1946:

> Dear Arthur,
>
> This is to introduce Mr. Stanley High of the *Readers' Digest,* an American journalist. He is over here to study Adult Education in U.K. Has been thoroughly indoctrinated by WEA who have never mentioned the NCLC. As Jim Millar is in Scotland will you take time to see him and explain.
>
> Yours,
>
> Ellen. (4)

The main features of the immediate post-war period were the continuing battle with the WEA, the unremitting struggle to increase trade union support, a campaign to obtain affiliations from overseas unions, the spread of foreign summer schools, the continuous process of revising postal courses and preparing new ones, maintaining the publishing output and, finally, the uphill struggle to transfer control of the entire operation to the TUC.

The NCLC and the IFWEA

The continuing antipathy of the WEA was shown by its attempt to exclude the NCLC from the international workers' education movement when it began to recover after the Second World War. Before 1939 the International Federation of Trade Unions (IFTU) had convened occasional international confer-

4. NCLC Corr.

ences on workers' education, but the Federation more or less collapsed as a result of the war. Millar's first inkling of the WEA's new activities was when he read in the press that a conference had been called on the Continent to found a new Workers' Educational International. Ernest Green, General Secretary of the WEA, was responsible for calling this conference, having got in touch with the continental bodies which, along with the WEA and the NCLC, had attended the pre-war conferences called by the IFTU. Although the NCLC had been represented from the beginning — that is, from the Brussels Conference in 1922 — it was not informed of the WEA's intention nor had the WEA sent it an invitation. All Millar could do when he learnt of the conference was to send a telegram wishing the new venture every success and indicating that the NCLC would be interested in the possibility of joining the organisation. According to Zachariassen, a Norwegian delegate, the contents of the telegram were not conveyed to the meeting.

Between December 1947 and June 1950 a series of contentious letters was exchanged between the NCLC and Green, over the failure of the latter to inform the NCLC about the formation and subsequent activities of the International Federation of Workers' Educational Associations (IFWEA). Green had become secretary of the IFWEA. The attitude of the WEA towards the question of the NCLC's membership of the international body was summed up in a letter dated 24 November 1948:

> As already pointed out in previous correspondence, the WEA was instructed by a recent Annual Conference to convene a meeting of the bodies it had been co-operating with abroad, with a view to further co-operation, and with the object of strengthening such organisations abroad as may have suffered during the war. The terms of reference were to invite organisations 'similar in type to the WEA' and to encourage their development. The Association must, therefore, be entitled to decide what bodies it considers are similar in type to the WEA and to take the initiative, as it has done, in bringing them together for consultation. With reference to your last paragraph, there has at no time been any proposal that representatives of your own organisation should be invited as I am sure you would

134

be the first to admit that you have never claimed that the NCLC is a bit similar in type to the WEA. (5)

The NCLC executive was in no doubt that the NCLC was being deliberately excluded from the IFWEA by the WEA despite the fact that most of the bodies invited were, like the NCLC, socialist in outlook. It was particularly incensed that the WEA refused to send a copy of the IFWEA's constitution or even to admit that one existed. On 7 April 1949 Millar wrote to Harold Clay, then chairman of the WEA:

> I have done my best and shall now have to report to my Executive that, despite their request, Mr. Green, Secretary of the International Federation of Workers' Educational Associations has not sent us a copy of the organisation's constitution and has not even replied to our question as to whether it had or had not a constitution. (6)

Eventually the NCLC received a copy of the vexed constitution and joined the IFWEA having the active support of the Scandinavian workers' educational bodies. The exchange of fifteen letters over a period of more than eighteen months serves to show how strained official relations between the WEA and the NCLC continued to be. For a time the WEA monopolised the offices of President and Secretary of the IFWEA. Some time after the NCLC joined, however, Millar made it clear at the International's conference that the NCLC was not prepared to accept an arrangement under which the two official posts were held by one organisation. The result was that a Scandinavian, Sven Arne Stahre, who later became head of UNESCO's education department, was elected president.

Support from Internationals

Little enthusiasm for the NCLC was shown by any general secretary of the British TUC, except Walter Citrine. Under George Hick's influence, he lectured at an NCLC summer school and had his book, *The A.B.C. of Chairmanship,* published by the NCLC. The position was different with regard to the Scottish TUC and many of the General Secretaries of International Trade Union organisations. Their socialism seemed to NCLC officials much more deeply rooted. Among the international general secretaries were Edo Fimmen, General Secretary of the International Transport Workers' Federation (ITF), the

5. NCLC Corr.
6. *ibid.*

135

strongest of the international trade federations and the one which, during the Second World War, broadcast to the sailors on Dutch, Belgian, French and other ships, following the Nazi sweeping victories in the West, not to take their ships back to German-controlled territory but to bring them to British or to neutral ports. Fimmen lectured at several NCLC schools. Another important international personality who lectured for the NCLC at home and abroad, was Walter Schevenels, General Secretary of the IFTU and subsequently General Secretary of the European Federation of the International Confederation of Free Trade Unions. J. H. Oldenbroek, at first General Secretary of the International Transport Workers Federation and afterwards first General Secretary of the International Confederation of Free Trade Unions, was another who helped the NCLC for many years, and who, after he retired to England, lectured at its summer schools in Britain and became an NCLC postal course examiner. The lecturers at the NCLC's foreign summer schools were nearly always outstanding figures in the Labour Movement of the host country and some of them also lectured at the schools held in Britain. Among these was Axel Zachariassen, General Secretary of the Norwegian equivalent of the NCLC. At Oldenbroek's suggestion the ITF provided a number of NCLC postal courses for trade unionists in British colonial territories.

Another Curriculum Development

During the War and after, the NCLC continued its policy of adapting old courses and introducing new ones to satisfy increasing and changing needs. In the early part of the War many active trade unionists had begun to realise that shop stewards were seldom trained to carry out their duties. If the War were to be won increased production was vital. An incompetent shop steward could not only do injustice to the men he represented, but material damage to the production line. Many shop stewards themselves began to feel that they should not be pitchforked into responsible positions without some form of preparation. In answer to the need the NCLC Postal Courses Department devised a course entitled 'Shop Stewards and Workshop Representatives and their Functions.' This course was originally drafted by Dr. W. McLaine, the assistant General Secretary of the AEU, who had experience as a worker at the bench, as a shop steward and as a Labour College tutor. Several other experienced trade unionists contributed to the final draft. The course was an instant success and was frequently used as a basis for class teaching.

136

When the war ended and the newly-elected Labour Government pledged itself to raise the standard of living, it became clear that increased productivity was absolutely imperative if living standards were to be raised. The TUC appeared to have the same view and therefore called a special conference in London of trade union executives to discuss the importance of encouraging trade unionists to take an interest in the problem of productivity. In 1950 the AEU asked the NCLC whether it could arrange two residential summer schools on Industrial Management for Trade Unionists for a number of selected active union members. The NCLC had not previously tackled Industrial Management and when Caddick, Assistant General Secretary of the Union and a member of the NCLC executive put the question to Millar on the phone, the latter swallowed hurriedly, not having the faintest idea how the NCLC could run a school on such a subject. However, he did not want to reject the suggestion and said 'Yes.' The vital question was How? He then recalled that a former member of the NCLC executive, Frank Chappell, a divisional officer of the AEU, who had represented an NCLC division, had been asked by Sir Stafford Cripps to set up a new government department which would advise the smaller firms on how they might increase production. Millar left Tillicoultry for London and ran Chappell to earth in his new department's office on the Thames Embankment. Chappell agreed to act as the main lecturer and recommended a socialist friend of his, Miss Nancy Hewitt, a senior industrial consultant, as another lecturer. Added to the list was Bill Hughes, who had recently lost his Labour seat in Parliament and was shortly to become Principal of Ruskin, and Dr. McLaine.

As the AEU Shop Stewards and other Union activists were to be brought from all parts of the British Isles it was necessary to choose a hostel in a central part of the country. Millar booked Holly Royde College, Manchester. The Executive Minutes of 19th September 1953 subseqently recorded that the College, which was attached to Manchester University,

> 'had broken its bargain by cancelling the let because of its objection to the NCLC. It had suggested that, if the Union would allow the University to run the school, arrangements could be made accordingly; but the Union was not prepared to have any outside body dictating the type of educational work it did.'

Fortunately a Co-operative guest house was still available

despite the fact that the season for booking was over. But for that the schools would have had to be cancelled. This experience contrasted with the fact that the NCLC on many occasions held summer schools in the hostels of Edinburgh University, St. Andrews University, Bangor University College and a London University College.

The two Industrial Management schools were regarded as successes and were followed in subsequent years by others in which the secondary subject was Workers' Control and Joint Consultation.

The first AEU schools on Industrial Management prompted the NCLC to arrange for a postal course on Industrial Management for Trade Unionists. This course and the accompanying publicity leaflet were prepared just as the TUC had called a special conference to discuss the question of productivity. It was the practice of the TUC office to distribute NCLC and WEA leaflets to delegates at congresses. A letter was therefore sent asking the TUC office if it would be kind enough to arrange to distribute copies of the NCLC's new leaflet, of which a sample was enclosed. The reply was not a letter of congratulation on having prepared such a useful course so speedily, but an intimation that the TUC office was not distributing any leaflets at the special conference. Millar, in Tillicoultry, telephoned and asked for Tewson, the General Secretary. He was told that Tewson was not available. Millar then asked for the Assistant General Secretary, but got the same reply. He then said he would speak to any deputy who was available. At this point Tewson himself came on the telephone. Millar reminded him of the discouraging letter he had received and pointed out that it was his responsibility to the NCLC executive, which largely consisted of trade union representatives, to see that such an opportunity for publicity was not wasted; that he had been in touch with his two London organisers and they had agreed that, if the TUC did not circulate the leaflets to the delegates by placing them on the seats in the usual way, they would themselves hand out the leaflets to the delegates as they entered the hall. Millar then went on to say that it had occurred to him that a number of his colleagues on the NCLC executive committee, including several general secretaries, would be attending the conference and that it was likely they would want to know at the next NCLC executive meeting why NCLC organisers had had to spend time distributing leaflets *outside* such a conference. Tewson hesitated and then said he would see

138

what could be done. When the conference took place the leaflets were not put on the seats as leaflets always were but left in a pile on a table at the entrance. Jack Martin, the NCLC Vice-President, who was one of the delegates and had been forewarned of the situation, said that as the leaflets were the only item on the table nearly all the delegates took one as they passed by.

Organising Problems

At the 1946 Annual Conference of the NCLC Millar reported that it had become exceedingly difficult to recruit organisers, partly because steady and better-paid jobs had become more plentiful. At that time the NCLC had 15 full-time organisers, 3 full-time tutors, 1 full-time winter tutor, a few honorary organising tutors and several hundred voluntary tutors. At Central Office the staff covering the work of the NCLC including the Postal Courses Department with a staff of 23 numbered 30. There were no postal course examiners at Head Office: they lived in various parts of the country and numbered 29.

During the post-war period the work of organisers became increasingly arduous over large regional areas. They continued to organise various activities, to campaign for support and to carry a teaching load without the benefit of paid secretarial assistance or, for the most part, adequate office space. During the period 1945-50 a single organiser in Edinburgh and District had responsibility annually for an average of 116 branch lectures, 70 classes and 30 day and weekend schools. In a typical year in the late 'fifties seven out of sixteen weekly classes in North Yorkshire were being taught by the organiser himself. Yet the loyalty of the organisers was remarkable. In 1955 five divisional organisers had served the NCLC for longer than twenty years. One of the main causes of the organisers' problems was the persistent shortage of funds.

The very success of the Postal Courses Department aggravated the problem ; more educational work could be done by adding new postal courses than by appointing new organisers. Thus, in 1949, less than one third of the total Central Office budget was allocated to the divisions. On the other hand, while the Central Office had to pay for nearly all of its assistance, a division paid for none of its services. Those services were given free by voluntary tutors, lecturers and by class, literature and college secretaries.

While NCLC headquarters ran the postal courses, publications and summer schools,the divisions ran the local classes, the extensive branch lecture service and the day and weekend schools. They also undertook all the local organising work and made a big contribution to the campaigns initiated by the Central Office. As with the federally organised WEA, some divisions were more active than others,depending largely on the composition of their populations and on their industrial character. But in general there was more conformity within the NCLC than within the WEA. Whereas the WEA Central Office exercised little control over its districts, which received direct grants from the State and collaborated with neighbouring universities on Joint Tutorial Committees, the NCLC, associated with trade unions through nationally negotiated schemes, was much more centralised.

In the early days the Scottish Labour College and its district colleges had a much larger income than any other division. This was partly due to the affiliation of local unions, as distinct from branches, which paid 2d. per member for free admission to classes. But when these schemes became national schemes at 3d. per member they provided additional facilities in the form of postal courses, the money being paid to Central Office. Moreover, as national union after national union affiliated on the 3d. per member basis their branches were no longer required to pay 2d. per member local affiliation fees to have free admission to classes. This reduced the incomes of many of the colleges, which were only partly made up by Central Office campaigns to get local co-operative societies to pay association fees, the bulk of which were passed over for work in the divisions.

The Participation Problem

Neither the impact of war nor the advent of a Labour Government with a handsome majority increased trade union enthusiasm for education. Speaking at the Durham Miners' Conference in 1943 about the apathy of workers towards education, Sam Watson declared:

> I can remember the day when a man would walk five miles to a meeting. Now some people want priority

tickets on the buses for a meeting only two miles away.
(7)
In his report to the 27th Annual Conference in 1948 Millar
wrote:

> The job of getting trade unionists to undertake educa-
> tional work in order to advance the trade union and
> Labour Movement was not an easy one. It was a great
> mistake to think that the affiliation fees paid by the
> Unions to the NCLC were used simply to provide
> educational facilities for trade unionists who volun-
> teered to take advantage of them. In fact, a very
> important part of trade union educational work was to
> stimulate members who had no desire to take up trade
> union education to do so and a substantial part of the
> NCLC's income had to be spent on that most vital
> activity. (8)

One way of arousing greater interest was to make use of the
trade union document that trade unionists had constantly to
handle — their membership card. Delegates to the Annual
Conference of the NCLC in 1946 passed a resolution to the
effect:

> That every trade union card should show that its holder
> was entitled to free trade union educational facilities
> just as every young citizen's birth certificate entitled him
> or her to free schooling. (9)

The Plebs League had been made up of individual members.
On its dissolution in 1927 no steps were taken by the NCLC to
establish individual membership. However, in 1948 it was
decided to bring such a system into existence. In return for an
annual subscription individuals were given the right to attend
local college meetings and to receive a copy of *Plebs*. 342 people
immediately took advantage of the offer and by 1962 there were
813 individual members.

The Residential College Idea Revived

In 1944 the NCLC got wind that the TUC was considering
providing after the War some form of residential training for
union officials. Still concerned about the need to offer residential
courses for its own organisers and tutors, the NCLC executive

7. NCLC MSS.
8. *Annual Report* in ECM, 1948.
9. *ibid.*, 1946.

committee instructed Millar to discuss with Citrine, General Secretary of the TUC, the possibility of co-operating in the running of a residential college. Although asked to submit a memorandum on the subject Millar gathered the impression that the TUC was not keen to collaborate. This memorandum, which was published in *Plebs*, took the form of a manifesto pleading for a comprehensive educational scheme for trade unionists to be sponsored by the unions themselves in collaboration with the NCLC. It attacked a TUC proposal to arrange courses under the aegis of the London School of Economics:

> The NCLC believes that the Trade Union Movement should not spend any trade union money on types of education which can be and will be satisfactorily provided by Education Authorities. The NCLC contends that, in the main, education for the personal betterment of the individual is the concern of the individual and the public education authority and not of the Trade Union Movement. On the other hand, education to equip individuals anxious and willing to serve the Movement should be provided by the Movement. Surely it is also true that the Trade Union Movement should do its own special educational work and not pass it out to the universities which have neither the trade union faith nor the hard-won experience that successful trade union educational work requires.

The new comprehensive scheme should include provision for a residential Labour College which

> ... could take the form of the Trade Union Movement's War Memorial and should be linked up with the activities and needs of the NCLC which does the bulk of Trade Union educational work. (10)

The TUC failed to react to this manifesto and the NCLC therefore wrote to the TUC Education Committee on 28 December 1944 (11) saying that it intended to launch an appeal for funds to establish a residential college on its own account and thought that the TUC should know of its intention. At this, the TUC replied that the training courses which the General Council proposed to initiate would develop to such a degree that it would become necessary to set up a permanent TUC training

10. ECM, 1944.
11. NCLC Corr.

college. Nothing was said, however, about collaborating with the NCLC. This did not surprise the NCLC since it was aware that the TUC intended ultimately

> to take charge of its own specialised education with quite undivided control and to have a residential college adequate for the purposes of the movement. (12)

In short, the NCLC had been rebuffed.

The Wortley Hall Development

In 1950 Vin Williams, the ebullient organiser for the South Yorkshire area, conceived the idea of transforming Wortley Hall, ancestral home of the Earls of Wharncliffe, which was standing empty, into a holiday home and summer school centre for the Labour Movement. A sub-committee of the NCLC executive committee visited Wortley Hall and discussed the proposal with Williams, who had formed the Wortley Hall Provisional Committee. The sub-committee decided that the NCLC could not possibly risk accepting the financial liability but agreed to encourage Williams to go ahead in his personal capacity. With the help of donations and funds raised by a variety of devices Williams and his voluntary helpers managed to turn the hall into a flourishing centre for education and recreation, much frequented by trade unionists. What made the centre possible was Williams' ability to persuade considerable numbers of craftsmen and other workers to devote a great deal of time to putting Wortley Hall into a useable condition without any payment whatsoever.

The NCLC's Structure

By 1949 a number of changes had been made in the NCLC constitution. The introduction of Divisional and College printed rules had standardised administration procedures throughout the country. The objects of the NCLC had been cut down to one phrase — 'To provide independent working-class education.' The reason for this change was not that the objects had changed, but that it was thought that the old-established objects might play into the hands of the state, by making it possible to argue that the NCLC was not an educational but a political body, with the result that the unions might be forced to pay the NCLC out of their political funds. This would mean that the 3d. per member would be paid only on the political membership, which was usually considerably smaller than the total membership.

12. ECM, 1945.

Another effect of retaining the original wording might have been to prevent unions which had no political funds from affiliating to the NCLC which would have cut the NCLC's work still further.

Eventually, the NCLC structure was stabilised as follows:

National Executive
One representative from:
1. British TUC
2. Scottish TUC
3. Irish TUC (Northern Area)
4. General Federation of Trade Unions
5. Labour Party
6. Co-operative Union
7. Each union with an NCLC Scheme

One representative from:
1. Each NCLC division
2. The NCLC Organisers' Association

Divisional Councils
One representative from:
1. Labour Party Regional Council
2. Co-operative Union Regional Council
3. Each Union with an NCLC Educational Scheme having branches in the division
4. Each Organisation with a Divisional Scheme
5. Each local College

College Committees
One representative from:
1. Each Branch of an Organisation with an NCLC Scheme
2. Each Trade Union or other Branch locally affiliated and each local affiliated Labour Party, Trades Council or Co-operative Society
3. One representative from each class

In 1948 Millar and Christine Millar celebrated the twenty-fifth anniversary of Millar's appointment as General Secretary of the NCLC. The burden upon them did not lighten as year followed year. Far from it. The last critical period for the NCLC was about to begin.

CHAPTER VIII

RATIONALISATION — THE LAST PHASE

Whereas during its earlier years the NCLC was mainly engaged in providing educational programmes for the local branches of unions, for Labour parties and other local organisations, by the Second World War most of its work was concerned with what it termed 'standard union education schemes,' financed and administered on a nationwide basis. Although it had a competitor in the WETUC, to which a few of its own member unions were also affiliated, it dominated trade union education. After the Second World War, however, both the NCLC and the WETUC had to face growing competition from a third source, when some of the bigger unions had begun to launch their own schemes, which proved to be expensive. To the NCLC it seemed that the existence of the WETUC with its inadequate education schemes lay behind the decisions of the other larger unions such as the T & GW and the G & MW to invest relatively large sums in creating their own programmes, for these unions were largely traditional supporters of the WETUC. The AEU was exceptional in restricting its own direct provision of educational facilities since it regarded the NCLC as capable of meeting most of its requirements.

Separate Union Schemes: A New Problem

Millar was acutely aware of the implications for the NCLC's future of the introduction of independent trade union educational schemes. He explained the position in a letter to Sam Watson, General Secretary of the Durham Miners — for years an NCLC voluntary tutor:

> In the course of our recent conversation you said, I think, that we would not need to consider rationalisation if we could get the G & MW and T & GW to affiliate on their membership. I can agree with you, but I have been trying for years to do that and there is not the slightest hope because these two unions have built up big education departments of their own, and their allegiance is divided between the WEA and the NCLC. The only way to bring them into purely trade union educational organisations is by means of rationalisation. The competition for trade union funds for educational

145

purposes has increased very greatly in recent years. This is because a passion has developed for unions doing some educational work of their own. Even some small unions now flatter themselves that they are doing educational work by running one week-end school that costs £200 a year for a handful of students. (1)

Following the new fashion for large unions to run their own education programmes the National Union of Distributive and Allied Workers (previously NUDAW) one of the biggest unions affiliated to the NCLC was tempted to follow suit. The immediate cause was a decision taken by the NCLC Executive at its last meeting in 1956 to raise the standard affiliation fee from 3d. to 4d. a member. Alan Birch, who had not long been the General Secretary, complained that his union could not afford the increase and proposed that the NCLC be asked to provide a limited scheme at lower cost. The USDAW also questioned the scale of payment 'in relation to' the extent to which members in the exercise of a free choice in using the various educational schemes, in fact, take advantage of the NCLC.' The NCLC was opposed in principle to limited affiliation schemes. Moreover, Millar suspected adherents of the WEA were responsible for this move and hinted that Birch perhaps wished to destroy the NCLC. Members of USDAW had actually taken full advantage of the NCLC's facilities. Millar believed that Birch really wanted to adopt an independent scheme like those of some other large unions but foresaw difficulties in persuading his Executive to find the necessary funds if it were to pay 4d. per member to the NCLC. Anxious to preserve the affiliation of USDAW the NCLC Executive Committee arranged for its sub-committee to meet Birch but that sub-committee failed to make any impression on him. His mind was made up and he was hardly even courteous.

In 1958 USDAW finally disaffiliated. Its loss was a bitter blow. The long relationship between the union and the NCLC had been initiated largely by John Jagger, A. W. Burrows and Ellen Wilkinson — all at the time important officials of NUDAW. Millar was deeply chagrined at the breach with the new leadership. His concern led him to take the unusual step of conveying his regrets in a circular letter to branch secretaries of USDAW:

This year the NCLC will be celebrating the golden

1. Millar to Watson, 18. May 1961, NCLC MSS.

146

jubilee of the Labour College Movement. I think you'll agree that for the USDAW — one of the NCLC's two foundation unions — to withdraw its upport . . . is a severe and most unmerited blow at working-class education. This blow is doubly severe because it comes at a time when the NCLC is trying to increase its income to meet costs and to provide long-overdue pay increases for its staff (2)

Shortly afterwards Millar was invited to speak on workers' education at a gathering organised by the Oxford Delegacy for Extra-Mural Studies. At question time, when asked to comment upon the recent trend for unions to establish education units, he pointed out that not even the biggest union could afford to provide educational facilities on as ample a scale as those provided by the NCLC. Recently, he said, one union had decided to pay for its own programme by the simple process of dropping its NCLC affiliation and using the money thereby saved to appoint a solitary education officer, who could hardly be expected to provide the same extensive service as the whole NCLC organisation. The statement provoked some laughter in the audience since the recently appointed education officer happened to be siting in the hall.

Bringing in the Laggards

In the face of the trend towards the establishment of independent educational schemes with narrow curricula the only obvious way of persuading the two biggest unions in Britain to make an adequate contribution to the NCLC's type of work seemed to be to prompt the TUC into taking over responsibility for that work. If this could be done, the recalcitrant unions would be required to pay the same subscription per member as the powerful AEU not to speak of quite a number of smaller unions. Furthermore, rationalisation of the organisation within the TUC would oblige every trade union affiliated to the TUC to make its contribution and this would bring in a number of laggards, especially from the textile industry. More money would become available for trade union education work, the WETUC might be expected to disappear and Ruskin College might lose its postal courses, leaving only one postal course department, of which the NCLC section would form by far the largest component.

2. Millar to branch secretaries of USDAW, 11.3.1958, *ibid.*

Millar himself had a further motive. He realised that the association he had served so faithfully for almost forty years might be hard pressed to survive his retirement for long and his retirement could not be deferred indefinitely. Millar had been involved for so many years in shoring up the NCLC and was known to so many trade union officials and executive members that he had come to exercise considerable personal influence in negotiating, retaining and extending education schemes. After the Communists had obtained control of the Electrical Trade Union and started a small residential college of their own which cost a good deal of money they began to take steps to drop their NCLC scheme. Millar then sent a circular to all the union's current and former postal course students drawing attention to the move. Shortly afterwards at Congress he was asked by the ETU Assistant General Secretary what business he had circularising his union members. Millar knowing that nothing was to be gained by temporising bluntly replied: 'The members that we circularised were NCLC ETU students.' That resulted in the plan to drop the scheme being shelved.

Millar knew that his successor as General Secretary could hardly hope to have anything like his range of contacts and might well have difficulty in obtaining additional trade union support in a field that had become much more restricted and even in obtaining increased affiliation fees to cover inflation especially as still more of the larger unions might adopt costly educational schemes of their own. In addition, the TUC education department might well seize the opportunity of Millar's not-too-distant retirement to extend its own educational work and, if that should require an increase in fees payable to Congress, the problems facing his successor in financing the NCLC would be compounded still further. Yet another explanation of the desire for rationalisation was that a large part of Millar's energies had always been devoted to trying to get new affiliations and to beating off union attempts to retrench by dropping or reducing their NCLC affiliation fees. Once the TUC had taken over the work, the man in charge would presumably experience few of the difficulties which Millar had wrestled with and he would be able, presumably, to concentrate upon promoting and extending the educational work.

Arthur Woodburn strongly supported the rationalisation idea. Three years older than Millar, he feared that when the latter retired the organisation would find it hard to stand up to the

148

combined competition of the TUC education department, union education schemes, the WEA and Ruskin College. He also considered that since the NCLC was now organisationally and financially stronger than ever before a more auspicious opportunity might never recur to negotiate for the continuance of its work and the protection of the tenure of its staff, a human problem of deep concern to himself as it was to Millar.

Ebby Edwards' Warning

The pressure to seek for rationalisation came not only from the NCLC's officials. At its Annual General Meeting in 1959 the Glasgow College urged that negotiations should take place with the TUC. The College believed, like senior NCLC officials, that the Organisation was so strong and had so many supporters on the General Council of the TUC that there was no risk of damaging the educational programme. Forgotten was the warning given in 1944 by Ebby Edwards, General Secretary of the NUM, that the NCLC must always be kept out of the hands of the TUC.

So for the fourth time the NCLC entered into negotiations with the TUC in the hope of at last producing a composite educational programme for trade unionists. The first and second series of negotiations had taken place in 1922 and in 1925. On those occasions rationalisation had been urged not by the NCLC but by active adherents of the WEA. Then, during the Second World War, Millar had mooted the idea of centralised control in a pamphlet entitled *Post War Education:*

> At present the situation is such that there is wholesale competition between the two bodies, and the State subsidises one body against the other. Moreover, while some trade unions treat their educational schemes with far-sighted generosity others allocate quite inadequate amounts for educational purposes. Many trade unions have no educational schemes whatsoever. Is it too much to hope that great weight will be attached to trade union educational work in the post-war world? . . . It is no doubt generally accepted that a modern State requires a well-planned State educational system. Is there not equal need for a well-planned educational system to meet the special needs of the Trade Union Movement? (3) (3)

3. *Post-War Education* (1943), p.16

149

The TUC had flirted with the possibility of introducing a comprehensive scheme in 1946 by appointing a Committee of Inquiry. W. E. Jones, representing the NUM, who moved the resolution, first praised the NCLC and then observed that in the view of his union 'there should be brought into the investigation the experience of the NCLC and the experience of the WETUC.' Among those who spoke in favour of a comprehensive scheme was George Cornes, who was to play a prominent part years later in the final negotiations between the NCLC and the TUC. The committee's report was considered by Congress at its Annual Meeting in 1948. The NCLC had proposed that its organisation should be amalgamated into one body with the WETUC under the direct control of the TUC. It emphasised that it was not seeking the abolition of the WEA, merely its withdrawl from trade union educational schemes. For its part, the WEA had proposed a tripartite arrangement in which the WEA — the WETUC having been dissolved — would provide trade union education alongside the NCLC and the unions themselves.

The TUC Rejects a Rationalisation Proposal

Plainly neither the WEA nor the NCLC was in a position to bring about a merger. Each, however, had shown an unprecedented willingness to seek an understanding. As one delegate pointed out: '. . . the NCLC had gone far beyond what anybody imagined they would in trying to meet the wishes of the trade union movement.' What the NCLC had in mind was that it would be by far the stronger section in the new schemes suggested. It believed that this would be reflected in the educational work if both the NCLC and WETUC were taken over by the TUC. In spite of what appeared a conciliatory spirit, the TUC committee virtually abandoned the search for a solution:

> The first possibility — the amalgamation of the existing bodies — does not secure the support of the bodies concerned and has practical disadvantages. The second — the provision of a comprehensive service directed by the TUC — is calculated to involve a permanent levy of 3d. per member per annum. On this ground, as well as others, the committee is unable to recommend such a scheme. The third possibility — that of the concentration of the finance of trade union educational work — is rejected by the committee because any advantages to be

achieved through such a scheme would be so partial and so conditional as to rob the scheme of practical value as a solution of the problem under examination. (4)

Thus, the trade union movement fumbled a chance to introduce a centralised scheme. It was very soon after this that Allan Flanders, at one time a TUC officer and later an Oxford University lecturer, commented on the neglect of trade union education in Britain.

> For this neglect the trade unions themselves carry the main responsibility. It is a task in which — until quite recently — they have taken little direct interest. Their financial contributions to the WEA or the NCLC might well be viewed by the cynical as the payment of conscience money. (5)

More competitive years loomed ahead for the NCLC and the WETUC, for which neither could be blamed. Nevertheless, at the time, Millar did blame the WEA for insisting upon a tripartite arrangement, and the WEA believed mistakenly that the NCLC was anxious for a rationalisation scheme because of its alleged financial problems.

The Labour Party Approached

The TUC having shown little interest, the NCLC therefore turned to the Labour Party with the same idea in mind. In the 'thirties, when Secretary of the Scottish Labour Party, Arthur Woodburn had argued in favour of the closest possible collaboration between the Labour Party and the NCLC. Instancing the Party's difficulties in publicising its policies in rural areas, he had pointed to the importance of postal courses. A postal course on agricultural problems, for example, could help to inform key supporters, who might then act as opinion leaders in their communities. In 1948, when Arthur Woodburn and Morgan Phillips were travelling together between Edinburgh and London, Woodburn proposed to Phillips, then the General Secretary of the Labour Party, that the Party should take over the NCLC's activities. Though personally favourable to the proposal Phillips was unable to carry his executive with him; they feared, so James Griffiths later told Millar, to antagonise some WEA supporters on the eve of a General Election.

4. *TUC Annual Report,* p.157.

5. A. Flanders, 'An American Experiment,' in Trade Union Education in *The Highway,* Vol 41, 1950, p.64.

In 1948 Morgan Phillips had issued a circular on behalf of the Labour Party urging the training of Labour candidates for the local government elections in the following year. 'Training schemes,' he said, 'will be essential in many areas and should be considered at once. Where there is no tutor available to the local party, classes can be arranged in association with the National Council of Labour Colleges or the Workers' Educational Association.' How significant this circular is when seen against the background of the Labour Party's attitude towards political education! A dominant feature of the Labour Party in the twentieth century has been its inability to perceive the need for anything resembling large-scale education in politics for its own membership. Delegates to the TUC also seldom showed much interest in that section of the General Council's annual report which dealt with trade union educational programmes. The Labour Party itself has done little to educate its own members, apart, for example, from issuing some pamphlets and running a few summer schools. In a recent study Dr. A. S. Barker makes clear that the Labour Party has always tended to ignore the vital question of the content of education. Its effects have been predominently concerned with ensuring that the State should provide equality of educational opportunity for the children of workers. And by equality of education they first meant opening wider access to the grammar schools and universities. More recently, as the grammar school opening remained restricted, Labour has put its shoulder behind the comprehensive school largely with the same objective — personal advancement. Only very occasionally, and as a result of the activities of the Teachers' Labour League and NCLC adherents, has the Labour Party conference debated the actual content of education for the workers themselves.

On the continent of Europe socialist parties usually attach great importance to the need among the rank and file for understanding of socialist concepts. Referring to the German Social Democratic Party, Alan Day, editor of the Socialist International Bulletin, wrote in 1970:

> In Germany it is the political education programme of the SPD which strikes the English eye. Annual expenditure under this heading is running at about one million pounds, and a substantial proportion of the Party's seven hundred full time officials are employed directly

or indirectly in the programme. SPD Headquarters in Bonn has a well-manned political education department and each of the Party's 21 regions has a full time educational secretary. This network is backed by 4 residential colleges providing courses for Party members and officers. The result is greater efficiency and ability at the voluntary official level and a highly articulate rank and file membership. (6)

In this country, although a considerable number of local Labour Party branches paid local affiliation fees to the NCLC in return for free admission to NCLC classes the Labour Party executive never paid more than £100 per annum, in return for which it held a seat on the NCLC Executive. This was the sum total of its commitment.

The Labour Party Fails Political Education

The Labour Party has tended, of course, to reflect the temperate character of the bulk of its supporters not to mention the fact that so little has been done for years to educate its members in socialist theory. As G.D.H. Cole once observed:

> . . . I think those who were at the head of the Labour Party machine failed to realise that there was any need for a body which would devote itself to the task of making and educating Socialists. They seem to have acted in the belief that the Labour Party machine itself could be made to serve this purpose, for which it was in truth disqualified both by its preoccupation with electoral affairs and, still more, by the fact that it was in essence a mass movement seeking to secure a mass-following rather than to train up a selective body of enthusiasts. (7)

The lack of a dynamic thrust from below and of a comprehensive theory of social change may explain the cautious policies of the Labour Party leadership. The failure of the Labour Party to educate its followers to political realities was noted by R. H. S. Crossman:

> Surely when it was faced by a tacitly hostile establishment in Whitehall and an actively hostile press in Fleet Street, the Labour Government should have felt the

6. *Socialist Commentary,* Oct. 1970.

7. G. D. H. Cole, *British Working Class Politics, 1832-1914* (London, 1941), p.252.

need for a politically conscious and politically educated rank and file such as was beginning to emerge in the '30s with the help of the WEA and the NCLC. Surely after 1945 the Party machine should have been instructed to organise a nationwide crusade of workers' education to give the rank and file the feeling that they were needed by the leadership not merely to man the electoral machine but to create that pressure of left-wing opinion required to combat Tory propaganda. If a Labour Government is to survive the attacks of its enemies and to make some advance towards socialism it cannot do so by treating the Party which put it into power merely as a useful vote-getting machine. (8)

This is the background against which we must see these activities and the very existence of the National Council of Labour Colleges.

The NUR Moves the TUC

In 1957 the NCLC again set out on a campaign for the rationalisation of trade union education programmes under the unified control of the TUC. Prompted by the NUR member of the NCLC Executive Committee the NUR submitted a motion for consideration by Congress at its annual meeting in September:

Congress approves the emphasis which is being laid upon improved working-class education, realising that only by a thorough understanding of the social sciences, new techniques and economic factors can the workers hope to achieve full emancipation. Congress, however, considers that much of the existing over-lapping of educational facilities should be eliminated to ensure that the maximum benefits can be derived from such schemes.

Accepting that the TUC educational arrangements now being developed will go a long way to meet the growing needs and demands of the Trade Union Movement, Congress instructs the General Council to try to bring about a co-ordinated educational policy with affiliated unions and other educational bodies, thus making better use of the total amount of money and facilities available. (9)

8. Quoted in *Socialist Leader*, 1. Aug. 1970.
9. TUC *Annual Report* (1957) p.389.

154

The motion at the annual Congress was moved by T. Holly-wood, President of the NUR and a former NCLC student, seconded by J. H. Wigglesworth, General Secretary of the Iron, Steel and Metal Dressers' Union and a member of the NCLC Executive, and supported by three other members of the NCLC Executive Committee: Jack Martin, W. Lindley and George Cornes. Martin stressed the wastefulness of competition:

> As I said, we have a number of educational bodies all competing for one thing — students. Education is a commodity that you have an awful job to sell. You even have difficulty in giving it away. Yet you have all these educational bodies competing for students who are not willing to be educated ... The Trades Union Congress is the only body that can co-ordinate the educational facilities of the trade union movement. No other body can do it. The NCLC has tried to get rationalisation, not just for a year or two but, as I know, for the last ten or twelve years and it has not been successful. (10)

Cornes distinguished between the type of instruction designed to improve the efficiency of trade union officials and the broader education of union members:

> . . . there are special jobs that individual unions should do for their own members in enlightening them about the work and structure of their own unions; a special work that Congress itself should do through its training college; and a special educational work to be done by the Co-operative Movement and the Labour Party. But for the general approach on the social sciences designed to increase the understanding of the membership as a whole the motion believes quite rightly that the responsibility is on the shoulders of Congress to stop overlapping and overspending and concentrate their energies in a unified way and thereby benefit the movement as a whole. (11)

No trade unionists associated with the WEA view spoke, except the Chairman of the TUC Education Committee, W. Beard, a long-time opponent of the NCLC. Beard poured cold water on the proposal. His antagonism to the NCLC was revealed by his snide way of introducing a review of the educational bodies concerned: 'You have first of all the NCLC.

10. *ibid.*, p.391.
11. *ibid.*, p.392.

It is an organisation which believes in independent working-class education, whatever that may mean these days.'

In general, the NCLC's enthusiasm for a composite scheme was warmly welcomed. As a result, Beard finally stated that the General Council would consider the proposal if it were referred to them. Hollywood, the mover of the motion, agreed to the referral with the proviso that 'we are not too happy in regard to his (Mr. Beard's) personal approach to this because he appears to be reasoning in the pattern of a decade ago . . . We want it examined in the light of 1957, not 1947.'

Previous attempts to bring about a rationalisation of trade union education had foundered on the rocks of the General Council's caution and the competition between the WETUC and the NCLC which arose out of their vastly different educational views. This time Millar felt that the strong position of the NCLC favoured the emergence of a satisfactory scheme. But seven anxious and finally disillusioning years were to pass before a scheme emerged. True to David Low's depiction of the TUC as a ponderous cart horse, the TUC took until 1964 to absorb the NCLC's educational work.

In 1957 the General Council passed to the TUC Education Committee the task of inquiring into the existing arrangements for trade union education. In 1959 the Committee recommended the creation of a national consultative committee, and urged a fundamental revision of the general educational provision and that co-operation with the WEA should continue. The agreement of the NCLC to 'sink its identity and merge its organisation' was welcomed.

In a letter to Harry Nutt, General Secretary of the WEA, Millar wrote:

> If the WETUC and the NCLC do not take rationalisation seriously I can see the time — although it will not be in my day — when the TUC and the unions will be spending practically all their educational funds on their own types of education, leaving the Education Authorities and the Extra-Mural Departments to provide the broader kind of education that there is no need for trade unions to finance. Such a development could leave no room for the WETUC or the NCLC. (12)

In a statement prepared for his executive committee publicly, Millar expressed the views:

12. NCLC Corr. 22.3.1958.

Naturally it is not easy for the NCLC to lose its separate identity and we appreciate that the same applies to the WETUC; but the two bodies could undoubtedly be merged with immense benefit to the whole British Trade Union and Labour movement, and a substantial increase in the work they have pioneered would result. (13)

What of the WEA? After the controversy over membership of the IFWEA there had been a steady and encouraging improvement in relations between the NCLC and the WEA. Harry Nutt, who succeeded Ernest Green in 1946, had taken steps to improve the relationship and each now reviewed the other's publications in its journal.

The NCLC's TUC Proposal

On 28 March 1961 the NCLC, weary of waiting for some sign of progress, wrote to the TUC recommending that the Unions should be asked to pay to the TUC 4d. per member (the NCLC's new fee) so that members of the unions could take postal courses and attend classes and day schools and have branch lectures free of charge. It further suggested that in addition to a national committee and regional committees the proposed new organisation should hold an annual conference, which would provide a forum for the discussion of both national and local trade union educational problems by delegates from various parts of the country. If the proposed new educational organisation was to work effectively it must provide adequate opportunities for discussion of trade union educational work and policy by active members of the movement. It was anticipated that the annual conference would attract only those specially interested in trade union educational activity. The same letter went on to claim that the National Committee would work under the supervision of the General Council and that at least two of the seats on the National Committee should be filled by former representatives of the NCLC.

The General Council's First Plan

In the 1961 TUC Congress Report the General Council proposed that a new organisation should be set up to take over the work of the NCLC and WETUC, that it should be financed by a compulsory payment of $2\frac{1}{2}$d. or 3d. per member, that the

13. ECM, 1958.

Committee should be broadly representative and that provision should be made for regional organisation. The new educational body was to

> take the form of a Joint Trade Union Education Committee consisting of members of the General Council (drawn from the Council's Education Committee). a representative of the TUC Educational Trust, representatives of Trade Unions (elected in a manner which would take account of the membership of the different unions), representatives of the Workers' Educational Association, a representative of Ruskin College, and a limited number of co-opted members. (14)

This proposal arose out of many discussions between Millar and Dennis Winnard, the Secretary of the TUC Education Department.

A small union which tried to refer back the recommendation because it was opposed to the idea that the educational scheme should be paid for by all the unions received scant support. Four other speakers took part in the debate and two of them, while welcoming the General Council's proposal, drew the attention of Congress to the fact that certain points which the NCLC had been stressing were missing from the report. Two speakers, Cornes and Smith, reminded Congress that their unions wanted more comprehensive provision together with more regional activity: a regional organisation and regional machinery for educational work. At the previous Congress the General Council had moreover given an undertaking that:

> we will call a meeting of all the unions, similar to the meeting which we called to deal with the college scholarships, when they were set up, so that we can put to the unions our ideas and plans, let them discuss the matter, and try to find some final agreement. (15)

That meeting had not yet come about. Smith hoped:

> that the new body will follow a missionary policy. The existence of the two competing organisations, the NCLC and WETUC, at least has the advantage that these two organisations, among their activities, were competing to sell the idea of trade union education to trade union branches and trade union members and we

14. TUC, *Annual Report* (1961) p.179.
15. *ibid.* (1960) p.426.

hope that the new body, when it comes into existence, will show equal missionary zeal in that respect. (16)
A vain hope, so it turned out.

In the course of a speech recommending the proposals, Beard, Chairman of the TUC Education Committee, declared that some of the places on the National Education Committee for co-opted members would be filled by people associated with the NCLC. So far, therefore, the NCLC's proposals had been taken seriously and negotiations with Dennis Winnard, the TUC Education Secretary, were proceeding reasonably satisfactorily from the NCLC's point of view.

At the NCLC Executive meeting in March 1962 it was reported that at a recent meeting with Woodcock, Beard and Winnard, the General Secretary and the President had sensed that the proposal to have a broadly-based committee, endorsed at the previous Congress, might be greatly altered.

Representative Committee Rejected

At the 1962 Congress the General Council announced that the cost of the new educational scheme would necessitate an increase in its affiliation fee of 3d. per member, which would be part of a total increase of 6d. per member. The General Council had decided, subject to approval of Congress, that, from the beginning of 1963, it should assume financial responsibility for NCLC work done for the TUC unions — not for the other unions affiliated to the NCLC — and for WETUC educational work with a view to maintaining their activities at roughly their existing levels pending the complete take-over. This seemed a reasonably satisfactory arrangement. However, the report rejected the proposal that the educational work should be directed by a representative committee and made clear that it would become the responsibility of the TUC Education Committee, of which Beard was still the Chairman. This new attitude worried the NCLC which found little consolation in the kind words of G. Smith the proposer of the motion, accepting the General Council's recommendation. He expressed

> sincere appreciation of the past work of the National Council of Labour Colleges and the Workers' Educational Trade Union Committee, and the recent Co-operation given by these two bodies without which it would not have been possible to see the introduction of

16. TUC, *Annual Report*, p.443.

a single co-ordinated educational scheme, under the control of the General Council at a reasonably early date. (17)

In view of the new policy now presented by the TUC Education Committee, influenced, the NCLC believed, by George Woodcock, the General Secretary, gloom descended over the NCLC. Up to this time it had continued to hope that a satisfactory educational scheme would be provided. The hope now largely vanished. Doubts about the TUC's good intentions were particularly strong in Scotland. Bob Scouller, one of the leading voluntary officials in Glasgow, who had attended the foundation conference of the Scottish Labour College in 1916, had as early in the negotiations as April 1961 written a letter to Millar saying:

> One point worries me a little, but I expect you are fully alive to it and are taking what steps you can to avoid its dangers. The College has built up a good body of voluntary workers especially tutorial but also adminis- trative — an enormous source of goodwill. The ten- dency of a highly centralised body is to become bureaucratic and my fear is if that develops in the new organisation we may lose that local enthusiasm which has been such a powerful factor in the development of the NCLC. (18)

The NCLC's Mistake

In 1962 the fatal die had been cast when the NCLC, still trusting in the good faith of the TUC, agreed that from January 1963 it would cease to draw affiliation fees from its TUC unions and instead accept a block grant from the TUC as the first step towards losing its identity. (It would continue for the time being to draw affiliation fees from non-TUC unions and other organisations). The NCLC did, however, take one important precaution. If, in 1963, the block grant was accepted and the NCLC's TUC unions ceased to pay affiliation fees to the NCLC they would cease to have any control over the NCLC as they would not be entitled to attend the 1963 annual conference. To prevent this the NCLC altered its constitution so that these unions which provided the great bulk of the NCLC's financial

17. TUC, *Annual Report* (1962) p.343.
18. 8.4.1961., NCLC Corr.

support would still retain their voting powers. The TUC Education Committee

> had apparently got the impression that, at an NCLC Conference their financial payment (the block grant) would give them sufficient votes to decide issues, irrespective of what any of the other bodies which own the NCLC's resources might wish. They were annoyed, therefore, to be told that the NCLC Executive responsible for the administration of the organisation does not need to call a conference unless it has some business that, in its view, requires the attention of a conference. (19)

The SLC's Fears Justified

The fears for the future of the Scottish Labour College seemed to be confirmed when in April 1963 the organiser for the East of Scotland resigned. The NCLC Executive proposed to appoint a successor to cover that very large area which included three of the four Scottish cities, for it had been an NCLC condition that the TUC would take over all NCLC employees who wished to be taken over. The TUC Office indicated that, if an appointment were made, it would take no responsibility for maintaining it. A complete collapse of the educational work in the East of Scotland ensued. After the take-over the Scottish Typographical Association made several attempts at the Trades Union Congress to get an organiser appointed for the East of Scotland but its efforts were stalled by the TUC Office.

In addition, the NCLC had difficulty in extracting from the TUC the full amount of the subsidy of £51,788 to which it was entitled. This contrasted with the fact, to which it drew the TUC Education Department's attention, that the WETUC was receiving from the TUC £6,000 more than it had received from trade unions. The reply to the NCLC's protest being unsatisfactory, Millar wrote: 'It seems clear that your letter indicates a deliberate attempt to avoid carrying out the understanding reached between us with regard to the financing of this year's NCLC work.' The letter went on to say

> there seems to be no reason why we should go to the expense of overdrawing our Bank account because your department has not lived up to the obligation undertaken by the TUC. Your letter of 29th October would justify us in advising the NCLC unions of the position

19. General Secretary's report to the Executive Committee, 21.3.1964.

in which you are putting us. It would justify, moreover, drawing their attention to the fact that this year they are paying not 4d. per member as before but only 3d. per member for our facilities and asking them to assist us for the time being by paying direct to us the additional 1d. per member. As for the TUC unions which were not affiliated to us at the end of December, 1962, but which are now getting the benefit of our educational facilities, it would be only fair to these unions to explain the situation to these 1963 unions also and to ask them to make us a grant. (20)

The threat, had the necessary effect, a cheque for £3,780 being received, a few days later from Victor Feather, the Assistant Secretary, without any explanation or apology. The NCLC did not believe that responsibility for its cavalier treatment lay with the Secretary of the Education Department but considerably higher up in the TUC Office.

Woodcock Takes Over

By this time the NCLC felt that further undesirable decisions would be enforced. It had now become apparent that the TUC Education Committee intended that the WEA would have at least one representative on each of the TUC's proposed regional education committees whereas the NCLC would have no spokesman. All trace of the NCLC was to vanish.

One seemingly unmistakable sign to the NCLC of the reality of the threat to its programme of activities was the appointment by George Woodcock, TUC General Secretary, of Miss Ellen McCullough to the TUC Education Department with the task of initiating the new educational scheme. The job was not advertised so that no other trade unionist had the chance to apply for it. Since Miss McCullough was the National Women's Officer of the TGWU, a leading WEA personality and a known critic of the Labour Colleges, this appointment was seen by the NCLC executive committee as a calculated affront. Its anger was intensified when it learnt that Woodcock wished Graham Horsman, who had joined the NCLC in 1945 and recently succeeded Christine Millar as postal courses supervisor, to join the TUC office in London simply as an assistant and at a loss in his real income. Responsibility for the Postal Course Department, with an annual enrolment of over 20,000 students, was to go to a clerk who had not previously worked in that department.

20. Millar to Woodcock in NCLC Corr.

The alarm of the executive committee was so great that Woodburn and Millar demanded to see Woodcock in order to present their strong objections to the TUC proposals and to confirm that, if they were not rescinded, their mandate to negotiate would have to be revoked. The NCLC's main objections to the TUC proposals were as follows:

1. Responsibility for the educational work was *not* to fall (as previously approved by Congress) to a 'Joint Trade Union Education Committee, consisting of members of the General Council (drawn from the Counil's Education Committee), a representative of the TUC Educational Trust, representatives of trade unions (elected in a manner which would take account of the membership of the different unions), representatives of the Workers' Educational Association, a representative of Ruskin College and a limited number of 'co-opted members.' Instead the work was to be handed over to the TUC Education Committee and NCLC views would not therefore be represented through co-option as intended. (21)

2. The College committees would not be replaced by district committees containing representatives of the Trades Councils and trade union branches. The grass roots of the trade union movement would thus have no voice.

3. There would be a small number of regional committees, each covering a very large area and consisting of a few busy trade union officials and a representative of the WEA.

4. There would no longer be an opportunity for the local Labour Parties, Co-operative Societies and other working-class bodies to benefit from the educational work, since they would be excluded.

5. There would be none of the district annual conferences which the NCLC had always encouraged as a means of stimulating local interest.

6. The publishing of special text-books was to be dropped together with the book service which the NCLC provided for its students.

7. There was to be no educational magazine to support the educational work.

21. TUC, *Annual Report*, 1961, p.179.

8. The extensive branch lecture service was to cease. (22)

A meeting with Woodcock was held on 28 November, 1963. The NCLC was represented by Woodburn, Cornes and Millar, who were accompanied by Horsman and Jock Haston, the senior London organiser. The two latter tried to bring home to Woodcock the importance of Horsman's role in the NCLC Postal Course Department and the value of the branch lecture service in stimulating trade unionists to attend classes and take postal courses. At the end of the meeting, the sole concession wrung from Woodcock was that in future Millar could attend those TUC Education Committee meetings that dealt with rationalisation. In the event, this promise was only partly honoured.

Early in March, 1963, Woodcock informed Millar by letter that there would be no further discussions with the NCLC about the nature of the TUC scheme. This abrupt intimation contrasted sharply with Woodcock's statement to Congress in 1963: 'We do not want to ride roughshod over people who have been doing the job, we want to bring them with us, we want to listen to their views, as we have listened to their views.' The letter bluntly intimated that the TUC would take over direct responsibility for providing educational services from 30 June, 1964, and thereafter cease to pay any monies to the NCLC. It concluded:

> In view of the apparent reluctance of the NCLC to accept the inevitability of changes in the educational work when it came to be conducted under TUC auspices . . . responsibility for the TUC educational service must rest with the General Council. (23)

NCLC Rejects Woodcock's Ultimatum

When it was presented to the NCLC Executive Committee, at its meeting on March 21st, this letter aroused indignation. Woodburn declared that Woodcock was requiring the Executive Committee to do something which under the constitution of the NCLC it legally could not do. He deplored the threatening tone of the letter and, on behalf of the Vice-President, the General Secretary and himself, moved this motion:

> The NCLC Executive, having considered the terms of Mr. George Woodcock's letter of 9th March headed 'Trade Union Educational Facilities,' accepts his pro-

22. ECM, 1964.
23. Woodcock to Millar, NCLC Corr.

164

posal to hand over its responsibilities on or before 30th June, 1964, provided that a mutually acceptable settlement of all the NCLC's legal and moral responsibilities to the staff, to its colleges, to its unions and to its other constituent bodies had been reached prior to 30th June.

To this end the NCLC Executive empowers a Committee consisting of its President, Vice-President, General Secretary and two other members of its Sub-Committee to enter into discussions with representatives of the TUC General Council and to report back to the Executive.

The Executive further draws attention to the fact that a handover of its responsibilities can be accomplished only by the appropriate conference.

The motion was carried by 48 votes to 3, the dissentient votes being cast by the two representatives of the General Council and the one representative of the T & GW. Cornes declared that if the TUC refused to meet the NCLC's new committee, his union would raise the issue on the floor of Congress.

All the NCLC organisers were summoned to a meeting in London so that they might be fully informed about the impasse which had been reached. On the evening before the meeting they discussed the situation among themselves and, despite the opposition of their chairman, George Clarke who wanted to wait until after the executive meeting, decided to approve a resolution accepting the very proposals to which the executive committee was opposed. Why did the organisers deliberately flout the executive committee? The reason was that, whereas a large majority in the executive committee now questioned the good faith of the TUC, they were persuaded that the new order promised to bring not only job security but higher wages and improved working conditions. They wished therefore to prevent the committee from adopting such a strong line that negotiations with the TUC would be ruptured irrevocably. Their action certainly undermined the authority of the executive committee.

At the meeting of the Executive the following day George Cornes, a national official of the Draughtsmen's Union, on behalf of the Executive's Special Committee on rationalisation, moved the Committee's recommendation that a special conference of the NCLC's constituent bodies be called to receive an account of the unsatisfactory nature of the form the TUC scheme was now taking and to obtain the conference's reaction.

He was seconded by another member of the committee, Arthur Pratt, the General Secretary of the Warwickshire Miners. After a long discussion during which some of the executive members became tired and others worried, J. C. Robinson of the Durham Miners moved a motion to the effect that, provided the staff were satisfied on certain points affecting their conditions, a conference should be called to hand over the NCLC to the TUC. This motion should have been treated as an amendment, but was treated by Arthur Woodburn, the chairman, as a motion. Moreover, he seemed to have completely and unexpectedly dropped his support of the recommendation of the Special Committee whose meeting he had chaired. This totally unexpected situation greatly upset Cornes, Millar and the vice-president, Jack Martin. Cornes and Martin were so taken aback that, when it was suddenly moved an agreed that the vote be taken, they both failed to draw the chairman's attention to the fact that the spokesman of the Special Committee, Cornes, had the right to reply before the vote was taken. Millar was, for the first time in his life, too upset to speak and he, too, failed to point out that Cornes was entitled to defend the Special Committee's motion. Robinson's proposal was then carried without any further discussion, at least some of the executive being aware of the motion carried by the organiser's meeting the previous day. The organisers' representative was himself at this fateful gathering.

Millar then recovered his power of speech and declared that no vestige of independent working-class education would be left under the new TUC proposals. He would take no part in such an organisation. Profoundly disappointed, he would resign and so cease to be employed by the NCLC in six weeks' time. Woodburn expressed his regret at this announcement and hoped that the General Secretary would continue in office. Martin said that, although he fully appreciated Millar's feelings, which were as sad as his own, it would be better for Millar to stay until the process of rationalisation had been completed. After the meeting, in response to requests by telephone and letter, Millar withdrew his resignation.

In May 1964, Millar went to Glasgow to address a meeting of the SLC and found the 150 delegates disturbed about the arbitrary control which the TUC intended to exercise. The SLC formally asked the national executive committee to make no agreement which did not safeguard the right of trade union branches and affiliated organisations to direct representation on the controlling body. Within the General Council of the TUC, George Lowthian, General Secretary of AUBTW, also voiced his concern about some aspects of the new scheme. But it was now too late for the NCLC to retreat.

At the very last conference of the NCLC, held on 22 August, 1964, George Cornes, on behalf of the executive committee moved that all the organisational machinery and assets required for the educational work should be handed over to the TUC except for those relating to the publishing society, the TUC having shown no interest in maintaining *Plebs* or any of the publishing activities. How different, said Cornes, was this conference from the one they had envisaged a year ago. Then the executive committee had firmly believed that it would be putting forward attractive proposals agreed with the TUC. Now it could only put forward proposals imposed by the TUC. In surrendering the right to draw affiliation fees from individual unions the NCLC had lost its independence. There were deep differences between the NCLC and the TUC Education Committee, none of which had been resolved. After Cornes had spoken, delegates from the Ayrshire, Sheffield, Belfast and Northumberland Colleges strongly criticised the TUC's proposals. J. W. Kitchen, representing the North Cumberland College, commented: 'This is the funeral service of the NCLC. I have been a voluntary tutor for 25 years; now I am being thrown on the scrap heap.'

The NCLC's Miscalculation

What had gone amiss? The NCLC had counted on many members of the TUC General Council being NCLC supporters but had over-estimated the amount of attention which these supporters were prepared to divert from their own parochial problems to planning trade union education in general. The NCLC had also overlooked the fact that, as a rule, General Council members found it advantageous not to challenge the General Secretary of the TUC unless over subjects vitally affecting their own unions. Thus, responsibility for moulding the new scheme fell into the hands of Woodcock, supported by Beard, who had boasted to Millar some years previously that he had prevented his own small union, the Pattern Makers, from adopting the NCLC scheme. Millar was convinced that if Woodcock, a former weaver, had been a CLC student and not a product of Ruskin and Oxford University, the TUC education scheme would have assumed a vastly different form. In the event, the TUC was unable, as planned, to take over the NCLC's work at the end of June. Instead its formal proposals were presented to Congress in September, George Woodcock countered objections by asserting that: 'If education has become a TUC activity, then the TUC must be absolutely in control of it.' A motion that the proposals should be referred back for consideration was defeated by a large majority. Congress was tired of the long drawn out negotiations.

TUC Office Wields the Axe

On the last occasion, before handing over to the TUC, that the NCLC collected statistics about its activities it produced the following figures:

1.   44   Postal Course Examiners
2.   587   Individual Members
3. 1,245   Plebs Annual Subscribers
4.   247   Plebs Agents
5.   70   College Secretaries
6. 5,548   Postal Course Enrolling Agents

Few traces of these activities survived the TUC take-over in 1964. Millar complained in *Plebs* that the NCLC had made 'a colossal mistake in handing over its education work to the TUC.' In Scotland both the Ayrshire and Fife Colleges decided to remain in being. The organisers, who had welcomed the change, were quickly disillusioned and turned to Millar for advice and assistance. All the organisers were instructed by the TUC Education Department to abandon class tutoring and limit their activities to organising restricted educational facilities for which there was little demand. Their financial and working conditions were not improved.* The vigorous publicity methods of the NCLC were dropped. As for the postal courses, the following NCLC subjects, all concerned with political and social matters, were among those also immediately abandoned.

Britain's Tasks Today
Electioneering
Labour and Election Methods
Labour Party — Yesterday and Today
Nationalisation and Social Control

* Years later under Len Murray, as TUC General Secretary, they were improved.

168

Parliamentary Candidates' Course
Questions affecting Britain's Future
Socialism
Towards the Welfare State
Trade Union Movements Abroad
Western Europe's Struggle for Unity

Since overall TUC membership increased by about 20% between 1964 and 1973 and since 45% more TUC members were entitled to free postal courses, the TUC ought greatly to have increased the total number of its postal students. On the contrary, during this period the number fell heavily. The figure for postal course students, quoted for 1973 in the 1974 TUC report was 10,087 compared with the NCLC's last figure of over 21,212 and Ruskin's figure of about 2,500. In 1974 the TUC figure fell to 9,019. The NCLC's trained staff at Tillicoultry were immediately stopped, without any decision of the Education Committee, so far as the records show, from keeping the courses up to date and introducing new courses, and that work was completely neglected at the TUC Office in London for years with unfortunate results.

What specially angered Millar, Christine and their colleagues was that immediately after the take-over, the TUC office dropped the NCLC's main course on economics, replacing it with an old Ruskin course which was thoroughly orthodox. There was no sign in the minutes of the TUC education committee that this was the result of any committee discussion. The action was apparently taken by the TUC office itself.

The Offer to the Labour Party

When it had become clear from its first leaflet that the TUC office had dropped many of the NCLC's postal course, class and day school subjects, the NCLC Executive Committee offered most of the dropped postal courses to the Labour Party but the offer was declined. Annoyed, the Executive Committee later repeated the offer; Millar went so far as to say that he was willing, for no payment, to establish a postal course department for the Party. Again the Party executive declined the offer without giving any reason. It may be that the Party felt it had not the necessary financial resources to run such a department effectively. The TUC took over from the NCLC alone 76 postal courses. These and the Ruskin courses were reduced to 46 and remained no higher in 1973.

The result of the narrowness of the TUC curriculum and the

continuing lack of drive in getting students is shown further by the 1974 TUC report which records that the number of classes throughout the country in 1973 was only 65 with 727 students, believed to be the lowest figure yet. What the TUC did show was an interest in Day Release Courses. In 1973 these had increased to 541 with 7,627 students. They, however, were not run by the TUC but mainly by over a hundred technical colleges. The reason why the TUC finds it much easier to get workers to go to day release classes is because these enable workers to escape from the daily grind. By 1974 most of the educational work recorded in the TUC 'Education Committee's report' consisted not of facilities run by the TUC itself but by the technical and further education colleges, the extra-mural departments, the London School of Economics, the WEA and Ruskin College, whereas the much more extensive educational work under the NCLC's auspices was all run by the NCLC itself. Even a year or two after the TUC took over the work of the NCLC and the WETUC and the Ruskin College postal courses, the fall in figures had become so obvious that at the TUC Jim Conway, a former NCLC tutor and then General Secretary of the AEU, complained to a former NCLC organiser, Jock Haston, that the Union was getting much less educational value for its money from the TUC than it had been getting from the NCLC. As for the NCLC extensive branch lecture service it has no successor under the TUC, and a great loss in rank and file education has resulted.

In 1974 Congress had authorised another move to hand union educational work very largely to other hands. It accepted a scheme mainly, it is understood, inspired by Sheffield University Extra Mural Department and supported by the BBC, under which the University, the BBC, the WEA and the TUC Education Department would co-operate in providing educational facilities including postal courses but on a very limited curriculum. That the BBC could be of use in approaching trade unionists is obvious but that it will be a party to providing the broad socialist educational material badly required by many trade unionists is something that neither the state-subsidised WEA, nor the BBC doesn't dream of, nor apparently does the TUC Education Committee either. As for the service provided by weekend schools for many years that is being wiped out as part of the campaign to push the cost of TUC education more and more on the state which does not provide education without conditions stated or implied (See TUC Report for 1975)*

The Millars Retire

Christine Millar had retired in 1963 for the purpose of strengthening Horsman's position when the postal course department would be controlled by the TUC. To mark their appreciation of her forty years of service to the NCLC as the postal courses supervisor and as deputy to the general secretary, the executive committee presented her with a typewriter, a movie camera, a cinema projector and a copy of the cinema film which she had made of the postal course work. The Scottish Divisional Council arranged for a dinner in her honour and raised £340 for a presentation.

When Millar's own date of retirement drew closer, the executive committee organised the J. P. M. Millar National Testimonial Fund. Graham Horsman sent out a letter inviting subscriptions, in which he praised Millar's devotion to the NCLC.

> From the First World War J.P.M. had devoted himself to building up the only National Trade Union and Labour organisation in the country. Under his remarkable leadership it grew from nothing to a federation for educational purposes of 109 British Trade Unions, 20 Overseas Trade Unions and nearly 100 colleges. In it Labour Parties and Co-operative organisations all over the country have also participated and through it for many years around 100,000 Trade Union and Labour people have studied every year. He has also given the trade union educational movement a marked international outlook, maintaining a close rapport with trade union educational organisations all over the Continent and in many parts of the Commonwealth.
>
> In 1920 J.P.M. was asked to allow his name to go forward as a Parliamentary candidate for Leith Burghs and he was later asked by the National Agent of the Labour Party to stand for other constituencies. He declined all these invitations because he felt that the Labour Movement had a special need for a strong educational organisation reflecting its own socialist philosophy and this he successfully set out to provide. (24)

24. NCLC Mss.
* As the proofs of this book are being corrected the TUC has been promised a state grant of £400,000 towards the cost of its educational work and is hoping for a bigger grant later.

171

The subscriptions to the fund totalled over £1,333, of which the Executive's contribution was £350. There was no donation from the NUR, AEU, T & GWU and G & MWU.

The presentation was made at a national dinner held in the House of Commons in 1965 when presentations were also made to Christine Millar, Arthur Woodburn and Jack Martin. Among the Speakers were James Griffiths, M.P., Secretary of State for Wales, Sir Richard Coppock, C.B.E., former General Secretary NFBTO, R. L. Marshall, O.B.E., Principal, Co-operative College and Chief Education Officer, Co-operative Union, A. L. Williams, General Secretary of the Labour Party, Aksel Zachariassen, former General Secretary of Arbeidernes Opplysningsforbund, H. A. Tulatz, Assistant General Secretary, International Confederation of Free Trade Unions, George Lowthian, M.B.E., General Secretary, AUBTW, and Walter Schevenels, General Secretary, European Regional Organisation of the International Confederation of Free Trade Unions.

When the year 1964 ended there remained one powerful relic of the past — *Plebs*. Towards the end of 1959 the Labour Party had ceased publishing its monthly journal *Labour Digest*, and soon afterwards the WEA published its last issue of *The Highway*. *Plebs* in its long life had seen other magazines come and go, including the only Labour daily newspapers *The Daily Citizen* and *The Daily Herald*, and the only Labour Sunday paper — *Reynolds News*. The TUC had greatly added to its educational work by taking over the NCLC and Ruskin College Postal Courses and the WETUC work, but it saw no need to publish educational text books or even to keep in print those already published by the NCLC. In a letter to Millar, Julius Braunthal, who had become Secretary of the Socialist International and in 1973 completed a three-volume *History of the International*, wrote:

> I have just got the July issue of *Plebs*, the last one under your editorship. I feel in all sincerity I should say how deeply I regret your resignation as editor of that journal which had been one of the very few papers in this country which kept alive the spirit and ideals of socialism. I was proud to contribute to it from time to time, and I wish to say how grateful I am to you for having given me the opportunity to do it. (25)

As we have seen, it was only in a limited way that the TUC

25. 9.7.1965., NCLC Corr.

took over the education work of the NCLC. True to its tradition it preserved only those activities concerned with the practical functions of trade union members in the narrowest sense. Arthur Woodburn has summed up the effects of its dead hand:

> Whilst it was to be expected that changes would result from the transfer of power to the TUC it was not expected that the possible and hoped for benefits of rationalising the overlapping and rival workers' educational bodies would be still-born by inactivity and discouragement. One of the essentials of success in trade union education was to attract students. It was an added bonus to the NCLC that it was run not by employees just doing a job but by people with an evangelical passion in a missionary enterprise — J. P. M. Millar and Christine (Director of Postal Courses) and their team, by ingenious and striking publicity methods had enormous success in recruiting students. Men and women often started as students in the expectation that they would obtain personal advancement, only to spend the rest of their lives as enthusiastic workers for the Labour Movement. At least one of Labour's best known Cabinet Ministers told me he was an example of this very process. The TUC took over a going concern with something like 100,000 students a year which had great prestige and goodwill. (26)

Democratic Roots Severed

During the negotiations leading up to the absorption of the NCLC Millar had proposed to Winnard that there should be a *national conference* dealing with trade union education, quite separate from the TUC itself. 'Such a conference is essential to keep working-class education a really live issue, and to give those who are playing some part in it an opportunity of meeting and discussing.' He further proposed 'that the Co-operative Union and the Labour Party should be represented at this Conference: ... a little standing committee that could be called now and again so that the three bodies could keep in step eventually.' No such conference was in the end established and, as A. J. Corfield has pointed out, delegates at both WETUC and WEA assemblies shared the disquiet of the NCLC 'that the democratic roots of the present educational system were being

26. NCLC Mss.

cut away. . . . The TUC was charged with creating a bureaucratic structure in which control was vested almost exclusively in full-time trade union officials who might have no direct interest in education.' How ironic that only when the NCLC had ceased to exist did its leaders find common ground with the WEA and the WETUC leaders, who also thought there should be a much more representative structure.

CHAPTER IX

ORGANISERS, TUTORS, VOLUNTARY WORKERS AND STUDENTS

When in 1921 the NCLC was founded the local colleges were employing only four organisers throughout the year: in Edinburgh, Glasgow, Liverpool and London respectively. In a few areas full-time organisers had been appointed solely for the winter session; in Scotland there were also a few full-time winter tutors. All the other work was voluntary and unpaid. The small full-time staff appointed before the formation of the NCLC had been the financial responsibility of the local colleges. However, as soon as the NCLC had negotiated an educational scheme with the AUBTW, it became instantly necessary to appoint more full-time tutor-organisers, especially in the south-east and the south of England — mainly agricultural areas in which the Labour College Movement was weak. Soon eleven organisers were being paid or supervised by the central office.

The Organisers

Although called 'organisers,' the full-time men divided their days between teaching and organising. One qualification for the post of organiser was a knowledge of Marxian economics. Other qualifications were past service in the Labour Movement and practice in speaking, especially as voluntary tutors or branch lecturers. For each vacancy there was as a rule a fair list of applicants, and candidates trained by the Central Labour College were necessarily in a strong position since they frequently possessed all or nearly all the required qualifications. In later years applicants for a full-time post who were put on the short list would be asked to sit a written examination before being interviewed by the sub-committee of the national executive.

Throughout the whole history of the NCLC the organisers

N.C.L.C. Organisers and Central Office Seniors of Coberhill in 1933

were always over-worked and underpaid but they were evangelists and willingly recognised that some sacrifice was part of the job. The first organisers appointed by the NCLC executive received a salary of £160 per annum together with their tram, rail or bus fares, and salaries were never greatly improved in real terms. Having to carry a large teaching load in addition to their heavy administrative and organisational duties imposed a constant strain, aggravated by the lack of secretarial assistance. A competent organiser required a strong character and many skills. He was expected to conduct courses, to give occasional lectures and to make frequent speeches. He had to learn how to type letters, cut stencils and prepare and keep record cards of students and address cards for the branches and other organisations in his area. He had to deal with a variety of different people and to be fairly adept at public relations; latterly, he was required to keep a book of press-cuttings showing the publicity obtained for the NCLC. He had to persuade busy men and women to give up part of their leisure time to serve as class tutors and as lecturers at branch meetings and one-day schools, to sell literature and to cajole others into doing the same, to help keep up the circulation of *Plebs*, to arrange for lantern and later film-strip lectures, to raise money locally and to help the central office with its task of getting local trade union branches to send resolutions to their head offices recommending affiliation to the NCLC. When there was a move in a particular union to drop its NCLC scheme, the NCLC organiser would see local members and ask them to help defeat it. Since most of the organisers used their own homes as offices their wives sometimes acted as unpaid secretaries, occasionally at the cost of domestic strain. Finally, assisted by the voluntary tutors, NCLC organisers ensured that class secretaries were appointed to help build up the classes, obtain enrolment slips from students and keep registers up to date.

Each organiser worked on his own in a very large area with nothing to sustain him but his own self-discipline, dedication to the cause and the advice and pressures coming from his colleges and from central office. It was certainly not their salaries which kept organisers in their posts. After 1931 organisers were not even allowed to stand for local or county councils precisely because too active a participation in local politics would have deflected their attention from their organising and teaching duties. As the only full-time officers in their area, they had to

175

ensure the functioning of the voluntary tutors, college secretaries and branch lecturers. The wonder was that the turnover of organisers did not become an insuperable handicap. That the great majority of them served the NCLC until they transferred to another sector of the Labour Movement, retired or died in harness, was a tribute to their selfless dedication. Even so, the problem of maintaining a cadre of experienced and efficient organisers was ever present.

Some indication of the quality of the organisers may be gathered from the fact that a high proportion of them became M.P.s. These included: Syd Bidwell, George Brown, Will Coldrick, Raymond Fletcher, W. R. Hatton, George Lawson, Edward Milne, W. J. Owen, W. N. Warbey and J. M. Williams. Their backgrounds and abilities may be illustrated by a few profiles.

Fred Shaw

One early enthusiast was Fred Shaw, an ex-engineer, a bookworm and a witty lecturer. His grammer was faulty but he knew his facts and how to conjure up vivid illustrations. One of his oft-repeated stories told how, after he had given a lecture explaining that *value* was determined by the amount of average, socially-necessary labour embodied in a commodity, one of his students asked: 'Suppose a cooper makes a first class barrel in the cellar of his house with the intention of selling it at a profit, and, when he attempts to get it into the street, finds that it is wider than the cellar stairs, has that barrel still got any value — does it embody socially necessary labour?'

After Fred Shaw's death, one of his students sang his praises:

Although a native of Huddersfield, Fred's name will forever be linked with Halifax, for much of his lecturing was done here, and many the comrades he won.

No one could have met Fred for more than ten minutes without being richer for the privilege. Some of us were more favoured. We listened to his lectures in the dim smoke-hazy rooms — usually on the uppermost floor of the Friendly & Trades Club.

Such was the richness of his personality that he always kept our interest despite our weary bodies and minds. We forgot the dingy atmosphere, the hard chairs and benches — under the influence of his verbal artistry. Whether his subject be history, economics, or just plain politics, he could weave and interweave his anecdotes and jokes — sometimes grim but always robust — and always enriched by the telling in his fine Yorkshire dialect.

And how he could play. He sang and romped at social gatherings with just as much enthusiasm and gusto as he poured into his lectures.

In his home life Fred's socialism dominated, but not to the exclusion of other interests. Last time we visited him he proudly showed us a home-made lantern-slide apparatus, operated in the kitchen — chiefly for the entertainment of the grandchildren, but appreciated also by the adults. We peeped through his telescope, which showed us the mountains of the moon. We scanned his albums which contained photos of his latest creative offspring — a self-illustrated album of castles throughout the British Isles. What variety! Never a dull moment!

Fred told us how he used to set off on Sundays (his day of recreation) to visit these castles. He would return **with photos, and in his leisure hours would write up the** historical data, and illustrate with beautiful pencil drawings. A truly remarkable hobby, puckered in amongst his more vital activities.

More remarkable still was his newest interest - a study of drama and dramatists throughout the ages.

Fred was an Historical Materialist — but a living refutation of the general assumption that materialists are drab and uninspiring. It was against this background that he judged all social phenomena. Indeed it was this philosphy that enabled him correctly to analyse the past and point the way to the future. Needless to say, his loss at such a time as the present is one the Labour Movement can ill afford. (1)

Mark Starr

Mark Starr, a former CLC student, was one of the first two organisers appointed by the NCLC executive. His territory was the Eastern Counties, which he managed to run from London with the aid of a small three-wheeler car. His area was largely agricultural but AUBTW members were scattered throughout it.

1. Appreciation by Florence Edwards of Halifax, Feb. 1951. (NCLC MSS.)

Starr was ambitious and had considerable drive. Like some CLC students, he had left school early and wrote poor English but he soon overcame the handicap. While at the CLC he wrote for the *Merthyr Pioneer* a series of articles, chiefly based on his lecture notes, which eventually formed the basis of one of the first Plebs small books, *A Worker Looks at History*. This was followed by *A Worker Looks at Economics* and a bigger book, *Lies and Hate in Education*. The latter was a study of bias in school books in Britain, France, Germany and other countries, written with the help of the Teachers' Labour League. Starr, when opening up his area, applied to a committee (largely made up of Conservative farmers) for the use of a room to run a class for bricklayers. 'What's to be the subject?' asked one farmer. 'Economics,' replied Starr. 'I move we give the use of the room free,' said the farmer. 'The workers are a wasteful lot and need a course in economics.' The course was to be on Marxian economics! Later Starr went to the USA and became the Educational Director of one of the best known and most progressive unions, the International Ladies' Garment Workers of New York.

Stan Rees

Stan Rees was born in Workington, where his parents had migrated from South Wales. Both his parents were socialists and ardent trade unionists. When only fourteen he became secretary of Workington Number 4 branch for members under twenty-one of the British Steel Smelters. At the age of nineteen he gained a union scholarship and went to Ruskin. The governing board at first objected to taking someone so young but finally agreed when his union insisted that the scholarship was for Rees or for nobody. He supported the Ruskin strike and as a result lost his scholarship, but managed to complete his two years at the newly-established Central Labour College.

When Rees returned to Workington, he found that instructions had been given not to employ him in the steelworks. The whole Rees family then returned to Wales where he immediately found a job. At twenty-five he was appointed a full-time organiser with the Union of Steel Smelters but was dismissed during the war when he was sent to prison as a conscientious objector. Soon after his release from prison he applied for and obtained a trade union appointment in north-east Lancashire with the Shop Assistants' Union. In 1924 he became Division 9 organiser of the NCLC and loyally served in that post until his deferred retirement. In retirement he became a well-known Newcastle City councillor and in 1975, at the age of eighty-four, he was still running the Durham Miners' Summer School, along with another long-retired NCLC organiser, Joe Crispin. He died in 1976 as this book was being printed.

C. L. Gibbons

C. L. (Charlie) Gibbons was born in London in 1888. When he was eight years old his mother died and he was placed in a home for destitute children, where he remained until he was sixteen. After two years as a farm servant in West Wales, he returned to London where he was successively a dairyman, a messenger for a millinery shop, and a plumber's mate. He then became a collier in South Wales and studied mining engineering at a continuation school. In 1909, he ceased to be a devout Christian and took up socialism, following chance attendance at a debate on independent working-class education. He became a member of the Plebs League and actively collaborated with Noah Ablett. In 1911 He won a two year scholarship at the Central Labour College. While at the College he served as one of the first provincial class lecturers. On leaving the college he returned to the Rhondda to work in the pits. With W. F. Hay he became joint editor of the *South Wales Worker* and wrote articles on current politics within the Miners' Federation. After the war he helped organise the South Wales Socialist Party and in 1921 became a colliery check-weighman. He spent a brief period as residential lecturer at the Central Labour College, then was appointed in 1924 as the Edinburgh and District organiser for the NCLC. When a serious ear infection made it impossible for him to continue lecturing he became a postal course examiner.

Vin Williams

Another miner and a Yorkshireman was Vin Williams. He too had walked miles through hill and dale to attend classes and later to lecture as a voluntary tutor. At NCLC summer schools he would keep a crowd of students in the lounge listening with fascination to his stories, often full of humour, about his experiences in the Labour Movement. After the Russian Revolution a number of socialists in the industrial countries made attempts to go to Russia, devasted by the war, in order to help develop modern industries. Vin Williams decided to make the journey, although travelling to Russia was at that time almost

179

impossible. He arranged for some sailors to smuggle him aboard a boat which was sailing from Hull to St. Peterburg. He was hidden in a big upturned barrel. As the ship left harbour it immediately struck rough seas whereupon Williams became violently sick. The captain soon spotted the rocking barrel, discovered its contents and headed back to port where he dumped Williams on the dock side. Vin Williams was a born organiser. He arranged mass week-end schools at holiday camps during the winter, to which the students were taken by a fleet of coaches. In 1948 the fees received for such schools amounted to £9,000 thereby breaking all divisional records. His initiative in founding a residential hostel has been described elsewhere.

Jock Haston

Brought up in an Edinburgh slum, Jock Haston went to sea and became a member of the Seamen's Union when he was fifteen. Among his subsequent jobs were those of butler and steeplejack. Early in his political life Haston joined the Communist Party. During the Second World War he was the secretary of a Trotskyist organisation, the Revolutionary Communist Party, a job for which he received less than a pound a week. Haston's political background provided a problem for the NCLC Executive Sub-Committee when they interviewed him for the post of organiser. He was by far the ablest and best-informed of the applicants. On the other hand, as a former Trotskyite he was notorious in the Labour Movement. The Committee wished to appoint him but feared the Labour Party might take strong exception to his gaining access to Party and trade union branches under the flag of the NCLC. It was left to Millar, therefore, to make two visits to the General Secretary of the Labour Party, A. L. Williams, in order to convince him that Haston was a genuine convert. On leaving the NCLC Haston wrote:

> It gives me no pleasure to tender my resignation. I owe a great deal to the NCLC and to the Executive for appointing me at a difficult stage in my own political evolution. It gave me a wonderful opportunity of turning my back on the sectarian battles and into straight-forward socialist educational work. During the last twelve years I have learned a great deal in the process of teaching others and have been grateful for

180

the loyal co-operation of head office and of your co-operation in particular. (2)

Haston is at the time of writing the Education Officer at Woodstock College — the college of the General and Municipal Workers' Union near London.

A. L. Williams

A. L. (Len) Williams started life as a barber's lather-boy and later found a job on the railways. Joining the NUR put him in touch with the Liverpool Labour College. While still very young he obtained a two-year NUR scholarship to the Central Labour College. After some years as an NCLC organiser, he became the Yorkshire divisional organiser of the Labour Party, later still National Agent and finally General Secretary of the Party. When he died he was High Commissioner for Mauritius. Earlier he had edited the Labour Weekly, published in Leeds and had written on NCLC pamphlet on Marxism.

Andrew Boyd

Among later NCLC organisers was Andrew Boyd, a member of the AEU. On 3 October 1964, three days after the TUC had taken over the NCLC organisers under the rationalisation scheme, Boyd wrote to Millar saying among other things:

> Although I shall no longer be working under your direction I shall try to keep in touch with you from time to time. After all I was a very young apprentice when I first came across the name of J. P. M. Millar twenty-five years ago and I don't forget that what I am today was because of the NCLC. I don't think that during the ten years I have been organiser that you and I have had the least disagreement about the work although the JPM I met in the flesh for the first time at Transport House in October 1954 seemed a very formidable gentleman and I said to myself I'll probably be terrorised. (3)

Boyd had a gift for writing. After taking the NCLC English courses he became an occasional contributor to a number of journals and newspapers. During this period he asked Millar if there were any objections to his studying in his spare time for a degree at Belfast University. Millar said 'No' and in due course Boyd became the only NCLC organiser of his period with a

2. Haston to Millar, 30. Sept. 1963 in NCLC Corr.
3. Boyd to Millar, *ibid.*

181

university degree. Hardly had he been taken over by the TUC than he discovered that the TUC office did not want to retain an organising tutor for Northern Ireland. Boyd was bitterly disappointed at the TUC's dismantling of the NCLC machinery in Britain and Northern Ireland and eventually resigned his post. He had by this time become a writer on historical subjects one of his books being *The Rise of the Irish Trade Unions — 1729-1970.* After leaving the TUC he immediately became a senior lecturer at the College of Business Studies in Belfast.

Joe Kenyon

Another organiser who became very unhappy under the TUC office and left was Joe Kenyon of Barnsley, a former Yorkshire Miner. Because of his age he was unable to return to the mines, and for a time he lived on unemployment benefit. Impatient with inactivity he started a union for the unemployed and other claimants to social security who often did not receive all they were entitled to, mainly through lack of knowledge. The Union was called The Claimants' and Unemployed Workers' Union and extended to places as far apart as Glasgow and Cornwall. Eventually he was appointed Welfare Rights Adviser to Batley Community Development Project, while continuing to serve his Claimants' Union. Later still he became a member of the Government's National Consumer Council.

On rare occasions the NCLC appointed a man who could not stand up to the responsibilities and tribulations of an NCLC organiser's life, but most proved to be outstanding personalities. George Aitken, for example, became head of the AEU's research department.

Walton Newbold and Tommy Jackson

The Labour College Movement, unlike the WEA, employed relatively few full-time tutors. During the early period there were a few men who conducted classes from October to March and who were known as winter tutors, but their number steadily declined, and not one was left when the NCLC was wound up. They had included some interesting personalities. Two of the best known winter tutors were Walton Newbold and T. A. (Tommy) Jackson, at one time a London compositor. In his autobiography *Solo Trumpet,* Jackson recorded that in the autumn of 1919 he was appointed the winter lecturer of the North-Eastern Labour College, centred in Newcastle, whose chairman at that time was Will Lawther. Jackson taught economics, history and philosophy.

'My work,' he wrote, 'consisted partly of addressing miners' lodges and trade union branches to urge affiliation to the Labour College, and partly in giving a series of lectures to such classes as were set up in the area of Northumberland and Durham — with a small overlap into the Cleveland district of Yorkshire. From Morpeth, Ashington and Newbiggin in the north my territory ranged to include West Hartlepool, Middlesborough, Stockton and Darlington in the south but the Chief activity lay in the mining villages in the neighbourhood of Sunderland, South Shields and Newcastle.

Overcrowding was such that I could find no other place of habitation near to Newcastle than a wooden bungalow in a field facing the seashore at Whitley Bay. Local transport to and from the villages in Durham was rudimentary in those days; and my journey to and from my classes often involved several changes as well as long walks. It was almost impossible to reach Newcastle before the last train for Whitley had left; though a tram might be caught to take me as far as Wallsend; the rest of the journey had to be made on foot — sometimes through a gale, or snowstorm, with the last mile of the journey illuminated by the recurring flashes of a "revolving" lighthouse lantern. It was in several respects hard going. But all the hardships were more than compensated by the genial and stimulating reception I received from the "Geordies".' (4)

Jackson wrote countless articles and a number of books, including *Dialectics: The Logic of Marxism* and *Charles Dickens: The Progress of a Radical.*

Walton Newbold had been brought up as a Quaker and had taken an Arts degree. He became a socialist pamphleteer, an itinerant propagandist and lecturer and, on winning the Motherwell seat he became the first British Communist MP. As 'missionaries' of socialism neither Newbold nor Jackson had a regular income. Instead they relied upon free hospitality in the homes of workers, eked out by occasional payments. Each became notorious for his scruffy appearance as they often lived a rough life. When Newbold brought up Jackson — one of the

4. *Solo Trumpet,* pp.153-5 (London, 1953).

wittiest speakers in the Labour Movement — to assist him during his second campaign for the Motherwell seat, Jackson declared to Newbold that Newbold's motive had been 'to show the electors that there is one dirtier man in the Labour Movement than yourself.'

The Voluntary Tutors

Above all, the NCLC relied upon voluntary tutors. They were initially paid nothing and later a 1/-d. per class night, provided they submitted a register for each class. This pittance was intended merely as a book allowance. From the beginning securing a regular supply of competent voluntary tutors was a serious problem. A very large proportion of the lecturers employed by the WEA were university lecturers or school-masters whereas only a minute percentage were manual workers. With the NCLC the position was quite different. There were very few university lecturers or school teachers and a very large proportion of self-taught and Labour College-taught manual workers such as miners, engineers, railwaymen, car-penters, shop assistants and clerks. There was never more than a small sprinkling of teachers, lawyers and members of other professions.

Students of the CLC were initially the main source of supply in some areas, many of them having conducted classes in the immediate neighbourhood of the Labour College while still students. Millar himself, when a student, had taught on Sundays at Chelmsford and Colchester.

Many students who attended local Labour College classes subsequently became tutors and thereafter Labour councillors, M.P.s or officials of such bodies as the trade unions, co-operative societies and the Labour Party. Ellis Smith, who was to become President of the Pattern Makers' Union and an M.P., was a voluntary tutor. A typical example of a student who became a voluntary tutor and finally a union official was Harold Child. He started work at the age of eleven for a wage of 2/6d. a week and then became successively a student at Labour College classes, a voluntary worker, and a voluntary tutor. Eventually he was appointed Assistant General Secretary of the Tailors' and Garment Workers' Union. Later on, he joined the NCLC Executive Committee and also became a county councillor.

Another student who became a voluntary tutor was Fred Lee of the AEU. After the Second World War, Lee was elected to

Parliament and eventually became a Cabinet Minister. Two other students to end up as Cabinet Ministers were Fred Peart, one of a small band of school teachers who served as voluntary tutors, and Jim Griffiths who became Secretary of State for the Colonies in 1945. James Conway became General Secretary of the AEU. Hugh Scanlon, President of the AEU, is another former student and tutor; Jack Jones, General Secretary of the Transport and General Workers' Union, recorded in an interview in 1973:

> I was drawn to the National Council of Labour Colleges, for example, because its economics together with economic geography was the clearest approach to economics that a young working class mind would absorb . . . At eighteen I was honorary secretary of the Liverpool College. The Labour College Movement took the 'learning by doing' method very much to heart and active students rapidly became voluntary tutors. I am not sure about the effect on the students, but I certainly learnt a lot as tutor. (5)

Vic Feather, former General Secretary of the TUC, attended classes on public speaking and economics. He had also been an NCLC postal student. His successor, Len Murray, wrote to Millar in 1973:

> My association with the NCLC has not been as long as yours with the TUC but one of my first involvements with the Labour Movement was as a voluntary tutor in an NCLC class on Economics in Wolverhampton soon after the war. (6)

Another voluntary tutor was an unemployed engineer and a former class student Walter Greenwood. He paid written tribute to the NCLC English Courses saying how much they had helped him. Later he wrote *Love on the Dole*, which became a best seller and was made into a film.

5. *Times Educational Supplement*, 4. Jan. 1974. Jones also referred to the role of the Labour College movement in the course of another interview:
   We badly miss the old Labour College movement which produced men like Len Williams and Nye Bevan. I never thought Bevan was a saint, but he was able to play an important role because of the Labour College tradition. It developed young trade unionists to the point where they could stand up to going into Parliament. (*The Sunday Times Weekly Review*, 25 March, 1973).

6. NCLC Corr.

Arthur Woodburn

Of all the earlier tutors who attained public eminence the most faithful servant of the NCLC was Arthur Woodburn. During the First World War as an anti-imperialist socialist he became a member of the Edinburgh District Branch of the No Conscription Fellowship of which Millar was the secretary. Being employed in an engineering factory he could have escaped conscription and avoided imprisonment as a C.O., but decided to take his share of the rough which befell those other anti-imperialist socialists who were not in reserved occupations. Shortly after the First World War Woodburn started to lecture to a small class in Edinburgh, which called itself the Marxian School of Economics. It contained several Members of the Local Branch of the Socialist Labour Party. Woodburn, who had a practical turn of mind, was quick to appreciate that the Scottish Labour College, Edinburgh District, provided better opportunities for independent working-class education and decided to join it. As a lecturer in Edinburgh he pioneered the use of illustrative slides. In the course of time he was to become successively Secretary for the Edinburgh District, Secretary for the NCLC in Scotland, a member, and finally President of the National Executive. His political career was crowned with success when in 1941 he became Secretary of State for Scotland.

"Professional Educators" Were Not Numerous

The NCLC could only occasionally recruit its voluntary tutors from the ranks of professional educators because few of them had any knowledge of Marxist theory or had ever been inside a factory or down a mine or had experienced the conditions of life affecting manual workers. Moreover the NCLC had no desire to try to match the mass of knowledge at the disposal of a university. Most university subjects, the NCLC officials thought, had no immediate bearing on the social problems facing working men and women and so were of small value in enabling them to carry on their political and industrial struggles. Another reason frequently given for the shortage of qualified tutors was that socialist-inclined school teachers were reluctant to teach under NCLC sponsorship for fear of being denied promotion. A third reason was that, whereas the NCLC did not pay its tutors, the university extra-mural committees and the Education Authorities were able to do so. The problem of tutor-supply became more acute after the closure of the CLC. Millar wrote in *Plebs:*

186

Rt. Hon. Arthur Woodburn, M.P., D.Litt.,
President N.C.L.C. 1937 to 1964

We, therefore, take the opportunity of appealing to those of our readers who could tutor NCLC classes, and who have not yet done so, to fall in for the educational front. We should also like to appeal to those who have in the past taken NCLC classes but have since dropped out, to dig out their lecture notes. (7)

The shortage of tutors of adequate quality was a disturbing problem. A report issued in 1924 admitted that some locally-appointed tutors might have inadequate qualifications. In future, it was urged, aspiring tutors should be given a test and, if necessary, some training. In the same year a memorandum on training was considered by the executive committee. It was recommended that 'teaching at the centre should be mainly by group tuition instead of the old lecture method.' In 1925, 'a National Summer Training Centre was held . . . and justified the efforts involved. It is hoped to extend the idea in the coming summer, but, for a very considerable time, the bulk of tutors will require to be trained at special classes run in the various localities.'

Since the CLC in London was not under NCLC control an NCLC training centre for tutors would have been desirable but this never came into being. The 1925 edition of *Education for Emancipation* urged that 'All NCLC tutors should make a point of encouraging promising students to undertake more intensive training in order to equip themselves for class tutoring.' Unless they had experience of public speaking, tutors were usually required to give a few branch lectures before being allowed to conduct even a short course. Postal course students figured substantially among those who trained as tutors, and new as well as experienced tutors could have the advantage not only of taking free postal courses or having the lessons as basic lecture notes. From time to time training courses were arranged in the districts. But the problem of securing tutors and turning them into effective communicators could never be fully solved, although a considerable role was played by the postal course on Public Speaking and the classes on this subject. Normally, however, those who became tutors had had experience of speaking not only at classes but at trade union branches, labour parties, trades councils and meetings of other bodies.

In 1933 *Education for Emancipation* again referred to the problem:

7. *Plebs*, 1930, p.195.

Some of the existing full-time men and most of the voluntary tutors have been trained locally and tutors' training classes have all along been a feature of the work of every effective division. To encourage this very necessary work the executive of the NCLC in 1930 decided to pay the fares of those attending tutor-training classes and to provide tutors or those definitely training as tutors with free correspondence courses. It also hopes to run a short-term training centre and to explore the possibility of a long-term training centre. The main problems lying in the way of the latter are financial, and the difficulty that many of the best students find in getting leave of absence from work. (8)

Opponents of the NCLC often referred critically but seldom with justification to the professional competence of its tutors. Thus, Professor Peers:

... no one is afraid of the propagandist activities of the NCLC as such; what one needs to fear is the cut-and-dried presentation of particular facts and ill-understood theories by teachers who themselves are not masters of the subjects they are teaching, who cannot for that reason deal adequately with discussion and who therefore encourage short cuts to limited knowledge without understanding. (9)

And again:

Classes are conducted either by the full-time organisers, who are few in number and therefore unable in the midst of many other duties to undertake any large number of regular courses, or by voluntary tutors who may have little qualification for the highly skilled work of teaching adults. . . It is strange that the trade union movement, with its exclusive attitude to the admission of unqualified persons to the ranks of skilled workers is prepared to use the service of those, many of whom have no direct qualification for work which demands a high degree of skill and knowledge — that of teaching adults. (10)

Sources of Knowledge

How did the tutors who had not been at the residential

8. *loc.cit.*, p.8.
9. R. Peers, *Adult Education: A Comparative Study* (London 1958) p.161.
10. *ibid.*, p.160.

College acquire their knowledge? The great majority were drawn from among the active members of the Labour Movement. They had, therefore, a good deal of experience in such bodies as union branches, socialist parties, trades councils and other working-class organisation, and they were usually of a naturally studious turn of mind. They were readers of socialist papers such as *The Labour Leader, The Clarion, Justice* and *Plebs.* They had read many of the pamphlets published by the socialist parties and books like *Merrie England* and *Britain for the British.* The latter was published in hundreds of thousands and the former sold over a million copies. Quite a large proportion had read the short books published in small type as pamphlets by the Socialist Labour Party. These included *Wage, Labour and Capital* and *Value, Price and Profit* by Marx, *Historical Materialism* and the *Development of Socialism from Utopia to Science* by Engels, as well as the *Communist Manifesto* by Marx and Engels. Many had also read Marx's *Capital, The Condition of the Working Classes in England in 1844* by Engels, as well as Hyndman's book on *Marxian Economics* and his *Commercial Crises in the 19th Century.* When such socialists came into touch with the Labour College Movement they were introduced to non-socialist books like De Gibbons' *Industrial History of England* and Thorold Rogers' *Six Centuries of Work and Wages.* Above all, Labour College supporters, if they had not read them before, were introduced to the library of classical socialist books published mostly by Charles Kerr and Company, the Chicago Socialist publishers, and to the Rationalist Press Association's books often republished in 6d. paper-covered editions. The latter included Darwin's *Origin of Species,* Hird's *Easy Outline of Evolution* and Haeckel's *The Riddle of the Universe.* The Kerr books included Labriola's *The Materialist Conception of History,* Engels' *Landmarks of Scientific Socialism,* Dietzgen's *The Positive Outcome of Philosophy,* Boudin's *Theoretical System of Karl Marx,* Marx's *The Poverty of Philosophy,* Lafargue's *The Evolution of Property,* Kautsky's *The Class Struggle* and *Ethics and the Materialist Conception of History* and Lewis' *Evolution, Social and Organic.*

During most ot the NCLC's history Labour supporters, especially manual workers, spent far more time reading books and pamphlets about social theory and social questions than they do today. In the early days of the Plebs Movement very few active members of the Labour Movement were elected to public bodies, of which there were many fewer than in 1963. Moreover, socialism was so unpopular that a socialist candidate usually came at the bottom of the poll. Keen socialists thus had plenty of time to come to grips with socialist theory.

When the Labour College movement began, few members of the teaching profession were socialists. A small number did, however, support the Labour College. One area where the NCLC received much assistance from teachers was the industrialised section of the West of Scotland where James Maxton and John Maclean were both trained teachers active in the Socialist Movement even before the first world war. On the North-east coast of England one of the leading NCLC tutors was Will Coxon who was headmaster of a small school. In Edinburgh a science master, John Maxton and Miss Jacob, a curator at the Royal Scottish Museum, served as tutors, as did one university student named Gray who afterwards became a professor. Patrick Gordon Walker, when an Oxford don, was another tutor.

Most Tutors Wage Workers

It was not educational theory that caused the Colleges to find the bulk of their tutors amongst wage workers. It's true that the worker-tutor had advantages when in the early days workers tended to feel uncomfortable in the presence of middle class accents and middle class vocabularies. The fact was that tutors could only be found in any numbers among workers because it was among them that socialist theories had won the bulk of their advocates.

As far back as 1853 the founders of the Working Men's College had discerned a need for workers to teach their peers. J. F. C. Harrison has pointed out: 'It was never the intention of the Founders, however, that the teaching should all be done by university professional men. In *Learning and Working*, and again in the original *Circular* advertising the College in 1854, it was emphasized that 'we hope, ultimately, to raise up teachers from among the working men themselves, who must receive regular salaries.' In 1861 Ludlow, one of the founders, wrote:

> . . . I have always been convinced that the teaching of working men by working men is the main ultimate work of these colleges; that the most imposing staff of teachers laden with university degrees and honours is worthless, except so far as it conduces to that end. Only

190

the working man can thoroughly understand the working men's difficulties, puzzles, bewilderments; only he can place knowledge precisely in that point of view from which his fellows can best grasp and handle it. (11) Some of the NCLC tutors were naturally gifted instructors, who, as Ludlow desired, could speak a language at once easily understood by the working man and who drew vivid illustrations from the working environment with which to enliven their lectures.

But if in principle it was a sound idea to depend overwhelmingly upon worker-teachers, in practice it meant that groups of students might sit at the feet of inexperienced men. Only very rarely did a letter of complaint appear in *Plebs*. A correspondent signing himself D.J.W. protested that lectures were all too often repetitive and cliche-ridden, no more than 'a series of denunciatory tirades against some monstrosity called capitalism, with oratory that descended to the commonplace and grammar which gave one the creeps.' Another correspondent complained:

> I have a long acquaintance with a certain college and can say that no tutor who has stuck to the job has been produced. Consequently this college is confined to the same old subjects repeated year after year by the same ageing tutors. All honour to the latter for their work, but cannot some way be found to throw the teaching gradually on to new and better trained teachers, including much needed women teachers? (12)

Postal Course Help

This letter was written before the Postal Course Department was able to play a substantial role in helping tutors, particularly by giving them access to new subjects. The same correspondent complained about frequent changes of tutors and their general lack of qualifications: 'Too many of our lectures are just that — lectures and not progressive studies.' Some of the tutors required more knowledge of their subjects and more training in teaching methods than could be given at infrequent weekend schools or classes specially run for tutors. Few workers have the ability or the time and surplus energy to persevere with the vigorous preparation required or the skill to initiate and objectively to steer fully effective discussion groups. But the NCLC had some

11. Quoted in J. F. C. Harrison, *A History of the Workingmen's College 1854-1954* (London, 1954), p.70.

12. *Plebs*, 1937, p.21.

gifted tutors even if, in the main, it relied mostly upon communicators who had had no formal training in teaching. That, however, is also true of many professional educators. An opportunity of taking an NCLC class gave many capable men an exceptional chance and incentive to increase their own knowledge and capacity. The raw tutor of one year could become years later very accomplished. The value of the voluntary spirit in teaching adults cannot be under-estimated. The NCLC held a secret which adult educators have so far sought in vain to arouse in the cultural deserts of the housing-estates of the sixties and seventies. In an article in *Highway* in 1950 Ernest Green once wrote:

> The WEA's main danger comes from without rather than within. It is all too ready to lay itself open to exploitation by providing classes for the type of tutor who views the movement as a racket and gives nothing in return. It should insist that tutors serve their apprenticeships by voluntary service . . . Twenty-five years ago no group of students would have been disappointed, however small. There were tutors who could be relied upon for some voluntary work. We have to recapture that voluntary spirit and it is worth organising our panels of voluntary tutors for the purpose. (13)

Teaching Methods

As far as teaching methods were concerned NCLC educational work during most of its existence consisted of lectures followed by questions and some discussion, but there was no particular stress upon learning through the medium of the discussion group — a recent conception which was not true of much teaching in any sector until after the Second World War. Latterly the NCLC made such more use of discussion-group work especially at its summer schools.

At first, there was a tendency for some tutors to feel obliged to use the technical vocabulary of Marx and other socialist theoreticians, thereby making full comprehension unlikely for many students. This did not last long. Horrabin and Millar themselves studiously used plain words both in their writings and speeches in an attempt to dispel the idea that the only way to explain socialist theories was by invoking a vocabulary outside the verbal experience of the average worker. The use of

13. 'Looking Backwards' in *The Highway*, vol. 42, October, 1950, p.8.

blackboards was encouraged and roller blackboards were supplied for use in makeshift classrooms when wooden ones were not available but at first the NCLC was handicapped in this respect for few Labour halls had blackboards. On one occasion when Christine Millar arrived at a new class in a mining village in West Lothian she asked the miners where the blackboard was. There was none she was told, but if she waited a few minutes, one would be got. Two miners disappeared and returned in a short time with a door removed from one of the outside privies — outside privies were all the miners' houses had as sanitary conveniences. That experience resulted in the NCLC supplying easily-carried roller cloth blackboards for its tutors.

The Horrabin maps reproduced in *Plebs* and *The Plebs Atlas* were often enlarged and used by tutors. Until superseded by film strips, lantern slides were popular teaching aids. Quite early, NCLC headquarters arranged for the Visual Information Service, inspired by an NCLC tutor Mrs. Clayton, to pioneer the use of film strips by making special ones for Labour College classes. In time every organiser had at least one projector at his disposal. It was not always possible to ensure that a tutor used visual aids, but supplies of books were always available at every class meeting. Practically all tutors regularly read *Plebs* and this kept them in touch with new books of interest and provided such periodic notes as Horrabin's Geographical Footnotes. Headquarters also frequently distributed lists of recently published books and pamphlets.

Who were the Students?

A vital part in the educational programme of the NCLC was played by college secretaries and class secretaries. Their work was entirely voluntary until the very last years, when they were paid a nominal allowance of 2/6d. for each register they returned. One Secretary wrote to Millar:

> When I tell you that I work for a living I am a Labour Party Secretary as well as Labour College Secretary, Secretary of a Works sports club and of a savings group, a member of a Co-operative board and of the Home Guard and in my spare time have an allotment and chickens to look after, you will realise that I sometimes wonder whether it is May or March.'

Who were the students served by the NCLC? It is possible to give an unambiguous answer. With few exceptions they were wage earners. A sprinkling of teachers and professional people apart, they were also nearly all either manual workers, clerks or shop assistants. This fact is no cause for surprise, especially for the early period, considering the socio-economic background of the prinicipal figures in the Labour Movement. As pointed out by R. S. Barker:

> Nearly all the trade union leaders and Labour politicians of the pre-war years, for instance, had left school at fourteen at the latest. Ben Tillett started work at the age of eight, Margaret Bondfield at thirteen. Ben Turner only attended school part time from the age of nine, and Robert Smillie was working by the age of nine. Of those Labour MPs not sponsored by unions in 1918, all but two out of twelve had received no more than elementary schooling. (14)

Between the wars the overwhelming majority of students who attended Labour College classes or who took postal courses had left school at the age of fourteen or earlier. A significant proportion of students later served the Labour Movement in more or less prestigious capacities. One example of class students later notable nation-wide illustrates this. In his own classes Arthur Woodburn numbered Margaret Herbison, a future Minister of Pensions, William Hannan, a future Labour Whip, John Robertson, a future Under-Secretary of State for Scotland, E. G. Willis, a future Minister of State for Scotland, James (now Lord) Hoy, a future Parliamentary Secretary of Agriculture, George Lawson, a future Deputy Chief Whip, Tom Oswald, a future P.P.S. to the Secretary of State for Scotland, and a number of future Members of Parliament. Other students who later became nationally known figures had benefited from postal course studies. Many had benefited from both.

Such was the keenness of the students during the earlier years that they would attend classes in the most uncomfortable rooms. Woodburn recalls one of his classes on economics held in the early 1920s at Tranent, a small mining village near Edinburgh The dingy hall where the class met was both lighted and heated by a smokey oil-heater with a glass funnel, placed on the floor Through the gloom he would hardly see his thirty students and they had to strain their eyes to read what was on the blackboard.

National Statistics

The first year for which there were national statistics was 1922

14. R. Barker, *Education and Politics, 1900-1951: Study of the Labour Party* (Oxford, 1972), p.122.

when 11,993 students enrolled for 529 classes. Postal courses began in the following year with an enrolment of 90 students. Neither in 1922 or 1923 were figures for day schools or branch lectures kept, but the number in attendance was certainly small in the case of day schools, larger in the case of branch lectures. By 1924 there were 71 day schools with 5,414 students: 976 lectures were provided for union branches and other bodies.

The peak total for classes was reached during the session 1925/26 when there were 1,234 classes with 30,398 students in attendance. After the failure of the General Strike and the long miners' stoppage, the militancy and self-confidence of the trade union movement collapsed. The 1929 slump further reduced the number and buoyancy of trade unionists. These two factors were reflected in a decline in NCLC numbers. In 1929 Central Office decided to accept from the organisers only those enrolment figures which were backed by the return of registers. This decision was taken after a union General Secretary, hostile to the NCLC, had persuaded his executive committee to demand the names and addresses of his own union's class students. A few colleges were unable to produce all the registers required to back up the figures they had reported. By 1929/30 classes had fallen to 810 and class enrolments to 19,275. Day schools had risen to a total of 164 with enrolments at 7,656, and branch lectures had increased to 1,105. In the thirties, in the wake of the economic slump, class attendance continued to dwindle but the steady decline of class enrolments was much more than offset by an increase in postal course enrolments. This compensatory growth led some organisers to infer (quite incorrectly) that Central Office deliberately built up postal courses and neglected class-work.

All the evidence indicates beyond any doubt that the over-whelming majority of those concerned with the Labour College Movement — executive committee members, organisers, tutors and students — were either wage earners, mainly in manual occupations, or had been wage earners before attaining office in various sectors of the Labour Movement. Whether or not the adventure was successful overall — a question considered in the last chapter — the NCLC practised what it preached: it relied very largely upon workers to help other workers further their education with the support of funds derived almost exclusively from working-class organisations.

CHAPTER X

COURSES, CLASSES & SUBJECTS

The NCLC provided instruction in nine different ways: weekly classes; branch lectures; lantern and film strip lectures; day schools; public interviews; week-end schools; residential summer schools; postal courses.

The Classes

The classes were held in the evenings or on Sunday mornings and usually consisted of twelve meetings. There were three sessions in each year which ran respectively, from January to March, April to June, and October to December. With the passage of time, six-meeting courses became quite common in NCLC work, as in WEA work. The national executive regularly enjoined organisers to stick to twelve-meeting courses whenever possible, in the belief that more demanding courses should be encouraged. At the same time, it did not seek to retain courses of twenty-four meetings — the duration of some of the courses offered by the Central Labour College and some local colleges in the early days, as well as of WEA-University tutorial courses. The reasons for discouraging twenty-four meeting courses were that the level of attendance tended to fall off during the second half, that in order to keep interest alive it was desirable to cover more than one major theme in a given year and that the more separate courses there were, the greater the number of people who could attend. Moreover, twelve-lesson courses were less strain on the tutors.

Originally, evening courses were planned entirely by the local colleges themselves but later much of the initiative passed to the full-time organisers who made use of the local secretaries and other activists. As a rule evening classes were held from 7 p.m. to 9 p.m. No minimum or maximum enrolment levels were fixed and as a result the number of participants varied greatly. Not infrequently a class might have a small enrolment on the first night but the tutor, by appealing to those who had enrolled, would usually be able to persuade them to act as recruiters so that a class would often grow considerably in size. On one occasion, after making a long bus journey to a small mining village in West Lothian, Millar found that only one student had turned up. Since this student had taken the trouble to travel from another town some five miles away Millar delivered his lecture as though faced by a full audience. The student subsequently helped Millar to build up the class enrolment to twenty. The policy of encouraging the first students who turned up at a course to bring their friends to future meetings always paid dividends. It brought home to the students that the expansion of educational work was not simply a task for the Labour College but very much a task for the existing students.

Clearing out
the
dust of ages

GOVERNING CLASS

IDEAS

J.F.H.

In advance of each session NCLC organisers sent out a printed leaflet to all affiliated trade union branches as well as to other branches when they had the necessary addresses, to the local Labour Parties and to Co-operative bodies in their respective areas. They also sent the leaflets to former students, which latterly they card-indexed. These leaflets contained a list of the evening classes arranged and offered a list of branch lectures. Sympathetic branch secretaries would so arrange the business at one of their meetings as to give the organiser or lecturer reasonable time to deliver a talk, to answer questions, to advertise the evening classes, to enrol postal students and to sell pamphlets. Occasionally, a class was run at branch meetings after the business was over but in the main they were deliberately arranged separately, so that they could be open to the members of all the local Labour bodies. While a number of the branch lectures were on the NCLC's work, most of them were on topics which would interest trade unionists and other Labour workers. Some were on trade union problems or trade union history, while others were on recent legislation affecting workers or on international affairs or proposed legislation or political issues.

Meetings had to be timed with an eye to the social habits of the students. On one occasion when Millar suggested to organiser Connell that he should visit the branches of the Lancashire Miners, which had just affiliated, to inform them about the work of the NCLC and to enrol students, Connell replied that it might work if the members knew him personally, but they were great people for protocol. Moreover, their meetings were held on Sunday mornings and ended immediately the pubs opened. Anyone who attempted to prolong a meeting was likely to see some of his audience disappear.

Week-end and Day Schools

Because they were expensive and those who attended had often to pay their own fees and fares, week-end schools were seldom arranged. Day schools, on the other hand, were a great success and continued to flourish when evening courses in the summer had difficulty in attracting students. These schools were sometimes held on a Saturday afternoon but usually on Sundays so as not to compete with shopping expeditions or football matches. Sometimes a school would be restricted to the afternoon period which simplified matters since the question of providing a meal would not often arise. At these schools there were always questions and discussions. The attendance at day schools was much larger than at classes. The lecturer at a two-lectures day school gave lectures, each of roughly one hour, and tea was usually served at the end of the first lecture. There was always a period set aside for questions and discussion after each talk. Students tended, however, to be more interested in obtaining information from the lecturer rather than engaging in discussion.

Written Work

The student was not asked to prepare for a class by means of selected reading. In classes largely or entirely composed of

198

manual workers it was not possible to insist upon written work. However, keen students were encouraged to become branch lecturers and eventually class lecturers. For them this meant not only much reading but careful preparation of notes. Although written work was seldom a requirement in an ordinary class, persistent efforts were made to encourage the reading habit. It was a standing rule that literature should be on sale at every educational gathering. As far as possible, the books and pamphlets on display were changed for each meeting. New pamphlets or books judged to be of particular interest were always on sale. In addition, college secretaries and the divisional organisers, who always carried stocks of literature wherever they went, sold books and pamphlets not only at their own meetings but sometimes at the meetings of other Labour organisations.

The NCLC central office made a practice of asking affiliated unions and other national bodies to allow the nearest NCLC organiser to have a literature stall at national conferences. These stalls served several purposes. They interested those present in the NCLC's work, provided an opportunity for enrolling postal course students and enabled the organisers or their deputies to make useful contacts for establishing classes and in other ways developing the NCLC's activities.

Accommodation

The NCLC did not expect Education Authorities (LEA's) to look with a kindly eye upon classes concerned with socialist education. So far as is known, only one LEA ever provided accommodation for an NCLC class. For several years up to 1926 some former Labour College students took classes under the auspices of two LEAs in South Wales. In 1926 an official of the Board of Education made it clear that from the beginning of the next session, *Plebs* text books were not to be used and that the class should become the responsibility of the WEA. In the event the LEA decided to make all the classes WEA classes. The Campsie (Stirlingshire) District School Management Committee refused an application from the Scottish Labour College for the use of a schoolroom for a course in industrial history and economic geography.

Local authorities were not invariably hostile to the NCLC. For instance, in 1931 the traditionally right-wing Edinburgh Education Committee took pains to consult at length with the local Labour College, which was quite influential, about allow-

199

ing it a room in a Corporation school, and the reason for finall'
refusing the request was that the College declined to agree t
have its class included in the Corporation's continuation schoc
programme. The refusal of a further request for accommoda
tion, made in 1935, led the College to ask the STUC to raise th
matter with the Scottish Education Committee, but the STUC
simply replied that the matter was a local authority responsi
bility outside its jurisdiction. In 1936 a third request wa
approved by the Edinburgh Education Committee by 7 votes t
3 but rejected by the Magistrates and the Town Counci
Nevertheless, the Magistrates agreed to see a deputation from
the College and after discussion allowed the Education Commit
tee's ruling to stand.

The lack of local authority support was not serious becaus
much of the LEA accommodation which might have been mad
available was in schools where the seats were unsuitable , fo
adults. At that time, too, the aversion from schools among man'
working men was acute. Most classes were arranged witl
advantage in Labour Party or trade union premises or i
co-operative halls, meeting places which working-men foun
more congenial than schools and which could usually be rente
for a small fee, or used free.

Very few of the Labour Colleges had permanent premises
Manchester Labour College in the early days rented a basemen
in the centre of Manchester, but Millar himself thought th
arrangement most unsatisfactory and persuaded the College t
vacate it, so that classes could be held in more attractiv
premises.

Summer Schools

At its first annual meeting in 1922 the NCLC indicated it
belief in the value of summer schools, by passing the followin;
resolution:

> That the Executive be instructed to arrange for th
> holding of summer schools wherever possible: that th
> offer of the use of the Kew premises made by the Boar
> of Governors of the London Labour College for thi
> purpose be accepted and that members be invited t
> send in names of students who are willing to attend
> that every assistance possible be given to the propose
> summer school to be promoted by the Scottish Labou
> College: that representation be made to the Midlan

200

and Northern areas of the NCLC inviting their undertaking the provision of a summer school in their areas.
areas.

Summer schools were much more expensive to run than other
educational activities. They involved fares for both students and
tutors and the cost of board and lodging. Such schools also
involved absence from work and that in turn often entailed loss
of wages or payment for lost time. Summer schools however
eventually played an important part in the NCLC's educational
programmes. The Plebs League first held a summer school in
1924 at Cober Hill Guest House, Cloughton, near Scarborough.
Very soon afterwards the NCLC assumed responsibility for
summer school work. Its first school took place in 1925 in a
hutted co-operative holiday camp in Rothesay. The school
immediately followed the annual meeting of the Council which
was held at the weekend to suit the convenience of delegates and
to avoid lost time and the losing of jobs through absence. Until
1930 the NCLC continued to combine its annual meeting and
summer school so that those who were attending the school need
pay for only one journey, for most of the students then paid their
own fares and fees. In that year, however, following Millar's visit
to Ireland, the largest Irish trade union — the Irish Transport
Workers — sent twelve students to the Rothesay school;
students were also sent by the Irish Labour Party and TUC.
Although some British trade unions awarded scholarships to the
school these were fewer than those awarded by the Irish unions.
The majority of the students were still paying their own fees and
fares.

Summer schools were intended not merely to provide students
from different parts of the country with an opportunity to attend
lectures by well-known personalities in the Labour Movement
such as George Lansbury, but to enable them to exchange
experiences and pool their knowledge. The value of the cross-
fertilisation was illustrated when a member of one professional
association attended a school at his own expense in order to see
what went on. He reported to his association's executive that,
informative as the lectures had been, he had gained equal
benefit from meeting engineers, bricklayers, electricians and
other manual workers, and from participating in discussions
during and outside lecture periods.

Initially, since students were all keenly interested in socialist political issues, sessions tended to take the form of prolonged ideological discussions and arguments, particularly about current political problems. With the passing of time, however, more and more unions began to award scholarships to the increasing number of students until eventually self-financing students became often a small minority. As this change took place the interest in sustained political arguments decreased. At most schools discussion periods became shorter and question periods longer, as though the students were anxious to pump the maximum amount of information out of the lecturers. Discussions with the lecturers sometimes continued informally after the formal meeting, but usually the students continued the discussion among themselves when sitting outside or exploring the neighbourhood. Latterly, organised group discussions were introduced at most of the schools (such as those run for the AEU) as an integral part of the programme. Each discussion group appointed a spokesman who, at a joint meeting of all the groups, submitted a report on the main points which had been raised.

Summer schools did more than amplify the knowledge of the participants through information dispensed at lectures and in discussion groups. The students represented a great variety of occupations, ranging as they did from dockers to draughtsmen, and the informal discussion they entered into about practices in their unions and other organisations, and the special problems they faced in their own industries and localities was a vital part of the educational experience.

Chance meetings often resulted in practical outcomes. On one occasion, for instance, at a summer school held in Bangor, a group of miners from Fife, whose local parliamentary constituency party was searching for a suitable candidate, were so impressed by one of their fellow students, a young voluntary NCLC tutor, that they nominated him. This student was William Hamilton who was duly elected to Parliament in 1950 and subsequently became well-known as the M.P. who kept a close eye on State expenditure on the Royal Family.

On another occasion, George Shepherd (subsequently Lord Shepherd) National Agent of the Labour Party, was persuaded to give a lecture at a summer school. He brought his wife, and once among the students he liked the ambience so much that the Shepherds stayed to the end of the school. Each year thereafter he attended a summer school for one week, though not always as a lecturer. As Shepherd confided to Millar, he found active members of the Labour Party were more inclined to approach him at a summer school than when he paid official visits to his constituencies. Since he encouraged the participants to treat him as a fellow student, he was able to come by information he could not have gathered in any other way and to make arrangements and drive home points which a formal initiative from head office would not have produced. When the Labour Party was rent with discord, he said that his faith was restored by his discussions with keen young trade unionists.

Summer School Students

Even when the unions began to award scholarships on a large scale, the proportion of very young workers in attendance was normally just as low as at evening classes and day schools. Their spare time was spent in attending technical classes in further education centres or courting or looking after a young family. As a rule, it was only when workers had reached the age of about twenty-five or thirty and had begun to feel the weight of the economic system that they could be presuaded to take an active interest in Labour College education.

Only once was the NCLC asked to run a summer school for apprentices alone — the request came from the AEU. Millar realised that such a school might well require some special handling and he selected Organiser Haston as the Director. On retiring to his bedroom on the first night Haston carefully examined his bed, and was rewarded by finding underneath his lower sheet a selection of carefully placed sprigs of holly. On rising in the morning to breakfast and start the first lecture he found his door had been so treated that it would not open. He made no sound of protest. Ten minutes later, the young bloods, who thought they had imprisoned the Director, walked into the breakfast room to enjoy, not just breakfast but their huge success. They could, however, hardly believe their eyes, Jock Haston, quite unruffied, was calmly tucking into his meal. As an ex-steeplejack Jock had opened his bedroom window, climbed on to the roof and descended the three storeys of the mansion house by means of the rain pipes. His place as Director was now secure.

Summer school Directors took care that no students treated summer schools as an excuse for enjoying a relaxed holiday. A school register was introduced in 1952 and ostentatiously marked during each lecture period. In consequence it was very rarely indeed that any student was not present at every lecture. Students were also encouraged to take notes, although many of them found it too difficult simultaneously to listen and to take notes. Even clerical workers found that dual task difficult. Notes taken by students were often jotted down from memory after the lectures, questions and discussions, except in the case of some special schools.

At the end of a summer school the official in charge was expected to ascertain from each student what he was prepared to do on behalf of the NCLC on his return home. Towards the conclusion of each school a talk would be given about the NCLC's aims and policies, followed by an appeal for active assistance. It was explained that the jobs to be done included not only lecturing or organising or campaigning for affiliation in their union and co-operative branches and in the constituency Labour parties, but also selling 'literature,' promoting the circulation of *Plebs* and giving branch lectures. Millar was not beyond suggesting that, as everyone could be of some service, even the mentally lethargic could always circulate leaflets. To capitalise on such exhortations, the official in charge issued each student with a form inviting him or her to indicate the jobs he or she was willing to do and to give, name, address, union, local Labour Party and co-operative society. These details were then distributed to NCLC organisers for appropriate action.

Foreign Summer Schools

Managing summer schools, especially the foreign ones attended very largely by mature trade unionists ranging from representatives of the rank and file through shop stewards to members of national executives was by no means easy. The directors of such schools had to ensure that the educational excursions were carried out without hitches, that notes were not only taken but latterly handed in for examination, and that the students went to bed at a timely hour so that they did not sit half asleep during the first session on the following morning. Diplomacy was often called for in dealing with union executive members, who on rare occasions, behaved as though the prescribed rules did not apply to them.

There was always in residence for help a liaison officer — a member of the foreign Labour movement with a good command of English.

J.P.M. and C.M. settling up after a Norwegian summer school excursion

The first foreign summer school was held in 1937 at the
Belgian Labour College on the outskirts of Brussels. The school
coincided with a conference of the Labour and Socialist
International, the delegates to which were the afternoon guests
of the Belgian Labour Movement at the College, so that the
students met Arthur Henderson, George Lansbury and other
leaders.

After the Second World War foreign schools were resumed
and became an important feature of the educational programme
of the NCLC. Some of the foreign schools were partially
subsidised by UNESCO, and a lecture was given on its work and
policy. It was the general practice to arrange educational
excursions. Usually one of these was to a residential college run
by the Labour Movement, others to a great ironworks, a motor
car factory, a glass works, a coal mine or a porcelain factory. In
some of the German schools the students went down a coalmine.
As the schools were usually held in or near the capital city, there
were visits to the Parliament building and to the TUC head
quarters and perhaps the headquarters of the Socialist Party and
the offices of the Labour daily newspaper.

On the last evening of the foreign summer schools a dinner
was usually held in a big restaurant; sometimes this meal was
paid for by the NCLC and sometimes by the local Labour
Movement. Occasionally the guests included the British Labour
Attache. On one occasion the NCLC's function collaborated
with a similar function held by the local branch of the
Policemen's Union.

The NCLC held foreign summer schools in Belgium, Holland,
France, Germany, Austria, Switzerland, Norway, Denmark and
Sweden. These were often organised by Christine Millar who,
unlike Millar himself, had a gift for learning languages. When
the language of a country in which a school was to be held was
unknown to her she took a Berlitz course beforehand so that
when the liaison officer was not available she could serve as a
interpreter. The actual running of the schools, because they were
more difficult than the home schools, fell to the two Millars.
When foreign schools were resumed after the Second World War
the first two were run in Paris. Each foreign school lasted only a
week to increase the number of students who could take
advantage of the facilities. At the Paris schools the students each
week numbered about a hundred. This figure was too great a
strain and subsequent schools were reduced to a more manageable
205

able figure. The two French schools were officially opened by Leon Blum, the French socialist leader who had headed the Popular Front Government before the second world war.

Soon after this war the NCLC took financial risk of chartering planes to take the students to and from their summer school destinations. This cut down the lost time for which unions paid and had the advantage that the students didn't arrive as tired as they did when travel was by train, boat and train. The NCLC was, in fact, the first British Labour body to use chartered planes. Fortunately, no foreign schools had to be cancelled and so there was no loss for cancelled planes — a risk for which insurance was not available.

The lecturers at the foreign schools in addition to being nearly all leading members of the Labour Movement of the country visited, were able to speak excellent English and so had no difficulty in dealing with the students' questions.

The lecture on the historical background of the country visitor was usually given by a socialist academic. A general secretary of one of the international trade union organisations was frequently one of the lecturers and usually spoke on the international trade union movement.

As the course covered a wide range and dealt with subjects about which many of the students knew little it was by no means easy for some of them to absorb and understand all the facts. In consequence, in the latter years the first morning session in each of the six days was entirely devoted to the school director putting questions to the students on the previous day's lecture. These questions covered all the main points and sometimes additional ones. This method made very lively sessions and enabled the students to clear up many misunderstandings. Occasionally students would volunteer the opinion that interesting as the lectures and the question sessions at the end were, the morning revision question session was even more interesting in that it provided an exceptional amount of student participation.

Whereas today it is commonplace for manual workers to spend holidays abroad, until about the 1960's few workers had been out of Britain except on military service. Most workers came to NCLC schools with little or no knowledge of European history or of the structure of the European trade union and Labour movements. The object of holding summer schools on the Continent was accordingly to shake British workers, who were often leaders in their own movement, out of their insularity by introducing them to new countries, new histories, new socialist parties, new socialist trade union problems and practices. It was also hoped that, like most of the leaders of the NCLC, those who attended would begin to develop an international socialist outlook. A typical lecture programme included:

> The Historical Background of Denmark
> The Danish Trade Union Movement
> The Danish Political Parties
> The Danish Workers' Educational Movement
> Danish Economic Problems Today
> Danish Political Problems Today

The instructional value of foreign schools was demonstrated on one occasion in a very practical way when a group of students were staying at Egmond-on-Zee in the Netherlands. On the second day some students expressed the wish to see Millar in order to complain about the food they were getting. Millar agreed to see them later on and informed the hostel manager about their complaint. The manager said he in turn had a complaint against the students, so it was decided that Millar and Christine and the manager would together listen to the group. The deputation agreed that, as they were the guests of the Dutch Movement, the manager would speak first. He was a little man who had catered for NCLC schools before, but he spoke with real passion on this occasion.

> Mr. Millar, he said, before this school came I thought all Englishmen were gentlemen. But now I've changed my mind. Some of the students are throwing their cigarette ends on the beautiful floors of the corridors. Others are throwing cigarette ends out of their bedrooms on to the sand dunes. Do your students know that but for those dunes a large part of Holland would be flooded by the sea? Do your students know that every little root of grass has to be planted by hand so that it may grow to protect the dunes from being washed away so that the country won't be flooded?

Before he could go any further the deputation looked thoroughly discomforted and assured the manager that only a few students could be blamed and that steps would be taken to see that their conduct improved.

It was now the deputation's turn to raise the question of food. Their spokesman was a very able young trade unionist, who had started life as a barber's lather boy and later became an internationally known figure in the Labour Movement and later still represented the British Government abroad. He said they objected to what they were getting for breakfast. It was no doubt all right for Dutch workers but it was not good enough for British workers who enjoyed a higher standard of living. They particularly objected to being asked to eat raw fish. Millar in reply, invited them to look at the facts. For breakfast that morning they had been provided with cold boiled eggs, boiled ham, two kinds of bread, ginger bread as well as cheese. The 'raw fish' was in fact smoked salmon. One of the reasons why the capitalist class in Britain exploited the workers was so that the capitalists could afford to patronise the Savoy grill and consume such a delicacy. As for the relative standards, Dutch workers at the time, Millar said, were enjoying the highest standard of living in Europe — higher than that of British workers. One of the reasons why the NCLC ran summer schools abroad was precisely so that British workers could see how other workers lived. One way to do this was not to provide British meals at continental summer schools. In fact, the breakfast they were getting was more expensive than the breakfast they ate at home. The group left the meeting a little wiser and undoubtedly had their legs pulled by the other students.

The Curriculum

Changes took place in teaching methods; the subject-matter of courses also evolved with the years. The Labour Colleges had originally confined their attention largely to economics and history, especially to industrial history, Marxian economics and the materialist conception of history. At the Central Labour College a key subject had first been called 'Philosophic Logic' and subsequently renamed 'The Science of Understanding.' So as to improve the students' command of English and the ability to speak in public, a few classes on public speaking had also been arranged. Thus, initially, the emphasis was unequivocally placed upon socio-political issues. In an address on working-class education at the North of England Education Conference in 1924 Craik stated:

> The Labour College was compelled to concentrate, and it continues to concentrate on the study of sociological phenomena precisely because the problems of the Labour Movement are social problems. It does not despise physical science. Rather does it seek, in the field

of sociology, to emulate the fruitful achievements of physical science, and to the end that the fruits of the knowledge of natural force, shall lighten the labour and lengthen the leisure of the collective working community instead of being a means for individual aggrandisement on the part of a few. (1)

But as the Labour Movement began rapidly to enlarge its membership and as some of its members attained positions of responsibility, the curriculum had steadily to be widened so as to embrace not only new subjects but also functionally useful subjects. The NCLC tried constantly to develop its curricula in line with necessary needs.

Courses introduced at an early stage included Britain's Economic Problems, Local Government, Secretaryship, Economic and Political Geography. A specially important subject was Imperialism. This subject was of great use in helping the Labour Movement to appreciate the growing problem of the break-up of the British Empire and to understand and help the struggle of colonial peoples to attain self-government.

Publications, postal courses and summer schools — all of which were controlled by the central office — reflect this widening of emphasis. In the 1932 edition of *Education for Emancipation* the leading article entitled 'The Crisis and Education' contained a clarion call for linking education and socialism:

> . . . although economic conditions cry aloud for a change of social system, the workers as a whole show no signs of being able to seize the opportunity provided for them. What is the reason for that? Is it that they are still mentally wedded to the existing social order (2). Again, in 1933, under the heading 'Hitler Reads Labour a Lesson,' *Education for Emancipation* warned that the tactic for seizing power used by Hitler of seeming to be socialist could by used in other countries. In fact Fascism was not something peculiar only to German and Italian capitalism . . . Surely, the moral that our own Movement must draw is that its strength, in the event of its being put to the test, will depend on the number of members it has who do not think simply in

1. *The School Chronicle and Education Authorities Gazette*, 2 Feb., 1924, p.96.

terms of slogans and sentiments, but who have had a sound independent working-class education — in other words, who have been trained in Socialist economic and historical theory. (2)

Even as late as 1937 *Education for Emancipation* maintained that 'the struggle between the new system and the old is in a sense an educational struggle, now that the economic system is ripe for change. It is a struggle of ideas for the possession of the minds of the People.' (3)

When the leaders of the NCLC talked about Marxism, they were far from implying that the scope of the education provided was limited to Marxist knowledge at the beginning of the century. Rather Marxism implied a way of looking at phenomena. The Marxist view of social change was born simultaneously and obviously associated with the Darwinian view of natural evolution. The very fact that Dennis Hird was a leading exponent of the theory of organic evolution and that the books of the Darwinians were treasured possessions of the pioneers of the Labour College Movement shows how closely the two theories of evolution were not only linked but mutually supported each other in what was seen as a battle for the human mind against the old conceptions of man and society. Dennis Hird himself did not know a great deal about Marxism. Among those who did were Craik, Noah Ablett and George Sims, to mention three of the students at the time of the Ruskin strike. It was Marx's economic theories including the materialist conception of history as well as Dietzgen's *Positive Outcome of Philosophy* and a number of Kautsky's books including *The Class Struggle* and *Ethics and History* which formed some of the basic tools which enabled the Labour College Movement to attack orthodox views of history, economics and philosophy and to show how forms of society had changed and that the then existing social system could also be changed.

Why "Independent Working Class Education"

The NCLC did not advertise itself as a Marxist educational organisation nor even as a Socialist educational organisation. It advertised itself as providing independent working-class education. The label was not at once Socialist in conception and was therefore calculated to give the new movement an opportunity

2. *op.cit.,* p.3.
3. *op.cit.,* p.3.

of gaining support from trade unions and other working-class organisations who would have been disinclined to give support if the words Marxism and Socialism had been used, for, unlike the German Social Democratic Party, which made no bones about its attachment to classical socialist theory, the British Labour Party was inclined to scoff at theory even though during the first decades of this century it had a substantial Marxist character through the influence, for example, of the Social Democratic Federation and certain sections of the ILP. Here, as in many other respects, the British Labour Movement seemed self-contradictory. The ILP carried on its work on the basis that, as Marx taught, socialism evolved out of capitalism, yet it talked of capitalism being destroyed and of socialism as a rival system. The small revolutionary parties often repudiated Marx in practice by preaching revolution where the essential conditions, according to Marx, did not exist.

It was easy to see in the early days that the NCLC's education was based on classical socialist theories. Its main subjects were Economics, History and, on a smaller scale, the Science of Understanding. When the curriculum became very much wider that basis was not nearly so obvious, yet it was there all the time. When the NCLC started courses on Local Government and National Government, these naturally did not talk about Marx but they were courses intended to equip the worker to achieve local government and national government power. In the same way, when subjects like Trade Union Branch Administration and Public Speaking were taught, these were also regarded as educational weapons in the class struggle. It is quite true that the class struggle was very rarely referred to in such terms in any of the courses. There was a solid reason for this just as there was a solid reason for talking about independent working-class education and not socialist education. The reason was that just as the Tory Party claimed to be the guardian of the interests of all sections of the population when in fact it was fundamentally a class-party largely financed by the well-to-do and the wealthy, the Labour Party also claimed, and had to claim if it were to get the maximum support amongst a poorly politically-educated electorate, that it was not a class party but one that set out to look after the interests of the population as a whole, including the millionaire! The Labour Party made that claim particularly at election times, although it was largely financed by the trade unions which mainly represented manual workers.

Political and Industrial Power

The NCLC's educational work was planned as a working-class educational effort to win political and industrial power, recognising that this could not be won without new ideas and new social conceptions. As the early issues of *Plebs* claimed: 'The class that fights against the workers thinks against them.' When the Labour Government came to power after the Second World War, Woodburn realised at once how important it was to give members of the Labour Movement the education which would help them to use the power that Labour now had to bring about important changes in the social system's treatment of its working population. He played a large part in shaping the NCLC's new curriculum with that end in view. The class struggle now required a great deal of informed practical activity, which had not been possible in the early days of the Labour College Movement, when it had been its job simply to break the intellectual bonds which tied nearly all wage workers to capitalist conceptions.

Speaking on this subject at a final meeting of the NCLC staff at Tillicoultry on the day before the NCLC's work was to be taken over by the TUC, Graham Horsman referred to the

> new turn in the subject matter of trade union education initiated by Mr. Millar in 1948, when ex-Provost Heathwood and the late Doctor McLaine and he had together planned a postal course on Industrial Management for Trade Unionists. At this time this was quite a revolutionary departure in trade union education. In introducing it, Mr. Millar showed sensitivity to the new needs of the Labour Movement at a time when the Attlee Labour Government was trying to grapple with the problem of raising productivity in order to provide the people with a bigger economic cake to share. The TUC had convened a special conference to consider how the Trade Union Movement could best help the Labour Government in this major task, and the joint efforts of himself, Mr. Heathwood and Dr. McLaine, under Mr. Millar's leadership had made it possible to have the first lessons available by the time the conference opened.
>
> This was not an isolated effort but the first step in a new policy which resulted during the subsequent years

in the NCLC's taking the lead in providing essential education for trade unionists — postal courses, classes and schools on such subjects as costing, time and motion study, work study, arithmetic and statistics and maths. . . .

Horsman went on to say that the NCLC's example was followed by others providing some trade union education, for example Ruskin College and the Extra-mural departments of some of the universities. Much of trade union education reflected Mr. Millar's 'personality, his preferences and even his prejudices.'

The policy symbolised by the Management Courses was only one example of this. The great scope allowed to Postal Courses was another, but perhaps most characteristic was the very important place always accorded by Mr. Millar in the NCLC's attitude to education about the Movement in foreign countries and to close contacts with the trade union educational movements of other countries. The marked internationalism of Mr. Millar's personal outlook had greatly coloured the work of the NCLC. The Summer Schools held on the Continent every year for something like a quarter of a century were both a symptom and a symbol of this outlook. (5)

New Subjects

The additions to the subjects taught were clearly reflected in the new postal courses introduced, which in turn reflected themselves in the class, branch lecture and day school work. Here are a few of these new subjects:

Britain's Tasks Today
Labour's Achievements and Future Policy
National Insurance
Shop Stewards' Functions
Trade Unionism and Industrial Management
Parliamentary Candidates' Course

The urgent need for such new subjects and the desire to cater for the interests of active trade unionists, as well as to offer subjects which would attract sufficient students to satisfy the unions that they were getting value for their educational payments, resulted in some neglect of the NCLC's fundamental subjects. In what may be called the Nazi period the NCLC had introduced a new postal course of the Science of Understanding. That course

5. Speech given on 30. Aug. 1964. *(ibid.)*

depended greatly on the illustrations to explain the subject to the students. It had been written by a refugee German socialist and in a few years some of the illustrations became decidely out of date and the course had to be suspended for revision. Unfortunately Conze, the author, was no longer available. C. L. Gibbons undertook to revise the course but the second reader never completed his revision work because of his share in producing the new courses on practical subjects which were required.

The constant pressure to provide the practical courses for the unions and the fact that the NCLC's editorial staff was limited had another unfortunate result. The NCLC was never able to provide a postal course on the Materialist Conception of History, although pamphlets and books on the subject were sold. Unfortunately, too, the lessons on the Materialist Conception of History written by Craik, were not found until after the postal courses had been transferred to the TUC. Had more ample funds been available to the Postal Courses Department it would not have been without these two courses during the latter period of its existence. The surprising thing was that the limited staff were able, with the help of many voluntary contributors, to arrange for the provision of as many courses as they did.

CHAPTER XI

POSTAL COURSES DEPARTMENT: A SINGULAR ACHIEVEMENT.

The reasons for using postal courses as a means of supplementing the traditional programme of evening classes, branch lectures and day schools are evident. The NCLC could not provide classes all over the country on the various subjects with which it dealt. There was neither sufficient money available to pay for organising tutors nor a sufficient number of voluntary tutors to cover adequately even the industrial regions. Thanks to the Postal Course Department the educational service was made available to isolated workers and extended as far as the Shetlands and later to Commonwealth countries. It was also realised that postal courses might help in preparing voluntary tutors and in broadening the range of topics they might teach. Then there was the large proportion of workers interested in Labour College education who also had numerous responsibilities in the Labour Movement. It was quite common for a local trade union official to be simultaneously an honorary officer in a constituency Labour Party, a member or official of a co-operative society and a member or official of a trades council. Such a man could not regularly earmark even one evening a week to attend a class. The high incidence of shift work did not help.

Permanent Sources of Reference

Another advantage of the postal course is that it furnishes students with information in an accessible form. Once a course was completed, the lesson notes and model answers, as well as the student's own notes, served as a permanent source of reference. Postal courses also obliged the student to express his ideas in writing and thereby to clarify his thoughts. The great majority of students attending NCLC classes, day schools and branch lectures did not take systematic notes; many, indeed, did not know how to do so, and, instead, concentrated on listening. No test was applied as a rule to discover how much of a lecture a student had understood or remembered, apart from the question-and-answer period at the end of each lecture.

Postal courses provided a reliable means of certification. The students were prepared to work hard in order to obtain a tangible award. There is considerable evidence that many students framed their certificates and hung them in the home or in their trade union office. Some trade union officials exhibited their certificates, not so much out of pride as in the hope of stimulating their visitors to become students themselves. When visiting his branches one new General Secretary, George Lowthian, for a time made a point of displaying at the branches he visited the twelve or more certificates he had himself been awarded.

A Wide Choice of Subjects

As time passed it became clear, too, that whereas it was not practicable in any one session, even in a large local college, to offer trade-unionists a choice of subjects from a broad curriculum the Postal Courses Department could build up a range of syllabuses to meet almost every individual educational need. But it must be recorded that a member of the National Union of Funeral Workers applied — unsuccessfully — for a course on embalming!

As new demands emerged, so new courses could be designed

215

to meet them whereas, initially, a modest list of only three subjects had been offered — Economics, Social History and English language. The provision of courses on English grammar was vital; few of the NCLC's voluntary tutors were competent to teach English grammar; working men would not attend classes on English grammar run by Local Education Authorities where the students were almost exclusively young people just over school-leaving age. Working men also tended to believe that teachers of the Local Education Authorities' evening classes were not seriously interested in helping people like them to improve their capacity for self-expression about subjects which were of primary importance to the working class. The barrier for such men was well nigh insuperable.

Christine Millar, who not only wrote uncommonly well but had had experience of school teaching and of teaching English to young 'veterans' of the First World War, designed three English courses. Their success was made manifest immediately in high enrolments and a large number of certificate awards. Raymond Postgate invited Christine to write a series of twelve articles on the teaching of English for *Lansbury's Labour Weekly*. The readers of these articles included delegates preparing speeches, a great number of the NCLC's voluntary tutors and other Labour activists. This really was workers' education. The academically trained should remember that it was not after all intelligence but above all instruction that working people lacked, particularly in those days of limited education. Articles such as Christine's fed an urgent desire to know how and how not to use English among poorly-educated people of ability and energy, who had an important contribution to make to society and who wished to be able to say, in acceptable language, what they felt so deeply.

During the first three years of the Postal Courses Department, there was a rising demand for postal courses. There is no question but that they filled an immense gap. Later the General Strike brought a fall in members occasioned partly by the temporary cancellation of postal courses for the AEU's large membership. Then between 1929 and 1931 came another dramatic increase, mainly caused by the affiliation of the NUR in 1930. NUR students were for a time enrolling at the average rate of 35 per day. Additional examiners and an additional clerk had to be appointed. But later the economic slump forced many unions to suspend or reduce their payments for their education schemes; the number of postal students declined by almost 2,000

Christine Millar, founder of the N.C.L.C. Postal Courses Department

Thereafter, between 1933 and 1939 increases from year to year brought the total to 12,300 for one year.

An enquiry by Christine Millar had shown in 1932 that of the total of 7,413 students, 7,225 belonged to affiliated unions, whereas only 188 students from non-affiliated unions were paying their own fees. The NCLC policy of seeking union affiliation was thus known to be highly effective. During the second world war the number of enrolments necessarily dropped, but immediately the war ended there was a surge of enthusiasm which, within four years, took the grand annual total of postal students up to over 21,000. An increase in the number of union schemes accounted for only half of the upsurge. Members of long affiliated unions enrolled in greater numbers. The ten year period 1949 to 1959 saw no change, but it would appear that the Labour Party's failure to win the General Election in 1959 had a salutary effect, for again enrolments began to rise. One feature of the post-war period was a growing overseas demand for courses, thanks to a campaign to interest colonial trade unions in providing NCLC postal courses for their members.

Students who took postal courses represented a broad cross-section of the Labour Movement. They covered an age range from fifteen to sixty and included, among other workers, shop assistants, bricklayers, clerks, engineers and miners. In any one year some very small unions were occasionally represented by a solitary student — the NCLC's smallest union was the London Jewelcase Makers which had only about 40 members. Other unions had more than two thousand students — the AEU had over four thousand. The main consumers were the NUR, NUDAW, NUM, C, & AW (now APEX) and the AEU. Women were always greatly under-represented partly because most unions had few or no women members. Christine Millar drafted a leaflet for circulation in unions with a high total of women members. She illustrated the leaflet herself with three drawings with the three captions 'Yesterday, in the East, women couldn't show their faces. Yesterday, in the West, women couldn't show their legs. Today women can show that they have faces, legs and BRAINS'.

Student Quality

As the years passed, the quality of the students improved. Christine Millar commented as early as 1935:

In bygone years a small section of the students were

217

semi-literate; today the semi-literates are under a score; at the other extreme are exceedingly able executive members of trade unions having up to a quarter of a million members. (1)

Christine always eschewed the pursuit of numerical growth for its own sake. In her eyes expansion was justified only if quality could be maintained or enhanced. In her regular column in *Plebs* on postal courses she stressed from time to time that the students were on the whole of high calibre. For example:

I have already referred, in these columns, this year, to the Department's card index, recording what present and recent students are doing in the Movement. Today the index contains approximately 2,000 cards. Postal students in the trade union section include approximately 300 secretaries — *i.e.* secretaries of Branches, District Committees, Joint Committees, and Federations — and a further 800 cards bear the names of Branch Chairmen, Treasurers, Minute Secretaries, Shop Stewards, Delegates, Executives and other committee members, etc. Labour Party office-bearers and other Labour Party workers are also classified under their offices and under Ward, Borough and Divisional Labour Parties and Federations. The Labour Party section of the index contains approximately 400 cards. In the section dealing with 100 co-operative office-bearers and other co-operative workers, students are classified under their committees — Management, Education, General, etc. and under Political Councils, Men's Guilds, Comrades' Circles, etc. The postal students on Trades and Labour Councils who have advised us of their offices number over 200. (2)

A minority of students were erratic in their despatch of answer

1. Christine Millar, 'Workers Education by Post' in *Plebs*, 1936, p.46.
2. *ibid.*, 1938, p.20. In 1938 the card index of postal students revealed the following categories of active workers in the Labour cause:
   70 regular contributors to the Trade Union Labour and Co-operative Press
   100 Co-operative Office bearers
   130 Municipal Candidates and Councillors
   200 Trades and Labour Council officials
   400 Labour party office-bearers
   1000 Trade Union branch officers.
   (ECM, 1938).

papers. But the great majority worked purposefully despite such handicaps as family opposition, industrial accidents, lack of study facilities at home and lack of a public library in the neighbourhood. Nervousness about expressing themselves on paper also led many students to put off answering papers. In 1929 one student wrote to the postal courses department:

> At long last I have completed my course. I have taken more than the three weeks for each lesson because I am a widower with five school children. I have to help the eldest with housekeeping when I get home at night and when that is done and home lessons are done and school lunches are made up for the next day and I have read the paper it is time for bed. I have only time at week-ends for studying, but I want you to enrol me now for the Advanced Course. (3)

New courses were usually introduced as soon as evidence of a need had been discerned. Thus, a course on Safety and Health at Work was introduced at a time when figures were published showing a rise in industrial accidents. The first course on Arithmetic and Statistics was the result of the representations of a former NCLC organiser, Sam Pollock, who was employed to go round coal pits, railway workshops and other workshops to enrol students, after making a short speech. He found that many shop stewards asked for a course on arithmetic because they were handicapped by a weakness in that subject.

Arthur Woodburn suggested several courses which would prove of practical importance to the Labour Movement. Old courses were regularly reviewed, sometimes to be modified but

3. Quoted in *Plebs*, 1936, p.67. Another student apologised for not keeping up to scratch:

I have now time to write telling you why I haven't sent in any more Exam. papers, since the first lesson. Well when I first applied for your free course I had quite a lot of comrades here to help me with the hard work but as time went on they began to get "fed up" and dropped by the wayside, as some dropped out others found the work more tedious or hard or I was only left with one faithful comrade, or also the work of ten had fallen on two. Just prior to these comrades falling away or just as I started your course I was asked to take on work for the YCL including League training, this I did and soon I found that I had bitten off more than I could chew, now you will understand that I had not time for everything and I decided to do the necessitious work first. Then through wet feet and being underfed I recently contracted a severe attack of "Flue" and was just getting better when I received the First lesson of your new course.

(S. J. Bullen to J. P. M. Millar, 11. Nov. 1926, NCLC MSS.)

occasionally to be dropped, In 1936 there were sixteen subjects in the prospectus:

Chairmanship
Economics
Economics—Orthodox and Marxian
Economic Geography and Imperial Power
English—Elementary (Grammar)
English—Intermediate (Composition and
           article-writing)
Esperanto (Elementary)
Esperanto (Advanced)
Finance
History of the British Working Class
Industrial History of Modern Europe
Local Government
Public Speaking
Scientific Way of Thinking
Social History
Socialism

The Character of the Courses

At first, courses normally consisted of twelve lessons. They were all written in as simple a style as possible, free from all but indispensable technical terms. Christine Millar set great store by *plain* English:

> The simplicity of the style in which NCLC text books are written has set a good example to working-class educationists, but the polysyllabic style of many conservative socialists is evidence of their respect for erudition for its own sake. (4)

Relevance was also essential. In the English courses, for instance, the illustrations were drawn from daily life. Often they were deliberately related to social questions which encouraged students to go on to the social science courses.

In the preparation of postal courses each lesson was made self-sufficient, *i.e.*, independent of reading-matter other than the material in that lesson and any preceding lessons. Students with previous experience of the teaching methods of other bodies sometimes wrote that to obtain the recommended books was far from easy. The Postal Courses Department occasionally received letters from trade-unionists complaining that their wives objected to their spending money on books. By making each course

4. *Plebs*, 1936, p.149.

completely self-sufficient the NCLC deprived students of the excuse that essential supplementary material was not procurable. However, supplementary reading lists were often included for the benefit of those students who did have access to books and the necessary free time to consult them. It was also found expedient not to ask for essays. The very word 'essay' intimidated many students, making them feel that they were being constrained to undertake a mammoth task far beyond their capacities. Posing short, unambiguous questions for the student to answer seemed to be the best way of eliciting a prompt response and ensuring that the student had grasped the content of a lesson.

Sustaining the Student's Interest

Like some commercial correspondence schools the Central Labour College had sent the student, at the onset of a course, merely a complete list of reading and written assignments. The method adopted by Christine Millar was to despatch no more than two lessons on enrolment to students resident in the U.K. and three to overseas students. Thus, when the student had completed and despatched the work set in the first lesson he had at hand the second lesson to study and work on. When a student received back from his examiner the corrected first set of answers, the third lesson was attached, so that the student had always one lesson in hand. This system also helped to sustain the student's interest by giving him something to anticipate. At the end of the course the NCLC issued a certificate indicating whether the performance had been fair, good, very good or excellent. Students whose work had not reached a satisfactory level were not awarded a certificate. If they pressed for one, they were invited to repeat the course.

Preparing Courses

When a demand for a new course had been discerned, the search would begin for a suitable author. The ideal author of postal courses was one who knew his subject well and could explain it in simple language, preferably making his points by means of a series of short sentences rather than long paragraphs. Once a draft had been submitted — sometimes the work of several authors — Christine Millar and, later, a second reader, selected from a panel, would comb through it, simplifying difficult sections, shortening sentences that were too long, removing inessential matter, replacing abstruse words by easier ones and making other improvements. The amended draft would then be read by the original author and at least by one other reader who had expert knowledge of the subject. The course was then re-edited and tried out on a small batch of students. The examiner, often the original author, was asked to look out for students' difficulties and misunderstandings which re-drafting could avoid. Then it was a question of periodic revising to keep the courses up to date.

Long before other voluntary organisations were doing so, the NCLC was keeping meticulous student's records. In general, its recording techniques were highly sophisticated. One reason for its efficiency was that it had to produce complicated quarterly statistics for the executive committee, largely consisting of representatives of affiliated unions, showing the number of students from each union taking each subject. Moreover, similar annual detailed statistics were submitted to the NCLC annual conference and to each of its constituent bodies.

The Reminder System

Great importance was attached to reminding students when they were in arrears with their work. Many students obviously needed constant encouragement and prodding if they were to complete a course, and the NCLC set great store by achieving a high rate of completions. The Department's reminders were graded: mild and encouraging, then more vigorous. The final reminder was most effective. It was a slip of yellow paper measuring 6″ × 3″ and bearing in large red letters **P L E A S E.** One student, harried by several calls to duty replied:

> I am sorry to have caused you so much trouble but now I hope to make amends.
> Trouble came my way but unlike the pioneers to whom you referred in your reminder, I allowed my enthusiasm to die down. I am keeping your letter as a medicine.
> Yours fraternally,
> H. SCORER   (5)

Many students persevered against many odds. One earnest postal student wrote to say that his wife had died leaving him with six children to look after, and that he could rarely start upon his exercises much before midnight.

Reminders took the form often of humorous notes, not of formal strictures, and were often illustrated by funny drawings

5. H. Scorer to J. P. M. Millar, 5. Nov. 1926 (NCLC MSS.).

in the style of the cartoons in the popular press. Long before he
became a Minister of the Crown and Chairman of the National
Coal Board, Lord Robens was a NUDAW postal course student.
Returning on one occasion from speaking to the STUC he
encountered Arthur Woodburn in the House of Commons and
told him he had met Jim and Christine Millar at the Congress.
'Had it not been for the reminders, especially the humorous
ones, I got from Christine Millar,' he observed, "I'm sure I
would never have finished my courses.' In being so punctilious
about sending reminders the NCLC was unusual, for it was
notorious that the profits of some commercial correspondence
schools were largely made out of the large proportion of
students who dropped out.

New Methods of Publicity

In order to enrol the maximum number of students Christine
Millar had constantly to devise new methods of publicity.
'Before the Postal Department can teach the members of the
affiliated trade union, it must first entice them with attractive
reasons for studying.' One method was to issue groups of
duplicated quarto sheets stapled together to make a brochure.
Each brochure presented a selection of students' opinions about
the postal courses they had taken. The brochure for each
affiliated union contained the appreciative comments of that
union's students. Many a postal student acknowledged that it
was because of the usefulness of the postal courses which he had
studied that he had qualified to take office in his union branch or
district, or to write for his union journal. These brochures were
sent out to each union's officials, executive members and branch
secretaries to encourage them to enrol students. In later years
the Postal Courses Department sent out to over 30,000 former
students, three times a year, cartoon-illustrated coloured circulars drawn up and often illustrated by Christine Millar. These
encouraged further enrolments, listed the increased number of
courses available and gave details of the latest new course.

The NCLC's opponents often tried to belittle the value of
postal tuition by suggesting that few of the students finished
their courses. In reality as high a percentage as 62% of NCLC

223

postal students completed their courses (6), despite the fact that very few of them were in search of better jobs. Courses on subjects of immediate practical benefit had a higher percentage of "completions." When a student ended his course, it meant that he had completed every single lesson, whereas students attending evening classes sometimes missed many meetings.

On a number of occasions NCLC organisers asked for the names and addresses of enrolled postal students so that they could be encouraged to attend locally based classes. The Central Office soon declined to provide addresses, however, explaining that the students would then have an excuse for dropping their courses — a student now and then offered the excuse that he could not complete a course because he was already attending an NCLC class or was about to attend one. The organisers did receive details, however, of the students who had performed particularly well on Postal Courses. This information was given in order that the organisers might approach these successful students to see whether there was any prospect of their becoming tutors.

International Interest

The NCLC Postal Course service attracted some international interest. During the early years the Norwegian Workers' Educational Movement sent a staff member to spend a week studying the methods of the Postal Courses Department and thereafter there was a close relationship. From Australia came a request from the Labour College* at Melbourne for permission to use NCLC courses and adopt its methods *in toto*. Brookwood Labour College in the USA also studied the NCLC's methods and courses and paid a tribute to them when it started its own department. Such distinguished experts on correspondence education as Miss Renée Erdos visited Tillicoultry to study

6. Although its rate of completions was high compared with that of other organisations the NCLC was not keen to publicise its figures.
cf. 'I am very chary about giving the percentage of students who complete correspondence course for various reasons which I need not go into here. Taken over a period of five years the percentage is 49.6%. You will appreciate that this percentage in the hands of people who have little knowledge of educational work can be misued . . . I would not wish the figures to be used in any context which might be misinterpreted and if you use the figure it is on the understanding that we don't object to the context in which it is used.' (Millar to B. Macleech, 17. Nov. 1951, NCLC MSS.). The proportion of completed courses greatly increased subsequently.

* The Victorian Labour College.

NCLC techniques. Christine Millar herself felt that her efforts had been vindicated when, in 1962, she was invited to address the conference of the International Federation of Workers Educational Associations on Education by Post.

Within recent years postal courses have come to be regarded with more respect in British academic circles. Throughout most of the earlier period under review, however, they were viewed in Britain with suspicion, bordering on contempt in some circles. The value of postal courses was sometimes called in question by the NCLC's own supporters, usually by those who had not themselves taken postal courses. For example, the following statement appeared in an article in *Plebs* in 1951

> The correspondence course is certainly of great value for 'pioneering work,' when potential students are anxious for assistance, but tutors are not available where they live. This probably accounts for the limited development by the NCLC of this method; It is now being used by the British TUC for trade unionists in the colonies. As a normal method of education, however, I believe the postal course, unless associated with class discussion or personal work with an experienced tutor, has serious limitations. One of its weaknesses is the difficulty in maintaining the continued interest of students who have once started a correspondence course, and the high proportion of starters who usually fail to complete it. (7)

Millar commented:

> Mr. Turner, no doubt is one who has little or no experience of postal courses (and certainly he has none as the NCLC does it) does not do justice to that work. The postal course requires much more work from the student than the average class does.
>
> Mr. Turner falls into the common error that a Trade Unionist who attends a class gets a better grasp of the subject than a Trade Unionist who takes a postal course. We would suggest that often the contrary is the case. (8)

What those who decried postal courses in order to laud class work often overlooked was one factor of considerable importance. When a student attended a class whether at a university, an evening class or at school, it was a matter of chance whether he was taught by an excellent, a fair or a bad teacher. For postal

7. H. A. Turner, 'The NCLC, the WEA and the Unions' in *Plebs*, 1951, p.273.
8. *ibid.*, p.274.

225

courses, however, the NCLC could always find really competent authors, editorial readers, and examiners. As a result, even the first draft of a postal course lesson was of considerably higher standard than that of the average class lesson.

A great deal depended on the quality of the examiners. Here again the NCLC had to depend on the examiner's interest in NCLC work. The NCLC's fees for examining and correcting students' answers were nominal — never exceeding 1/- and as low as 6d. In order to help the examiners the NCLC, after the early days, attached model answers to each lesson sent out for correction. This enabled the examiners to concentrate their attention on the individual student's special difficulties.

A factor of great importance in retaining a student was to return his corrected work promptly; even if he had been weeks behind in submitting written work, he was no less anxious than the punctual student to have his corrected lessons back quickly. (One new elementary English student, who had been very slow in sending in his first answer-paper, apologised by saying, 'I'm sure I must be one of your most laxative students.') The NCLC therefore asked its examiners to return corrected answers to the students within three days of receipt.

Check on Examiners

To ensure that an examiner was dealing effectively with his students' answer-papers and was not, as month followed month of correcting answers to the same questions, losing his enthusiasm for making encouraging comments or giving helpful advice, the Supervisor regularly recalled from students their examined and corrected papers. Every examiner was told on appointment that papers examined by him would, from time to time, be recalled to the Postal Courses Department. Very occasionally, one examiner or another would be asked if he were growing weary of examining and correcting, since it was recognised that examining answers to the same questions time and time again, could become monotonous. It was very rarely that an examiner gave up of his own accord, and only once or twice in over forty years did the supervisor deem it advisable to appoint another examiner in place of one who confessed that his spirits dropped to zero when he saw the postman arriving with yet another collection of students' answer-papers. According to letters which the supervisor received occasionally from students who had taken commercial college postal courses the NCLC examiners returned the students' marked papers more promptly than the commercial institutions returned theirs.

As for the examiners themselves, it was essential that they be committed to the NCLC's educational goals. Courses dealing with legal matters were usually examined by lawyers or tutors specially interested in Labour law questions. Courses on subjects associated with industry such as Work Study or Industrial Management were examined by industrial consultants interested in the Labour Movement, or professional lecturers on those subjects who admired the aims and achievements of the Postal Courses Department and allowed themselves to be enlisted as examiners.

Finding specialists to draft new courses and finding others who could help to keep the courses up-to-date was an unending task. Much of the work of keeping courses up-to-date was done in the Postal Courses Department. In 1946 a young socialist Oxford graduate, Graham Horsman, was appointed as an editorial assistant in the Department. He had been one of the youngest Labour councillors in England. While his university training enabled him to be of service he knew little about the subjects taught by the NCLC, but quickly began to handle them with skill, and greatly lightened the burden of the Supervisor. As the Postal Courses Department grew in size a second editorial assistant — a Polish refugee graduate — was appointed. He was succeeded by David Pringle, an Edinburgh University graduate.

The unique achievement of the Postal Courses Department has not in this country received the acclaim which it deserves, mainly because it operated during the period before correspondence courses became academically respectable in Britain. Throughout four decades tens of thousands of working men and a few women, some already trade union and Labour Officials, were enabled to broaden their knowledge and improve their skills thanks to taking NCLC postal courses.

N.C.L.C.

the Trade Union and Labour Movement's Educational Organisation

supported by the British T.U.C., the Scottish T.U.C., the Co-operative Union, the C.W.S. Ltd., and the Scottish C.W.S. Ltd. The N.C.L.C. conducts the majority of Trade Union education schemes, and schemes for Co-operative Societies, Trade Councils, Labour Parties and other working-class organisations.

This is to Certify that

having taken the N.C.L.C's postal courses on

under the education scheme of the

is now awarded the   Group Certificate.

Christine Lillar
Supervisor, Postal Courses Department

J. P. M. Millar
General Secretary, N.C.L.C.

DATE:
C.D.M.   CERTIFICATE No.

CHAPTER XII

PUBLICITY AND PUBLICATIONS METHODS

The NCLC was forever striving to provide an efficient service for what was in general a resistant clientele. If students were to be numbered not by the hundred but by the thousand, intensive and skilful publicity methods were required. It was vital not merely to draw attention to the learning resources which were available but to persuade workers that they would be interesting and beneficial to them for, if workers saw the need to send their children to school, they were not moved on the whole to educate themselves. Study would entail considerable effort and to many the education offered by adult education organisations seemed unrelated to the practical aims of trade unions and allied bodies. In order to attract attention the NCLC relied mainly upon four methods of outreach; securing a wide circulation for *Plebs;* designing eye-catching pamphlets and posters; circulating regularly thousands of union branches and other Labour bodies as well as tens of thousands of shop stewards and former students; providing a large-scale branch lecture service, advertising and latterly exhibiting a coloured motion picture. For some years it also made use of a mobile exhibition.

Plebs and Plebs Pamphlets

At first, *Plebs* was the main publicity weapon of the Labour College Movement. *Plebs* set out, in season and out of season, to state the case for independent working-class education, backed up by pamphlets on the same subject, to win support for the NCLC throughout the Labour Movement, to help build up an efficient organisation, to create a market for *Plebs* and other publications, to provide material for both lecturers and students, and to encourage the reading of books and pamphlets on economic and social questions. Its technique was to combine lively articles with news items, both liberally illustrated by cartoons. In a letter published in *Plebs* in 1925 the late Jimmie Maxton, MP, wrote:

> The *Plebs* is practically the only journal that approaches working class problems with the students in mind and without sectarian interest. I could wish that every I.L.P. student of economics and sociology was a regular

reader. It can be read with interest by any member of the working class movement. (1)

Cartoons

Horrabin's cartoons were a uniquely telling way of expressing ideas with point and humour. His genius inspired the NCLC to make a feature of cartoons in all its advertisements, leaflets and pamphlets. Harold Batho, brother of Winifred Horrabin, together with Charles Marchington, Stuart Boyle and 'Barlow', three NCLC students, were among those who also regularly supplied cartoons. Amateur cartoonists submitted drawings, some of which were extraordinarily good. Readers with no sense of design sometimes sent Horrabin ideas which he was able to use. The best known of Horrabin's cartoons was widely reproduced outside Britain (see facing page.); it summed up Labour's view of the policy of the detested National government headed by Ramsay Macdonald.

The success of the NCLC's publicity was partly due to its realisation that most working men regarded education as a dreary process. That's why much use was made of bright colours both in papers and ink for leaflets, circulars and covers. Horrabin and Millar always tried to introduce some humour into their writings. On one occasion Horrabin prepared for *Plebs*, some potted biographies of well-known NCLC personalities. Of Redfern (organiser of Division 12), a very earnest man, plagued with ill-health, he wrote: 'E. Redfern, most serious man in Movement. When he laughs, it's put down in the Minutes.'

Slogans and Posters

Slogans were used to jolly along postal course students and to extract written work from the dilatory. One slogan intended to attract new students ran: 'Your union card is a season ticket for free educational facilities worth many guineas.' A publicity scheme devised by Christine Millar involved producing a series of posters showing different types of workers actively engaged on their jobs. The caption in each case read: 'In their spare time they take NCLC postal courses.' To obtain good photographs of all types of worker whose unions had NCLC schemes the files of the press photographic agencies had to be searched. In the poster illustrating transport workers there was a photograph of a handsome bus driver sitting in the cab of his bus. Only after the

1. *Plebs*, 1929, p.36.

229

IS HE GOING TO PUT THEM ON?

poster had been widely circulated did it come to the ears of the Millars that the photogenic driver was a well-known communist who was very unpopular among the T & GW union's senior officials and equally unpopular at Transport House. When posters were exhibited at TUC and other union conferences, it was noticeable that many delegates were anxious to see whether their particular trade was represented among the photographs. One TUC delegate who sought out Millar to complain that there was no photograph of his craft at work was taken aback on being told that his union had no NCLC educational scheme.

The Branch Lecture Service

Realising that the majority of affiliated union members were never likely to attend classes or to enrol for postal courses, unless directly enjoined to do so, the NCLC made use of an extensive branch lecture service. It sent speakers to union branches and to Labour Party and Co-operative organisations all over Britain and Northern Ireland. The speakers lectured on the NCLC's work and on current political and industrial issues so as to pass on information and interest their listeners in attending or organising classes or enrolling for postal courses. When any new legislation affecting workers was passed, speakers were sent out to explain its effects. During strikes or periods of mass unemployment speakers were in great demand. Such branch lectures helped to spread information and enliven trade union branch meetings.

Union Journals and Advertising

The NCLC arranged to obtain from the unions copies of their journals so that it could monitor the amount of space given to publicity about the educational scheme or to the short educational articles or advertisements circulated by the NCLC. Illustrated advertisements with amusing drawings were latterly regularly sent out to the editors accompanied by free stereos. These were designed to catch the attention of readers and to encourage members to enrol for postal courses and attend classes. Many unions made use of them, whereas others seemed to have no idea of the importance of constant publicity if they wanted to obtain the best results from their education schemes. Sometimes a union official who supported the WEA's point of view would give scant space to the NCLC's activities in his union's journal.

Circularisation and Card Indexes

Aware that the vast majority of trade unionists did not read their union journals, the NCLC occasionally took space for its illustrated advertisements in *The Daily Herald, Reynolds News* and in the socialist weeklies. Three times a year it sent to the head office of unions with NCLC educational schemes supplies of printed letters drawing attention to the free educational facilities and particularly to any new courses. These printed letters incorporated an enrolment form and a humorous illustration intended to catch the eye. Unions were expected to distribute these circulars to their full-time officials and to all branch secretaries. The printed letters were meant to be read at local branch meetings. Three times a year NCLC organisers circulated details of local educational facilities to nationally affiliated union branches and to the local affiliated branches of other unions and associated bodies as well as to as many as possible of the non-affiliated local organisations. These local circulars, which were often illustrated, listed the classes which were opening and the day schools and conferences which were soon due to be held. The organisers in later years were required to keep card indexes of their past students and to send them a printed circular giving details of the classes arranged for each of the two winter sessions. Circulars were also sent from time to time giving former students particulars of the day schools in their areas.

Not all the branch secretaries who received circulars took the trouble to read them to their branches or even to summarise their contents. Some ten years after the Electrical Trades Union had affiliated to the NCLC, a branch chairman buttonholed Millar after he had given a talk at a summer school. 'I'm glad,' he said, 'the NCLC has wakened up.' 'What do you mean?' Millar asked. 'You're at last, through the head office of our union, sending out circulars describing the free educational facilities.' 'How do you know?' asked Millar. 'Because recently I have been elected branch chairman and have been going over the correspondence with the secretary before the meetings.' 'Well,' said Millar, 'you can take it that your branch secretary has been receiving circulars ever since the union affiliated ten years ago but he has apparently not drawn attention to them because he was not interested in educational schemes or because he couldn't organise his business to find time to mention the new courses or to point out that an enrolment form was available.'

Social Functions

As a means of attracting new students, in addition to maintaining contact with old students and raising local funds, the NCLC encouraged its colleges to organise social functions during the winter months. For example, the district committees of the Scottish Labour College arranged annual Burns suppers which served the important purpose of publicising the NCLC's work throughout the local Labour Movement. These lively social gatherings attracted large attendances and not infrequently attracted welcome press publicity. The chief speaker at the last Burns supper arranged by the Edinburgh District was Herbert Morrison — a cockney who loved Burns.

Forty Thousand Chief Shop Stewards

Driven by its perennial need to recruit more affiliated unions and other bodies, the NCLC was constantly on the look out for novel publicity methods. Each week the *Advertisers' Weekly* was carefully scanned in search of ideas. Latterly, Christine Millar hit upon the idea of obtaining from the Post Office copies of classified telephone directories covering the whole country. These were combed through for the addresses of big companies likely to have a large number of employees. Stencils were then made, addressed to 'The chief shop steward' of what appeared to be all the main industrial firms. A post office sorter generously arranged the stencil cards according to postal areas and thus enabled the NCLC to pay postal charges at a reduced rate. For the country as a whole the number of stencils reached over 40,000. Periodically, a circular was sent out inviting the chief shop steward to inform his shop stewards of the educational facilities which were available including any new course and to advertise them on works' notice boards. A few firms which had no shop stewards wrote blistering letters to the NCLC office at Tillicoultry. A big advertising agency, whose address had slipped on to a stencil by mistake, replied that it kept special records of the kind of firms in which the NCLC was interested and that if the work of circularisation was entrusted to it — at an unspecified price — it would ensure that no circulars would be wasted on firms like itself which hoped never to have to put up with a shop steward.

Postal Courses — Student's Role

Publicity directed at former students played a key part in

Herbert Morrison at Edinburgh Burns Supper

getting them to enrol for new courses and persuading fellow workers to enrol. Besides keeping a course record card for each enrolled student, the postal courses department kept a master card for every student, which, among other items, recorded the name of his union and a list of all the postal courses he had taken together with his results. These cards were used to circularise details of new courses as well as a list of old courses so that the recipient might not only enrol for a new course himself but encourage his friends to enrol for one of the old ones. Several times a year tens of thousands of circulars were sent out with the help of the master card stencils. The master cards also came to be used to record the jobs being performed by students in the Labour Movement. This enabled the NCLC to provide fairly accurate statistics of the remarkable number of postal students holding official positions.

Another major means of publicity was to arrange NCLC book displays and to circulate leaflets at trades councils and at Labour Party and other conferences throughout the country. From time to time the NCLC central office sent out news to the press and to the press agencies. As a means of inducing them to court publicity, divisional organisers were required to keep a press cuttings book containing cuttings referring to NCLC work in their areas.

Filmstrip Lectures

Film strip projectors, issued to each division and to some of the colleges, were also used as a means of publicity. Lantern and film strip lectures attracted much bigger audiences than classes. Projectors were sometimes used to assist other sections of the Labour Movement. In a small mining town in West Lothian one enterprising tutor decided to use the film strip projector to ensure a high turnout at a municipal poll. He had a film strip prepared limited to a single picture, which read 'Be sure to vote Labour tomorrow.' Armed with the projector, he shone the picture throughout the evening on any surfaces light enough to show up the image clearly — including a miners' shirt hanging on a drying line.

From 1921 the Edinburgh District of the Scottish Labour College printed a vest pocket booklet which not only gave details of all its classes, including a list of the lectures to be given to each class, but details of the college itself including a list of

233

the many affiliated organisations. It was sold to class students at 6d. a copy. Soon other colleges also printed similar booklets.

The NCLC Exhibition

In 1932 the NCLC took the important step of giving its educational work national prestige by planning an exhibition which would illustrate the origins, history and activities of the Labour College Movement. Christine Millar was mainly responsible for the planning and artistic presentation of the exhibits. So that the exhibition might be mobile, special display boards were designed which, when opened out, would hang from picture rails and when travelling would fold up and fit into specially made cases. The exhibition itself partly consisted of mounted leaflets, letters, photographs, pamphlets and extracts from biased school books. In addition, large coloured, wooden cut-outs of cartoons by Horrabin and other illustrators were made together with coloured graphs showing the progress of the NCLC in obtaining union support, postal course students and class students. Bound volumes of *Plebs* were on show as were busts of Dennis Hird and Karl Marx. The exhibition was a great success and was shown in halls in London, Edinburgh, Glasgow, Newcastle and other cities. The exhibition was also shown in one of the two halls in Transport House at a time when an international conference on workers' education was being held in the other hall. It enhanced the reputation of the NCLC and dealt a blow against those critics who cast aspersions on the NCLC's efficiency.

Lack of the Right Books

In a telling passage Baroness Stocks had drawn attention to the desperate shortage of reading matter facing working men at the beginning of the present century:

> When the Oxford Committee issued its famous report in 1908, such was the meticulous thoroughness of its author, that they added an appendix on suggested courses of study with recommendations for reading. Contemplating the list of books in the history section, one is struck by the lamentable paucity of material relating to the economic and social aspects of the subject. How did the English peasants come to be excluded from the land? What conditioned the revolutionary ferment of the Chartist Movement? How did the technical advance of the industrial revolution period

A section of the N.C.L.C. Exhibition

affect the day to day lives of the workers? There was, of course, Cunningham's great pioneer economic history there were the Webbs, there were others — but compared with the response made by generations of historians to the requirements of constitutionalists, and military technicians there was precious little. Yet these were the very kind of questions which most vitally concerned working-class students. They wanted to know something of the forces which had made them what they were. They wanted to guage the possibility of controlling and directing these forces, so that they might become what they wanted to be (2)

Before the foundation of the Central Labour College, classes in economics arranged by such bodies as the SDF sometimes took the form of reading paragraph by paragraph a chapter of say, Marx's *Capital* with the class tutor or leader trying to help the students tease out the meaning. This method incidentally enabled students to see how English could be used and to pronounce unfamiliar words. Reading Marx was a painful task for workers who had left school at the age of eight or nine or at best twelve, and who had little time to spare for prolonged study.

The Labour Movement was mainly borne along by manual workers who were seldom writers and who, even when they had the requisite skill, were so busy organising and agitating that they lacked the time to write. They therefore rarely set down their thoughts except on those occasions when journalists put together their recollections.

The Part Played by Pamphlets

Pamphlets were immensely influential in the Labour Movement and in the educational work of the Labour Colleges especially during the formative years. A pamphlet was not only easier to prepare than a book or monograph, but far cheaper to produce. This was crucial because low wages put the price of books out of the reach of workers who wanted to buy them. In 1914, for instance, railway surfacemen were paid only 15/0d. per week. Moreover, many an untutored man who would be intimidated by the sheer length of a book, would make an effort to read a pamphlet, The Socialist Labour Press kept in print year after year, a number of classical socialist pamphlets — some

2. *op.cit.,* p.46.

equal in length to a small book — such as *Wage Labour and Capital, Value, Price and Profit* and the *Communist Manifesto.* The socialist publishers, Charles Kerr and Company of Chicago, issued simple pamphlets such as *Shop Talks on Economics* by Mary Marcy. The SDF, the ILP and *The Clarion* also issued a large number of pamphlets but these were little used in the Labour College Movement's educational work, although they were read by many *Plebs* supporters. (3)

The First Plebs Books

The first three books published in connection with the Labour College Movement were W. W. Craik's *Outline of the History of the Modern British Working Class Movement,* Noah Ablett's *Easy Outline of Economics,* and Mark Starr's *A Worker Looks at History,* each being half-way between a pamphlet and a book. They were short and had paper covers in order to keep down the price. Later the Plebs League started to publish its own text books, which were fi. it sold at 2/6d. each (limp covers) and were considerably longer. The first print was usually 5,000 to 10,000. Most of the text books were repeatedly reprinted after being brought up to date and published by the NCLC in both hard board and cloth. The first was *An Outline of Psychology* written by Lyster Jameson and illustrated by Horrabin. This was the first book on the subject written by a Marxist. It was followed by *An Outline of Imperialism* by T. Ashcroft; *An Outline of Economics* by W. McLaine; *An Outline of Economic Georgaphy* by J. F. Horrabin, *An Outline of European History* by Maurice Dobb; *An Outline of Finance* by Arthur Woodburn; *An Outline of Man's History* by Patrick Gordon Walker and *An Outline History of Unemployment* by W. T. Colyer.

Great influence on Labour College students and members of the Plebs League was exercised by two works of Joseph Dietzgen, a socialist German tanner, the *Positive Outcome of Philosophy* and *Philosophical Essays.* W. W. Craik expounded Dietzgen's views under the rubric of *The Science of Understanding* and on 9 December, 1928, the Central Labour College published a leaflet to mark his centenary.

The publishing firm mainly responsible for providing books in English on classical socialist theory was Charles Kerr and Company of Chicago. Most of the classical socialist books were

3. The titles that appealed to the tutors and many of the students may be gauged from the list of books in the NCLC library in 1925. (see ECM, 1925).

written in German, although some were written in Italian and French. They included works not only by Marx and Engels but by Karl Kautsky, the German socialist scholar, August Bebel, Antonio Labriola and Paul Lafargue.

NCLC Books

Generally speaking, the NCLC's own publications took the form of books and pamphlets. Occasionally a pamphlet was published by a local Labour College. The first edition of W. W. Craik's book on the British Working Class Movement was published by the London District Council of the NUR and later reissued by the Plebs League. Like the authors of nearly all the pamphlets issued by the British Labour Movement during the early part of the present century those who wrote for the Plebs League and the NCLC Publishing Society received no royalties, with the exception of Lord Citrine, author of *The ABC of Chairmanship.* Among other NCLC publications were reprints of four classical socialist works: *The Economic Doctrines of Karl Marx* by Karl Kautsky, *Commercial Crises of the Nineteenth Century* by H. M. Hyndman, *The Life and Teaching of Karl Marx* by M. Beer and *The History of British Socialism* also by M. Beer.

Although the NCLC received little help from intellectuals with its class work it did receive a good deal of help with its publications. Marxist intellectuals had difficulty in finding publishers for books on Marxism and so were often enthusiastic supporters of the Plebs Movement. The first three books published by the Plebs League were written by an ex-railwayman and two ex-miners respectively. Then the pattern changed. Subsequent books were written by a journalist (Frank Horrabin), an ex-engineer (W. McLaine), a Cambridge University lecturer (Maurice Dobb) a journalist (Raymond Postgate), a scientist (Lyster Jameson) an ex-railwayman (Tom Ashcroft), a clerk (Arthur Woodburn), book translators (Eden and Cedar Paul). The Pauls wrote a volume entitled *Proletcult*, which was too esoteric to make much appeal to the NCLC's working-class supporters. Especially for the Plebs League they also wrote *Creative Evolution: A Study of Communist Ergatocracy;* no other Plebs publication had such a recherche title. Patrick Gordon Walker, at the time an Oxford don, provided one of the Outlines already mentioned; V. Gordon Childe, who subsequently became a professor at Edinburgh University, wrote *Man Makes Himself;* Ellen Wilkinson and E. Conze were joint authors of
237

Why War? and E. Conze wrote *An Introduction to Dialectical Materialism*. The NCLC book with the biggest number of readers was Horrabin's *Outlines of Political Geography*, next came Citrine's *The ABC of Chairmanship*, a book that is still being reprinted.

Using Commercial Publishers

Sometimes, in order to tap a wider market, Plebs and NCLC books were published in two editions; a hard board NCLC edition and a commercial publisher's cloth bound edition. The most interesting commercial publication was *Socialism's New Start: A Secret German Manifesto*. It was pseudonymously written by 'Miles,' the name adopted by a small group of young German socialists who, after the Nazis seized control of Germany, relentlessly exposed the sudden collapse of socialism, trade unionism and communism in Germany and set out to re-state a socialist solution. The book had already been circulated secretly in Germany in what was described as a thumb-nail edition. It was printed in microscopic type on India paper as a tiny booklet under the disguised title of *Schopenhauer on Religion*. The first page or two was genuine Schopenhauer but after that it became *Neu Beginnen* — the German title of *Socialism's New Start*. A representative of this group escaped to England and unsuccessfully tried to persuade commercial publishers to issue an English edition. She eventually came to the NCLC office, which arranged not only to publish a stiff-board edition on its own account but for Allen & Unwin to issue a commercial cloth-bound edition; subsequently, American publishers issued a transatlantic edition. H. M. Brailsford wrote the introduction to the NCLC and Allen & Unwin editions, and the American publishers added a foreword by the American socialist, Norman Thomas.

Foreign Editions

The American print of *Socialism's New Start* was not the only NCLC book issued in a foreign edition. Other publications included an Italian edition of the *ABC of Chairmanship*, a Swiss edition of *An Outline of Man's History*, a Danish edition of *An Outline of European History* and a French edition of *An Outline of Modern Imperialism*. Horrabin's *Outline of Political Geography* was published in half-a-dozen foreign languages as well as in Esperanto.

Right up to the time of rationalisation in 1964, the NCLC

kept most of its text books in print by re-issuing edition after edition and bringing the material up to date as necessary. Not many new books were issued during the latter part of the NCLC's history, for two reasons. The first was that commercial publishers began to appreciate that there was a market for socialist books which had not previously existed. The second reason was that the greater part of the NCLC's activity had to be concentrated upon providing postal courses on new subjects and bringing old courses up to date. Suggestions that these postal courses should be published in the form of books were not adopted because if students could obtain their material in that form they might have an excuse for not doing any postal course work. In consequence, not one NCLC postal course was published as a book. Moreover, it was much easier to keep postal courses up to date when run off from stencils then to update books. Only one postal course was printed — Chairmanship.

The NCLC used the Publishing Society as a way both of economising on its purchases and occasionally making a little profit. For example, the Society bought teaching, organisational and other aids which it sold at cost price to the divisions but at a profit to outside bodies. It bought the first Stenorette when Grundig opened up in London. The NCLC's first order from a union came from the Boilermakers, whose representative on the NCLC executive explained that, under the union's rules, no one but the General Secretary and the committee members were allowed to be present at an executive meeting. The Boilermakers' General Secretary, therefore, had had to take his own notes. As the Stenorette was not human the Executive Committee agreed that its presence could be allowed. When the first tape was played back there was considerable concern about some of the language coming back from the machine. In consequence, said the NCLC's Executive member, there was afterwards a substantial improvement in the Executive's vocabulary.

An important result of the Publishing Society's becoming agents for the Stenorette was that the NCLC was able to provide its organisers with these small light tape recorders for their public speaking classes, in place of the extremely heavy tape recorders which preceded them and required a strong man to carry them about.

Plebs and the Fabian Society

When, in 1964, the TUC was about to take over its work, the

239

NCLC Executive Committee assumed that the TUC would realise that its greatly expanded educational programme would need the support of a monthly magazine and the publication of books specially written for workers' classes. That assumption turned out to be entirely misplaced, so when the NCLC Executive Committee realised that the TUC intended to cease publishing *Plebs* as well as text books it took steps to preserve the NCLC Publishing Society. Millar was empowered to find an alternative arrangement for the NCLC's publishing activities. Several possibilities were considered, but since the Fabian Society was anxious to publish a magazine with a working class readership, its offer to take over control of the Publishing Society was accepted. The NCLC agreed to provide an initial two-year subsidy of £5,000 to keep *Plebs* going. A new Publishing Society committee was formed composed of three NCLC representatives, Woodburn, Cornes and Millar himself, together with representatives of the Fabian Society.

Shortly after the transfer of the Publishing Society to the Fabian office, Millar resigned as editor and a new editor was appointed. Tom Ponsonby, secretary of the Fabian Society became secretary of the Publishing Society. The Fabian Society was not in a financial position, however, to subsidise *Plebs,* and only two years later the NCLC Trustees provided a further subsidy of £1,500.

Attempt to Preserve "Plebs"

Prior to the transfer of the Publishing Society to the Fabian office, Robert Maxwell, M.P., the publisher, had already been approached by Millar and had offered to take over financial responsibility for *Plebs* provided Millar would continue for some time as editor and Christine Millar would act as sub-editor. This offer had not been accepted when the Fabian Society expressed a desire to take over the publishing Society. When the NCLC Trustees were no longer able to continue the subsidy Tom Ponsonby approached Maxwell, who agreed to support *Plebs* for some months and eventually to transform it into a new magazine called *The Trade Unionist.* A dummy of the new magazine was prepared and an editor appointed but at about this time Maxwell lost control of Pergamon Press and its directors refused to finance the publication of the proposed new journal. Tom Ponsonby was willing to make further efforts to find a group which would provide the necessary money but the NCLC Trustees decided to advise him that *Plebs'* honourable

240

history should be closed. The editor, Dick Leonard (later an M.P.) appointed to replace Millar had resigned some time previously and was succeeded by a former NCLC organiser Frank Ward, a senior member of the head office staff of the Amalgamated Society of Woodworkers and now the Labour Party's Information Officer. Ward saw to it that the last issue of *Plebs* still flew the flag of independent working-class education its main article, 'The Struggle for Socialist Education' being written by Millar himself.

"Plebs" is Reprinted

Plebs had been published without a break from 1909 to 1969 that is for a longer period, it is believed, than any other general Labour monthly. It had not only played an outstanding part in independent working-class education but had provided a platform for many leading British socialists as well as for outstanding members of the Labour Movement abroad. It was fitting therefore, that at about this time, thanks to the enterprise of Tom Ponsonby, Kraus Reprint, a division of the Kraus Thomson Organisation Limited, decided to republish the first forty volumes of *Plebs,* that is those from 1909 to 1948 and to offer them cloth bound for $556 a set. In 1974 it proposed to offer the remaining volumes at $325.50. The first reprint resulted in a substantial payment to the NCLC Publishing Society which still continues to function on a limited scale in the Fabian Society office in London.

It should not be forgotten that the Plebs League and afterwards the NCLC Publishing Society sold other publications in addition to their own. An important function of the NCLC and the League was to encourage worker-students to read pamphlets and books. The NCLC enforced a rule that every class, day school or summer school must have a 'literature stall. Books were supplied directly not only to postal course students but also to organisers, college secretaries, tutors and branch lecturers. In order to encourage regular reading habits the NCLC frequently sent out to its officials lists of recommended new books and pamphlets and the Publishing Society made every effort to supply its students with any book they wanted even though the discount on a book sale often failed to meet the cost of the service. Under rationalisation the TUC ended this service.

The Colour Movie

The last publicity method aimed at obtaining postal course

ENTHUSIASM

"That's all right by me, but I don't think the Boss will like it."

students and advertising the NCLC's work generally took the form of a colour movie film planned and directed by Christine Millar and photographed by a Polish refugee camera man.

In the 1970s the problem above all others exercising adult educators is how to attract a larger and more socially diversified clientèle. (4) One of the achievements of the NCLC was to make some impression on that section of the population which is almost entirely absent from adult education programmes in most communities. Its success was mainly due to the fact that it never lost sight of the practical needs of its target group and the necessity of providing regular information in a lively and always up to date fashion. The pragmatic approach of the NCLC to the problem of outreach is worth studying by all those agencies currently striving to attract a clientèle that is resistant to education in its traditional forms.

4. cf. 'One of the difficulties with which the NCLC has to contend with in getting every Union, for example, to appreciate the importance of providing independent working class education for its members arises through a misconception. The misconception is that the purpose of an educational scheme is only to provide educational facilities for those members who are anxious to have the education and ask for it. Such members form but a small percentage in any union. Actually the main purpose of the NCLC educational scheme is to get at the very much larger body of members who do not appreciate the need for an education planned to help the Working Class Movement and who, in many cases, take very little interest in the organisations of which they are members.' *(The War of Ideas,* 1939, p.10).

CONCLUSION

When the history of the Labour College Movement is considered in the long perspective of over sixty years it emerges that overt attacks upon its educational provision were surprisingly few. There is no doubt, however, that its teaching methods, academic standards and alleged communist standpoint were the object of a persistent undercurrent of denigration. In the view of a few trade union leaders and Labour Party politicians and of virtually all other educational bodies, what it offered was not really education at all but socialist propaganda. Why was there so much private and relatively so little public criticism? Millar and his colleagues believed that their critics were simply being prudent since every overt attack gave Labour College spokesmen a valuable opportunity for expounding their educational philosophy. This belief was largely justified with regard to the WEA but it did not account for the silence of other educational bodies, Silence on their part was rather explained by sheer indifference or the conviction that the NCLC was a fellow-travelling organisation best ignored. Less easy to explain is the short shrift given the NCLC by historians, some of whom ignore its existence altogether or show an imperfect acquaintance with the range of its activities, especially its large programme of postal courses.

An Orthodox Critic

In a letter to Millar, John Mack, Stevenson lecturer in Citizenship at Glasgow University, blisteringly encapsulated the kind of criticism levelled at the NCLC by those steeped in the traditions of orthodox adult education:

> It is not the case that the NCLC has made a major or even an important contribution to the education of the trade unionists in this country. It is not the case that the NCLC contribution is at all comparable with the work which the Workers' Educational Association and the Workers' Educational Trade Union Committee has done from the beginning. It is true, I gather, that the NCLC provides courses for a greater number of trade unions than does the WEA. But what kind of courses? And what is the effect of these courses on the people who take them? I don't find your statistics impressive. You don't give the duration of your classes nor any indication of the degree of student duplication. The main criticism I have to make of your case is however

243

on the ground of the quality and thoroughness of the work done. Here I am prepared to grant that, as the writer of the article in *Scottish Adult Education* for August, 1954 (No. 11), points out, you may be doing a good job with the technical organisational-training courses for trade union officers, which now form the bulk of your work. But that could be done by any competent technical training college. The test of any trade union or non-trade union educational work is the range and quality of the general ideas discussed in the liberal studies of philosophy, politics, economics, history, literature and the arts and so on. In these studies the NCLC has always been deficient. In the early part of the century they were misled by the belief that wisdom and understanding lay in a rigid adherence to the more useless parts of the writings of Karl Marx, and particularly the theory of surplus value. (By the way, my remark at the conference was not that this was all you taught, but simply that you taught it with great vigour in the 1908-1938 period, that it was valueless then, and that is valueless now.) In more recent years the NCLC has been less doctrinaire and more objective in its teaching of the liberal studies, but it has been greatly handicapped by its continuing adherence to what it calls the 'principle of independent workers' education.' This means in practice the making use of teachers who have not studied these subjects at University level, or of only such beliefs and ideals of the British Labour movement; and it means, moreover, making use of even those qualified teachers without paying the rate for the job. As a result the quality of the work done in liberal studies by the NCLC has been consistently inadequate. Your boast that you do not make use of the Universities (as the WEA has always done) emphasises to me the main weakness of your position. To neglect the thinking that goes on in the Universities on the ground that it is 'capitalist' and therefore tainted is simply to use 'Smear' tactics — a kind of inverted McCarthyism. What is worse, it has served to confirm the prejudices and the dislike of hard thinking, that characterise the rank and file trade unionist in this country. You have certainly succeeded in shutting off a great many unions from exposure to WEA and University thinking, but in doing so you have served these unions very badly indeed. The results are seen in the present plight of the British trade union movement - never more powerful as regards numbers, never more intellectually muddled. It may be unfair to blame this entirely on the NCLC — the native reluctance of the ordinary trade unionists to undertake the unpleasant task of criticising his own prejudices might have prevented rapid enlightenment even if the NCLC hadn't been there to justify his intellectual laziness. But that has been the NCLC's historic role, as I see it. (1)

J. F. C. Harrison is also critical of the NCLC's determination to march alone:

The problem, stripped of political aims and talk of social purpose, was essentially the practical one of how to provide opportunity for learning for people earning their living by hard work. It was primarly a problem in teaching and educational organisation. To its solution the NCLC approach contributed practically nothing; to maintain a purist attitude of independence, to refuse to co-operate with the university and the State educational system was simply to cripple the workers' educational movement indefinitely. Working men could not, and their trade union would not, afford the full cost of higher education; the only practicable way to get it was by co-operating with the university and the Local Education Authority. (2)

And Baroness Stocks observed:

Its proud boast from the first was that it received no financial assistance from State or capitalist sources and that its teaching was — and is — unconstrained by any obligation to serve the interests of those in power. It has, however, been argued by its unkinder critics that this financial independence and the freedom from official inspection inseparable from grant-aid, is not uncon-nected with the unorthodox qualifications of its tutors and the lack of any precise record of its class atten-dances. (3)

Then there was the propaganda slur. Here are two statements separated by some thirty years. The first was made by Mans-bridge in 1920:

1. Mack to Millar, 3 Dec. 1958, NCLC Corr.
2. J. F. C. Harrison, *Living and Learning* (London, 1961), p.297.
3. *op.cit.*, p.51.

It is obvious that no one but a 'class-conscious' student who is willing to accept at the outset certain dogmas (couched in pseudo-scientific language), would find opportunity for development in the Labour College. . . . The members of those Unions, who do not accept the dogmas and wish for freedom of study at a residential college, would have to turn, of necessity, to Ruskin College, or, better still, to the Universities themselves. (4)

The second comes from a press report in 1949 made by Mr. Bullock, Chairman of the TUC:

When Councillor M. Webb said that enmity existed between the WETUC and the National Council of Labour Colleges, Mr. Bullock said this should not be so, but because he believed in education rather than propaganda, he backed the WETUC. (5)

The Propaganda Slur

How justified was all the criticism by orthodox educationists and the propaganda slur? Whether or not the Labour Colleges were wrong to adhere to a narrow interpretation of workers' education, it must be stated that its critics were themselves blinkered in failing to perceive that orthodox curricula and teaching methods could make little impact upon the vast majority of the working class population. In his book *Adult Education: Why this Apathy?* published in 1953 Ernest Green, himself an inveterate enemy of the NCLC, pointed out that there were indeed grounds for believing that the traditional forms of adult education failed to attract the interest of manual workers:

The real picture of manual workers' response to adult education in the past twenty years is dispiriting. In 1933 the percentage of manual workers in WEA classes was 34.25%. The figures for recent years are: (1949) 20.50%, (1950) 19.80, (1951) 18.89. As the figures show, the number of manual workers is not only deplorably low but has been on the decrease for twenty years. (6)

Right up to 1975 those who plan adult education programmes continue to be dogged by the knowledge that their clients are

4. A. Mansbridge, 'Organisation' in R. St. John Parry, ed. *Cambridge Essays on Adult Education*, (London, 1920), p.71.

5. *Evening Advertiser*, 10 Oct. 1949.

6. E. Green, *Why this Apathy?* (London, 1953), p.12.

predominantly drawn from the middle classes and that as the years pass by it becomes no easier to reach out to manual workers. The perennial problem is how to reach those with only a limited amount of education who feel a distaste for orthodox educational institutions. Over a hundred years ago many activists were suspicious of the education offered them and a good proportion have remained so:

> But many of the workers whom it was desired to attract, including some of the most active and serious minded of their number, were Radicals, seeking education as a means to the reconstruction of society. When they found that discussion of all the controversial issues of politics, economics and religion, was carefully excluded, they were apt to leave in disgust, suspecting (not without plausible justification) that the institutions were a put-up job designed to teach the worker obedience to constituted authority and to increase his skill for the benefit of the employer. (7)

J. F. C. Harrison has also pointed out:

> The plain fact was that a desire for higher (liberal) education for its own sake was no more widespread among the working than among other classes — an illusion of which successive generations of well-intentioned middle-class educationists have had to disabuse themselves. The prolonged effort and absorption of time that part-time study after an eleven hour work-day demanded, were such that for most men some *more compelling** motive than learning for its own sake was necessary. (8)

What 'compelling motive'? At the end of the day, the Committee of Inquiry which, in 1917, probed exhaustively and sympathetically into the causes of industrial unrest in South Wales recommended that the universities be entrusted with the task of civic education:

> We would suggest that continued education should be further extended, that the scope of studies should be widened to include courses bearing upon the duties and privileges of citizenship, and that due attention should be paid to proper physical development. We would further suggest that the University is the proper medium for the education of the adult and that

7. T. Kelly, *George Birkbeck*, (Liverpool, 1958), p.226.
8. J. F. C. Harrison, *A History of the Working Men's College*, p.129.

university tutorial classes should be established in every centre of industry in Wales in which political economy, industrial history, and such other subjects as bear upon the conditions and interests of the workers can be studied impartially under the guidance of skilled and recognised authorities. (9)

* Our italics.

A fundamental question arises here: who was to select, in this particular historical context, the 'skilled and recognised authorities'? So many educational organisations and so many teachers are more or less prejudiced, ordering and interpreting their material in the light of a subjective perception of the beliefs, attitudes and behaviour that people ought to adopt. At least one leading WEA supporter had no illusions. Writing in *Highway* in October, 1947, H. V. Wiseman declared:

Though the WEA professed to be 'non-political' it never was. In a democracy every influence has political significance, even that indifference or escapism which are the doom of democrats. (10)

And, in any case, what gave grounds for hope that the miners of South Wales would rush to sit at the feet of university teachers? The Committee diagnosed the ailment but recommended an inadequate, if not irrelevant, cure. The virtue of the NCLC was that it related its programme to the felt needs of trade unionists. Nor, in practice, was that educational programme biased to any significant extent. There is little tangible evidence that the majority of NCLC tutors forced all their material into a Marxist framework and the Executive Committee discouraged one-sided presentations. Thus, in 1931, on behalf of the Committee Millar issued a circular to Divisional and Area Organisers which contained the following statement:

A lecture that simply gives one point of view is not an educational lecture. It is not suggested that the lecturer must in all cases carefully refrain from suggesting what he thinks the right point of view, but it is suggested that he should give a reasonably fair statement of the case from any other point of view that is of importance. (11)

New Needs Demanded New Courses

Like any other educational institution the NCLC was contin-

9. *op. cit.*
10. 'WEA which Way' in *Highway,* Oct. 1947, Vol. XXXVIII, p.280.
11. NCLC MSS.

ually and positively affected by the consequences of social change, though the effects were almost imperceptible to those experiencing day-to-day events. But there was a time-lag between the introduction of new educational programmes and their embodiment in a modified theory. As time passed, the proportion of classes and postal courses explicitly dealing with Marxist theories decreased because the needs of the Labour Movement demanded new classes and courses designed to equip workers for practical problems and responsibilities arising from their industrial and political struggles and to help them in their efforts to improve their condition. The great majority of the subjects taught covered ground about which many workers had had experience as shop stewards or branch secretaries or chairmen of meetings and committees or public speakers. Conscious of the relative poverty of the trade unions and their abiding reluctance to spend much money on educational programmes, the NCLC concentrated singlemindedly on equipping workers with the special knowledge and skills required not only to combat social and industrial exploitation but to help them bring about a new social order. Adhering to the principle of first things first was all the more necessary in that the overwhelming majority in the Labour movement were inactive. To the NCLC it seemed that to have taught to the activists English Poetry or Painting in the Eighteenth Century would have been to divert meagre resources away from the primary goal of striving for better social and economic conditions. It seemed shocking, for example, that in the very year of the General Strike in 1926 Professor Peers could say in the course of a speech about the WEA:

> That the preoccupation of the movement with economic subjects was a thing of the past. Today in his own area, more students were studying English Literature than any other subject. (12)

In the article referred to above, Wiseman deplored the direction taken by the WEA classes: 'The farce of non-political must be abandoned even at the cost of losing the lukewarm. Escapist subjects must be rigorously pruned and only those which can be adapted to the social purpose of the workers' movement accepted.' That was precisely the view of the NCLC. In any event the NCLC saw no point in duplicating courses provided by other bodies. As Millar put it, in reply to Mack's strictures:

12. *Nottingham Guardian*, 19 Nov. 1926.

> A knowledge of economics can . . . be of considerable
> help in training trade unionists to deal with employers,
> whereas a knowledge of how to play the violin would be
> of no assistance. Nor would it be of assistance to be able
> to distinguish one school of painters from another. (13)

At the same time, so much importance was attached by Labour College supporters to the study of economics, social history and the social sciences generally that they did not always make it sufficiently clear that they were not thereby attacking all the other subjects taught by other educational bodies. To some extent it was, therefore, their own fault that they seemed philistine or mechanistic — the history of art can be anything but an escapist subject if taught with an eye on the influence of social conditions.

The NCLC's Figures

How much justification was there for the denigration of the NCLC's educational services as such? This took two forms: criticism of the numerically low class attendances and insinuations that the returns were in any case falsified. Yet if class enrolments were combined with postal course enrolments the aggregate enrolment was consistently high throughout its whole history. These reached a peak of 30,398 during the General Strike period in 1925/26, at the time when there was no national check against registers, which were not then always kept. The number of class students thereafter declined until the years 1940 to 1963, Thereafter no classes were recorded nationally unless registers were received. During this period the student figures fluctuated mainly between 11,000 and over 13,000. In 1962, the last complete year of entirely independent operation, there were 12,259 students. After 1925-26 the drop in classes and class students was more than offset by substantial gains in other forms of provision. Thus in 1963 there were 21,212 postal course students, 8,566 day and week-end school enrolments, and an attendance of 43,984 at 1,761 branch lectures. The reasons for the decline in class attendance have already been mentioned. Between 1918 and 1930 it was much easier to attract trade unionists to classes because most of them lived in the centres of cities such as Glasgow. When major housing estates spread into the suburbs, large numbers of trade unionists left the city centres and showed reluctance to attend centrally-based classes. Attempts to organise classes in the suburbs were not often

13. Millar to Mack, NCLC Corr.

successful; many of the men preferred to tend their gardens, listen to the radio or, after the Second World War, watch television. Moreover, when the stimulus of the First World War, the Russian revolution and the General Strike atmosphere had subsided, interest in political questions flagged and there was a general decline in attendance not only at NCLC classes but also at trade union and Labour Party meetings. A special factor affecting student attendance after the Second World War was relatively full employment and an increase in overtime. The very expansion of the Labour movement also meant that the activists, who would once have attended classes or served as tutors had become too busy serving on local councils and miscellaneous committees. The loss of tutors to political activity was particularly striking; on one occasion in an English borough all four NCLC tutors stood for the first time for the local council and were elected. The victories of the Labour Party in local and parliamentary elections had the effect of creaming off tutors and students, a majority of whom were more attracted by the challenge of active politics than sustaining an educational programme.

Allegations that the NCLC falsified its enrolment returns were unfounded. It has already been shown in Chapter XI that the drop-out rate from postal courses was surprisingly low precisely because rigorous measures were taken to maintain a high level of enthusiasm. Equal care was taken by the Executive Committee to ensure that class attendances were honestly recorded. To check registers is evidently not a foolproof way of checking actual enrolments but it does encourage punctilious habits. The minutes of the Executive Committee of the NCLC show that from the time when registers were first called in for checking in 1931 there were unremitting efforts to ensure that returns were not falsified.

Nevertheless, if one criterion of success is to accomplish more than any other agency in the same area of endeavour, then the NCLC's achievement is unique. The following enrolment statistics cover the total span of its existence, apart from the first year:

Year	Classes	Students	No. of Day & Weekend Schools	Students	Branch Lectures	Postal Course Students	Summer Schools
1922-3	529	11,993	—	—	1,125	—	1
1925-6	1,234	30,398	105	6,154	1,168	1,459	1
1928-9	931	20,520	138	6,688	1,259	2,404	1 & 1F
1931-2	704*	17,173	159	9,666	1,617	7,418	
1934-5	753	16,219	216	15,649	1,649	6,827	
1937-8	728	13,274	217	14,380	1,438	10,700	1 & 1F
1940	742	13,254	214	11,561	1,287	6,790	2(1)
1943	560	10,025	237	13,184	1,722	12,465(4)	4(2)
1946	748	12,514	206	11,747	2,776	16,276(5)	6(3)
1949	820	13,198	300	17,636	2,683	20,982	8 & 3F
1952	878	15,040	304	12,818	2,468	18,652	8 & 2F
1955	769	11,631	230	8,468	1,997	15,832	9 & 2F
1959	724	11,376	234	8,394	1,964	15,543	9 & 2F
1962	766	12,257	298	9,306	1,761(6)	17,751	9 & 2F
1963 (last year)	692(6)	11,032(6)	297(6)	8,566(6)		21,212	10 & 1F

From this year class figures were not nationally recorded unless actual registers were received
1) and (2) Second World War
3) Some of these and some of the subsequent schools were for individual unions
4) Enthusiasm for Labour Government
5) Enthusiasm for Labour Government
6) The figures could have been considerably higher had the TUC office not prevented the NCLC from replacing its Edinburgh and East of Scotland Organiser
* Foreign schools

Note: Film strip lectures, public interviews and brains trusts in later years not included in above figures. These were later developments.

The WEA's and WETUC's Results

By contrast, in respect of the WEA, as B. W. Pashley has pointed out:

> . . . in certain respects the (WETUC) results would seem to have been disappointing. It has already been mentioned that the WETUC did not bring about a rise in the proportion of manual workers in WEA general class provision, although during a period of expanding total numbers it may have put a brake on the decline. Even so, in its session 1925/6, for example, only 1,426 members of the four participating unions at that time claimed remission of their fees. The figure rose to 1,877

252

by 1936 but was still only 2,081 in 1938. After 1945 the members claiming remission of fees were not given in WETUC Annual Reports, and although the WEA claimed that about thirty thousand trade unionists attended classes in 1951 there is no indication that they were participating in WETUC schemes; in fact the number of trade unionists cited in 1951 included 10,000 teachers. Certainly some classes were arranged directly for the WETUC but these were difficult to organise and few in number. In general, trade unionists, even under WETUC schemes, were but one element of an ordinary class, and would thus most likely be studying subjects in a way not designed for their own sectional needs and purposes. (14)

It is even more instructive to compare the occupational categories of students served respectively by the NCLC and the WEA after the Second World War:

Analysis for the period 1st June, 1948, to 31st May, 1949

	NCLC %	WEA %
Manual Workers	86.37	20.5
Clerks, Draughtsmen, Travellers and Foremen	4.22	16.1
Shop Assistants and Shop Keepers	5.40	3.8
Teachers	.01	12.2
Civil Servants and Postal Workers	.01	4.8
Home Duties and Nursing	3.95	28.8
Miscellaneous	.03	8.5

The WEA's failure to appeal to manual workers was emphasised in a critical analysis of trends in enrolments prepared by S. G. Raybould in 1949:

> ... the fact which stands out most clearly is that manual workers are rapidly coming to occupy a much less important place in the ranks of the Association's students. In the decade before the outbreak of war one student in every three was a manual worker; or, if we exclude the category 'Home Duties and Nursing,' about three in every seven. By the end of the War, the

14. B. W. Pashley Role, Definition and fulfilment in English Adult Education. (unpublished thesis, Liverpool University, 1964/69).

253

proportion had fallen to one in four of all students. In each session since 1944-5 the figure has fallen until in 1947-8 it was only one in five of all students, and less than two in seven of all students excluding those engaged on 'Home Duties and Nursing,' in spite of the considerable increase in the latter group. (15)

In short, whereas the WEA was very far from fulfilling Mansbridge's desire that 'three quarters of its members should be actually labouring men and women,' the NCLC consistently unto the last catered overwhelmingly for manual workers.

The irony and the tragedy of 'the unfortunate quarrel between the NCLC and the WEA' was that the two rivals were competing for a very small if influential clientèle. At no time did more than a fraction of trade unionists show any interest in taking advantage of the educational facilities at their disposal just as the great majority very rarely attended their branch meetings. Thus during the session 1925/26 only 1,426 members claimed remission of fees for attendance at WEA classes. The figure was 1,877 for 1936 and 2,081 for 1938. Attendance at WEA week-end and one-day schools arranged by the WETUC was much higher, but still not impressive. For example, the attendance at such courses in 1939 was no more than 3,951. Pashley has offered the following student total figures for various years between 1924 and 1939:

Session	Weekend	One Day	Total
1924-5	734	—	734
1925-6	over 1000	—	over 1000
1926-7	1100	—	1100
1932	1109	3341	4450
1933	1322	3075	4397
1935	1605	2720	4325
1937	1900	1497	3397
1939	1429	3308	4737

Commenting upon such figures Pashley concludes:

It was quite clear that even when comparatively little burden was imposed upon trade union funds, when full adult educational facilities were made available, when every attempt was made to stimulate educational activity among trade unionists, there was no really enthusiastic response from the rank and file. (16)

15. S. G. Raybould, WEA, *The Next Phase*, (London, 1949) pp.5-6.
16. Pashley, *op.cit.*, p.183.

One charge levelled against the NCLC was that it failed to integrate its various educational activities; the students were not encouraged, it was alleged, to pursue a logical sequence of studies; each class or postal course was treated as an end in itself; even when an attempt to integrate was made, it was unsuccessful; the summer school programmes lacked cohesion. In practice, it was the experience of the NCLC's professional staff that many of their students did systematically pursue related courses. Thus, a student often followed a course on Industrial History in the first Winter session, went on to Economics during the second Winter session and attended a course on Economic Geography during the Summer session. The student who took up the study of English by post would frequently begin with the English Grammar course, next turn his attention to the course to Compostition and then to the course on Labour Journalism. Many who started with English were helped by the treatment of this subject to become interested in taking up other courses. One student wrote:

> You may wonder from a superficial glance at the courses I have taken how my outlook would be affected by English and Pre-History. Nevertheless the English courses alone are capable of changing the outlook of any fair-minded person by reason of the carefully selected examples which range from extracts from the best socialist writers to simple branch correspondence. I have never read of Bernard Shaw's works until I came across the tantalising extracts in the English postal course. Since then I have spent some happy and instructive hours reading his prefaces and plays. (17)

As for most of the summer schools, they were never in general intended to be cohesive but to attract as wide a spectrum of trade unionists as possible and to encourage them thereafter to enrol for classes and postal courses. The NCLC made no attempts, unlike the Central Labour College for a brief period, to provide long-term courses on the model of WEA tutorial courses, neither did the NCLC organise linked week-end schools, which were too expensive and inappropriate for the great majority of the people it wished to serve. The NCLC could do no more than conscientiously encourage students to take up complementary studies and this it did by a variety of methods.

17.   NCLC Minutes, 1940/41, p.218.

The State Education System

It is curious that critics of the NCLC have not commented upon its attitude to the State system of education, for in this connection it might have appeared vulnerable. Should it not have devoted more of its resources, as did the WEA, to agitating for the reform of the educational system as a whole? The NCLC was certainly anxious to see the school curriculum drastically modified. It published *What's Wrong with the Schools* by T. Ashcroft, *Bias in the Schools* by J. P. M. Millar and Arthur Woodburn and *Lies and Hate in Education* by Mark Starr, and after the Second World War it submitted a memorandum on the subject — afterwards published as a pamphlet — to a committee set up by the Secretary of State for Scotland. Anticipating by nearly thirty years the attitude of the European Economic Community, this memorandum, like a number of previously published NCLC pamphlets, advocated the removal from school text-books of nationalist propaganda and slanted history. But the main thrust of the NCLC was to build up its administrative machinery and its teaching programme. It had neither the staff nor the financial resources nor the time to engage in other activities on a substantial scale.

Two Charges Against the NCLC

The two most serious and interrelated charges levelled against the NCLC were that it was politically extreme and operated as a divisive force within the Labour movement. Its opponents often erroneously associated it with the concept of the 'class war' instead of the class struggle and hence with a desire for change by means of revolution. Some critics of the NCLC were genuinely convinced that it was a crypto-communist organisation. The misconception stemmed from the common assumption that to subscribe to Marxist theories automatically made one a communist. It was understandable that the uneducated would make this glib assumption but galling for the NCLC that leading educationists should give credence to it. Margaret Cole, who supported the WEA, once described *Plebs* as the 'parish magazine of the British Marxists,' although she never accused it of being Communist, and W. H. Marwick commented that the Council's affiliations were closer to the Communist Party than the Labour Party. In a letter to the *Manchester Guardian* of 23 December, 1949, a correspondent wrote:

> Motions on the publication of accounts of political

parties may be commendable but it is the ancillary political organisations that often supply the funds and facilities for undercover propaganda and these would probably remain undiscovered.

Without mentioning the NCLC by name the correspondent went on to say that he had seen copies of two postal courses which 'seem to be a more insidious form of propaganda than presenting a game of tiddlywinks with a packet of sugar.' One of the courses referred to was on electioneering and the other on the health service.

The NCLC was always overtly Marxist and therefore socialist in its educational orientation. This showed up most prominently in the lecture notes and textbooks that it produced. Thus the textbook, *An Outline of Economics,* first published in 1923, put forward as a basis Marx's Labour theory of value and other concepts related to the class struggle. This book went through numerous editions and it remained Marxist to the end as did another and more original textbook, *An Outline of Finance* covering a somewhat different field. Moreover, the NCLC appreciated that there was a certain ideological connection between the Communist Party and the Labour College Movement just as there was an ideological connection between the Communist Party and the Social Democrat Party in Germany, bitterly opposed to the Communists. The Labour Colleges, in common with the Social Democrat Parties in Europe, the Socialist Labour Party, the British Socialist Party and the Communist Party regarded Marx as having made the greatest single contribution to the emergence of socialist theory.

The view of the NCLC leaders was that social democratic parties were not revolutionary organisations in the commonly accepted sense of the word revolutionary and could only become so in revolutionary times. True, they wished to turn the capitalist system into a socialist system; true, also, they believed that force might be required to effect transition in some countries. But Marx himself, who had lived through an epoch of revolutions, did not consider that force would necessarily be required in Britain despite the evil social conditions of his day. Neither the Labour College movement nor the Social Democratic parties set out to destroy the fabric of capitalism by force; on the contrary, they considered that socialism could be ushered in by making use of the industrial and scientific fabric which capitalism had created. It is also significant that many of the most active

257

supporters of *Plebs* saw themselves as industrial unionists and categorically not as syndicalists. As for the early Labour College leaders, they played an important role in turning some railway unions into an industrial union — the NUR and the local miners unions in South Wales and elsewhere into industrial unions, but they had to cease to press the case for industrial unionism for they realised that, since nearly all the British unions were organised on a craft or general basis — one general union even accepted a picture house manager-proprietor as a member — the Labour College Movement could not extend its educational work if it used its machinery to advocate industrial unionism. During the Ruskin troubles, the Plebs leaders had already been wrongly accused by the college authorities of trying to break up the trade unions. The Trade Union Movement, Labour Governments and even Britain itself are still paying an enormous price for union failure to reorganise on an industrial basis. Even in 1976 there are still over twenty unions catering for workers in a steel mill and over twenty in a motor car factory. The result is that demarcation practices and disputes cause gross over-manning in both industries, two to three workers doing the job that one worker does in Germany, for example. The irony of the situation is that after the war, by which time the German trade union movement had long been destroyed by the Nazis, the advice of some British trade unionists* that the German unions should be rebuilt on an industrial basis was followed, so that in Germany there are sixteen unions whereas in Britain there are well over a hundred unions affiliated to the TUC alone as well as others outside it. The result is that in many British industries there is gross over-manning as compared with Britain's competitors such as Germany and Japan and the costly products and Britain's lower standard of life are in a substantial measure one consequence. Had the WETUC not been a competitor standing by to pick up unconsidered trifles, the NCLC's policy on teaching industrial unionism could well have taken a more courageous line, but it still would have had to be very careful. All it did was to take its students to foreign summer schools where the students could learn about industrial unionism in practice.

The idea that the early Labour College leaders favoured syndicalism was as far from the truth as it could be. The typical syndicalist had no time for politics. Labour College pioneers, on the other hand, attached great importance to political action; to

* Commenting on the death of Victor Feather, a former NCLC student and much later TUC General Secretary, the *Guardian* gave Feather the credit for this advice.

them syndicalism seemed a fatally narrow conception. Aneurin Bevan, for example, arrived at the Central Labour College as a student with syndicalist beliefs, but he soon dropped them.

The Communists and the NCLC

As for the communists' attitude to the NCLC, there was further irony. While Millar was a prisoner of the military in Aldershopt as a conscientious objector, another C.O. arrived, Palme Dutt. Millar found him a meek and mild guild Socialist and set about explaining Marx's theories to him. Dutt later became the communist party's chief theoretician and Millar regarded this result as hardly his good turn for the Labour Party. The NCLC itself, after its first ten months of existence, was not infrequently assailed as an enemy by members of the Communist Party and threatened by attempts at clandestine infiltration although a few, like Tommy Jackson, had a different attitude.

Consider the Following extract from a report submitted to the Annual Conference of the Communist Party of Great Britain on 7th Octobr, 1922:

> The present available opportunities for embers, such as the Labour College Economic and Industrial History classes, do not provide for the needs of the Party. Our members and recruits need to be trained in an understanding of the principles and policy of our Party, in the history and tactics of the international Communist struggle, and in our own work and methods of organisation. The Labour College classes, even where they are not actually hostile or indifferent to the Party, do not provide for these needs. Their teaching of economics and industrial history lacks the revolutionary political application which finds its realisation in the Communist Party. We cannot allow our members to be trained under alien influences, and we must be prepared to assume our own responsibilities . . . Labour College classes should be made use of wherever Communists are in Control but the classes have to be really revolutionary in character. (18)

In the April, 1923, issue of *Plebs,* J. T. Murphy, a leading communist, criticised the content of Labour College education. (19)

18. NCLC MSS.
19. J. T. Murphy, 'Wanted: The Marxism of Marx' in *Plebs,* 1923, pp.152-6.

The revolution, he said, has blown to smithereens the pedantic formalism of the so-called Marxian theorists of the epoch of the Second International. (20)

We are now faced with the challenge to give the revolution full play within the institutions of the working class and bring the Marxism of Marx to bear upon its problems, which means that the class struggle is the key to the interpretation of the educational needs of the workers. Without it there is no justification for independent working-class education, no justification for the existence of the Plebs and the Labour Colleges, and no fulfilment of the published aims and tests of these organisations. (20)

In the following issue Craik, Hamilton, E. Redfern, E. Turner, Coxon, Holder, Lawther, F. Silvester and Millar, all responded on behalf of the NCLC. Millar's reply contained the statement:

Such criticism, however, seems to arise from the fact that these critics have convinced themselves that at least a substantial minority of the workers know about the class struggle and are simply needing a practical programme to rush the revolution into existence in about twelve months. The painful truth is, however, that there is no such substantial minority of workers. The great bulk of the minority, for instance, that votes Labour recognises the class struggle no more consciously than it recognises the fact that at one time the sea divided Britain from the Continent. (21)

Palme Dutt, a leading Communist theoretician, in 1923 strongly criticised a Plebs text book on imperialism, finding fault with Plebs authors in general for being subservient to trade union officials.

The enduring hostility of the Communists was revealed after the Second World War at one of the annual dinners of the Central Labour College Students' Association, of which George Phippen, an NCLC Organiser, was secretary. Although not a former residential student, Arthur Horner, secretary of the National Union of Mine Workers and a well-known communist, had been invited as the guest speaker because of his South Wales connections with those who had been at the residential college. In his speech Horner launched into an attack upon

20. *ibid.*, p.156.
21. *ibid.*, p.207.

Millar, who was sitting among the guests. The gravamen of the attack was that Millar had used his influence to destroy the Communist soul of independent working-class education. Another unwitting tribute to the 'independence' of the NCLC was provided by Archibald Robertson when, in 1937, he decided not to renew his *Plebs* subscription saying:

> Four years' study of *Plebs* has shown me that it spends quite as much energy fighting communists as fighting capitalists. As I can get all the anti-communism I want from the Capitalist press, I see no use in supporting further a paper or an organisation which, I am convinced, is merely helping to confuse the idea. (22)

The Labour Party's Educational Weakness

The allegation that the NCLC was a divisive element within the Labour and trade union movement has frequently been made. Among those who condemned the NCLC for engaging in what some thought was a sterile conflict with the WEA was the late Professor Peers:

> But this largely factitious controversy has unfortunately bedevilled the whole approach to trade union education, has obscured the larger needs, and has hindered the formulation of any real policy, since neither the TUC nor the interested unions, in the interests of a peaceful life, are prepared to decide between their apparently conflicting views. On the other hand, it seems likely that many trade unionists to whom the partisan approach does not appeal are deterred from taking advantage of NCLC services which might be useful to them. (23)

The basic difficulty was that the Labour Movement as a whole had no particular concern for the education of its members. In reality educational activists were few and far between and fragmented into conflicting groups. Unity of educational purpose, like unity in other matters, could have been provided only by the Labour Party or by the trade unions or, ideally, an alliance of the two. As has been seen, neither one nor the other grasped the importance of giving their members a wide Labour education. Most trade unionists admired the State system of education and merely thought that it should be made more accessible to their children, in particular to enable them to get

22. *Plebs*, 1937.
23. *op.cit.*, p.161.

better jobs. For its part the Labour Party has signally failed to see to the political education ·of its keenest supporters; Its attempts from time to time to interest its members have all failed to strike a spark. Yet the same membership used NCLC facilities. Had not the Plebs League and the NCLC battled with the WEA it is possible that among trade unionists interest in education would have been even much less than it was and the stranglehold of orthodox content and methods, generally admitted now to have been regrettable even in the State sector, would not have been questioned. The conflict at least had the virtue of pointing to a need, a fact that G. Smith of the Post Office Engineering Union had noted at the 1961 Congress when the new rationalised educational scheme was being discussed.

> The existence of the two competing organisations, the NCLC and WETUC, at least has the advantage that these two organisations, among their activities, were competing to sell the idea of trade union education to trade union branches and trade union members, and we hope that the new body, when it comes into existence, will show equal zeal in that respect. (24)

The grave misunderstandings which arose between the Labour Government and the Unions during the period 1967 to 1970 might have been less serious had the TUC, the Labour Party and the Co-operative movement seized the opportunity to build up an educational programme designed to enable supporters to face up to the obsolescent structure of the trade unions, the vulnerability of the national economy and the possibilities offered by the European Economic Community. For the failure the Labour Party must share some of the blame. It missed the chance to take over the non-technical elements in the NCLC's work and to make it the basis of a nationwide programme. Though the Labour Party has now five times provided the national government, it still has no organised educational programme for its members, although two or three postal courses are now being run on a very small scale, with its blessing. A. L. Williams, General Secretary of the Labour Party and a former NCLC organiser, was himself, not surprisingly, conscious of the Party's remissness in the matter of education. On one occasion he wrote to Millar:

> . . . the Labour Party carries on a substantial educational activity, but this is largely unco-ordinated and unsyste-

24. TUC, *Annual Report,* 1961, p.443.

matic. We run four national weekly summer schools each year, as well as one ot two weekly schools for young people, and our Women's Movement and our Regional Councils also run schools, including some of a week's duration, but more often day and week-end schools. We have urged local parties to limit the routine business at meetings to provide time for educational discussions, and we have produced regular series of publications, including *Ammunition and Talking Points,* for the guidance of study group leaders.

Plans have been produced from time to time to pull all these activities into shape, but they have nearly always been frustrated because of an election cropping up or some other similar event. This is the basic difficulty facing the Party. . . .

All this is an argument for the existence of a body representative of the whole movement, specialising in the provision of educational facilities — and no such movement now exists! (25)

The NCLC's Achievements

In the present account the Labour College Movement has been described warts and all. Too many of its critics have had eyes only for the warts. Having stereotyped the Labour Colleges as the would-be *vox populi* of the working classes, obstinately peddling a misguided and increasingly misguided concept of education, too many critics of the NCLC have failed to see that the mainspring of its activities specifically after the foundation of the NCLC, was the pragmatic desire to extend its control over trade union education for a constructive purpose. Defects the Colleges certainly had — what educational organisation does not? — but the fact remains that they made a bigger quantitative contribution to working class education than did the trade unions themselves and the WEA put together. Through the pages of *Plebs* and their numerous publications they disseminated information otherwise unobtainable by their readers, and stimulated men and women to become active in the Labour Movement. Their students came from and remained attached to the active section of the Labour movement. All over Britain and Northern Ireland as well as in some overseas countries, they were responsible for recruiting and holding together a cadre of militant labour supporters. It was in 1950 that a trade union

25. NCLC Corr.

263

leader affirmed that the NCLC had not only helped to produce a vigorous and informed leavening of activists but also given their basic political education to many trade union and Labour Party notables. He might have been echoing Ellen Wilkinson, speaking years earlier in 1924 at the annual meeting in Stockton:

> Although I had taken a degree in History at Manchester University I was astonished to discover when I came in contact with the Labour Colleges how little real history I had been taught.

How did the NCLC stand during the last few years of its independent existence? After rationalisation, at a meeting of the Trade Union, Labour and Co-operative Democratic History Society, a well-known WEAer alleged that the NCLC had pushed rationalisation because its financial position had become shaky. The fact is that from 1957 to 1964 the NCLC grew considerably stronger. Its Report for 1963 submitted to its final conference in 1964 showed that eight British unions had affiliated for the first time and that eleven overseas unions had also affiliated for postal course facilities. Even in the first few months of 1964 a further British union and three overseas unions affiliated so that the non-TUC unions with NCLC educational schemes numbered 32. During the same period the Australian Council of Trade Unions (TUC) had ordered a substantial number of NCLC postal courses and arrangements were developing under which Australian trade unionists could receive NCLC courses as well as courses partially based upon them. The Turkish Metal Workers' Union had asked the NCLC for assistance in providing postal courses for its members and the Angola Workers' Union had also asked the NCLC to help it provide postal courses: the All Ceylon Federation of Trade Unions was also proposing to affiliate.

Like all social movements the NCLC fell short of the high expectations of its founders. In 1944 Will Coxon commented in a letter to Millar:

> Looking back on the movement, one must admire its tremendous growth in the trade union movement, but I think this too requires qualification. I must say that to me its influence has not been proportionate to its growth. (26)

26. *ibid.*

Two statements made as long ago as 1935 might well serve as the epitaph of the NCLC. First, Harold Laski wrote:

> This month, I hear, marks the coming of age of the National Council of Labour Colleges. I should like to offer it my good wishes. In the face of great handicaps, it has done bravely a pretty big job. Sometimes I think it has suffered from an excessive sectarianism; and sometimes, also, I have felt that its students required a higher standard of technical performance. But there are thousands of men and women in this country whom it has made politically conscious. It has published text books of which it can be proud; and its monthly journal *Plebs* has always been lively and stimulating. It deserves ten times the support it receives; with that support it might really persuade the Labour Party to accept a coherent philosophy. (27)

Secondly, Will Thorne, General Secretary of the GMWU, wrote:

> During the passage of years the NCLC has rendered to the Trade Union and Socialist Movement a very great service, the fruits of which can never be reckoned in time. . .(28)

Apart from its positive achievements the NCLC is worth studying for the sake of the many splendid people who gave their skills and energy to fostering it for but little or no material reward. Mark Starr is in no doubt about the crucial contribution of the Millars themselves:

> Likewise for J. P. M. Millar whose organising genius and dogged pertinacity made him literally Mr. NCLC as he welded together the widely diverse local activities into a nationwide movement based on the financial support of the unions, for whose practical needs the educational services of the unions were increasingly tailored. JPM was ably backed by Christine Millar who founded and ran the NCLC postal courses department which played an outstanding role in the NCLC's educational work. (29)

NCLC officials and organisers would have been the first to admit, however, that the NCLC could not have flourished had it

27. Praise for Pioneers (unpublished) NCLC Mss.
28. *Reynolds News*, 2 Feb. 1935.
29. NCLC Corr. 7 Jan. 1935.

not been for the devoted service of thousands of voluntary tutors, lecturers, college secretaries and postal course writers and examiners. It is time for the achievements of the Plebs League and the Labour College movement to be more widely known and, above all, high time for the British TUC to widen greatly its extremely narrow and inward looking educational curriculum.

NCLC EDUCATIONAL STATISTICS FROM 1938 TO 1963

Year	Classes	Students	Day & Week-end Schools	Students	Branch Lectures	Students	Postal Students	Summer Schools	Students
1963	692*	11032	297	8566	1761	43984	21212		
1962	766	12257	298	9306	1964	56493	17751		553
1961	734	11452	266	9406	2115	57621	15918	11	572
60	710	11242	226	7739	1818	45944	15543	11	591
59	724	11376	234	8394	1997	56255	15175	11	592
58	778	12200	232	8431	2400	61489	15935	11	578
57	782	11625	219	8163	2530	69804	14704	11	602
56	769	11631	230	8468	2468	66762	15832	11	576
55	787	11680	284	11184	2392	70763	16550	11	667
54	760	11919	290	11331	2527	69102	16646	9	629
53	837	13912	266	10459	2476	72131	17144	10	679
52	878	15040	304	12818	2623	79332	18652	9	656
51	817	13681	248	10402	2382	81103	17006†	10	656
50	900	15275	245	11434	2680	80591	18718†	11	636
49	820	13198	300	17636	2776	89360	20982	7	510
48	758	11999	244	13830	2681	84913	18521	7	392
47	668	10794	186	12308	1957	64797	15573	9	593
46	748	12514	206	11747	1722	52827‡	15835	5	475
45	759	13721	206	10775	1614		16540	5	296
44	680	11587	227	10136	1340		12465	4	326
43	560	10025	237	13184	1289		9973	4	370
42	600	10350	225	11061	1022		7500	3	297
41	580	9901	185	9142	980		7546	2	234
40	742	13254	214	11561	1438		11410	1	90
39	860	15611	260	14317	1902		12338		
38	728	13774	215	14380	1649		10700		

*TUC prevented NCLC from replacing East of Scotland organiser so work collapsed and figures fell badly.

‡Prior to this,figures were not recorded.

†In these years General Election work by prospective students brought down the figures.

For the previous years' class figures see *Education for Emancipation* p. 5 which gives totals for 1922-23 to 1936-7. At first the NCLC educational year was 1st April to 31st March. It was later changed to Jan.-Dec. In 1931 and after no class figures were counted unless they were accompanied by registers. These brought down the figures.

POSTAL COURSES DEPARTMENT

REPORT FOR YEAR ENDED 31st DECEMBER, 1963

COURSES IN FORCE DURING 1963

Unions with NCLC Schemes	Courses in Force Jan/Dec 1963	Courses in Force Jan/Dec 1962	Increase	Decrease
AEU	4290	4163	127	—
Amal. Moulders' Union	6	12	—	6
Amal. Slaters, Tilers & Roofing Ops.	6	9	—	3
Amal. Soc. of Lithographic Printers.	35	33	2	—
Amal. Soc. of Woodworkers.	41	20	21	—
Amal. Union of Asphalt Workers.	3	6	—	3
AUBTW.	230	250	—	20
ASLEF.	304	320	—	16
Assoc. of Govt. Supervisors & Radio Offs.	267	50	217	—
Assoc. Soc. Moulders & Foundry Workers.	3	1	2	—
Assoc. Correctors of the Press.	10	17	—	7
ASSET.	327	316	11	—
British Roll Turners' Trade Society.	13	7	6	—
Card Setting Machine Tenters' Society.	—	1	—	1
Chemical Workers' Union.	35	69	—	34
Cigarette Machine Operators' Society.	—	—	—	—
Cinematograph, Television & Allied Techs.	48	74	—	26
Clerical & Administrative Workers.	1019	1004	15	—
Cloth Pressers' Society.	—	1	—	1
Comp. Section (NFBTO).	22	18	4	—
Con. Health Service Employees.	374	413	—	39
Constructional Engineering Union.	83	124	—	41
DATA.	961	817	144	—
Electrical Trades Union.	1205	1022	183	—
Fire Brigades' Union.	806	702	104	—
General Iron Fitters' Association.	10	4	6	—
Heating & Domestic Engineers.	50	35	15	—
Hinckley Hosiery Warehousemen.	3	—	3	—
Iron, Steel & Metal Dressers' Trade Soc.	21	37	—	16
Laminated & Coil Spring Workers' Union	5	3	2	—
Leicester Hosiery Trimmers.	5	14	—	9
Liverpool Victoria Workers' Union.	17	37	—	20
London Jewel Case Makers.	—	—	—	—
London Typographical Society.	209	134	75	—
Managers' & Overlookers' Society.	47	63	—	16
Military Musical Instrument Makers' Soc.	17	2	15	—

Unions with NCLC Schemes (contd.)	Courses in Force Jan/Dec 1963	Courses in Force Jan/Dec ·1962	Increase	Decrease
Monotype Casters & Typefounders' Soc.	10	15	—	5
Musicians' Union.	44	35	9	—
NAU Life Assurance Workers.	10	10	—	—
N. Assoc. Coll. Overmen, Deputs. & Shotfrs.	285	363	—	78
Nat. Assoc. Operative Plasterers.	32	20	12	—
Nat. Assoc. Transport Employees.	12	10	2	—
Nat. Soc. of Brushmakers.	3	4	—	1
Nat. Soc. of Electro. & Stereotypers.	78	78	—	—
Nat. Soc. of Painters & Decorators.	265	210	55	—
Nat. Soc. of Pottery Workers (Scotland).	—	1	—	1
Nat. Union of Blastfurnacemen.	67	62	5	—
Nat. Union of Boot & Shoe Operatives.	57	38	19	—
NUFTO.	154	152	2	—
N.U. General & Municipal Workers.	1171	789	382	—
N.U. Gold, Silver, etc. Trades.	11	8	3	—
N.U. Lock & Metal Workers.	18	34	—	16
N.U. Mineworkers.	1249	1400	—	151
N.U. Packing Case Makers.	13	22	—	9
N.U. Pearl Agents.	15	27	—	12
N.U. Press Telegraphists.	31	24	7	—
NUR.	843	1041	—	198
N.U. Scalemakers.	40	32	8	—
N.U. Shale Miners.	1	1	—	—
N.U. Sheet Metal Wkrs. & Coppersmiths.	523	597	—	74
N.U. Tailors & Garment Workers.	56	76	—	20
N.U. Water Works Employees.	25	26	—	1
Nelson Weavers.	—	2	—	2
Plumbing Trades Union.	210	227	—	17
Power Loom Carpet Weavers.	2	2	—	—
Rosendale Valley Textile Workers' Assoc.	—	—	—	—
Scottish Brass Turners.	14	7	7	—
Scottish Carpet Trade Workers.	12	17	—	
Scottish Lace & Textile Workers.	1	1	—	—
Scottish Operative Glaziers.*	4	—	4	—
Scottish Plasterers.	19	16	3	—
Scottish Power Loom Tenters.	7	10	—	
Scottish Slaters, Tilers, etc.	5	10	—	
Scottish Transport & General Workers.	2	3	—	
Scottish Typographical Association.	60	71	—	1
Scottish Union of Bakers.	28	23	5	
Society of Litho. Artists.	87	99	—	1

269

Unions with NCLC Schemes (contd.)	Courses in Force Jan/Dec 1963	Courses in Force Jan/Dec 1962	Increase	Decrease
Society of Technical Civil Servants.	159	156	3	—
Springmakers & Toolmakers.	2	2	—	—
Transport & General Workers.	915	724	191	—
Transport Salaried Staffs' Assoc.	533	384	149	—
Typographical Association.	348	361	—	13
Union of Jute, Flax & Kindred Textile Ops.	2	1	1	—
Union of Polish Craftsmen.	—	—	—	—
United French Polishers.	—	3	—	3
United Rubber Workers.	11	15	—	4
U.S. Boilermakers, etc.	405	439	—	34
Watermen, Lightermen, etc.	10	19	—	9
Total NCLC Union Schemes	18321	17445	1819	943
Special Schemes.	11	33	—	22
Voluntary Secretaries.	2	4	—	2
Voluntary Tutors.	6	15	—	9
Commonwealth, etc.	131	129	2	—
Paying.	71	125	—	54
			1821	
			1030	
Total NCLC Schemes.	18542	17751	791	1030

Unions Added Under Rationalisation

	Courses in Force Jan/Dec 1963	Courses in Force Jan/Dec 1962	Increase	Decrease
Amal. Assoc. Beamers, Twisters & Drawers.	8	—	8	—
Amal. Assoc. Oper. Cotton Spinners & Twnrs.	1	—	1	—
Amal Soc. Leather Workers.	1	—	1	—
Amal. Soc. Oper. Lace Makers & Aux. Wkrs.	1	—	1	—
Amal. Soc. of Textile Workers.	9	—	9	—
Amal. Soc. of Wire Drawers.	16	—	16	—
Amal. Soc. of Woodcutting Machinists.	62	—	62	—
Amal. Union of Foundry Workers.	95	—	95	—
Amal. Union of Oper. Bakers, etc.	30	—	30	—
Amal. Weavers' Association.	5	—	5	—

Unions Added Under Rationalisation	Courses in Force Jan/Dec 1963	Courses in Force Jan/Dec 1962	Increase	Decrease
Assoc. Blacksmith's Forge, etc. Soc.	5	—	5	—
Assoc. of Building Technicians.	6	—	6	—
Assoc. of Post Office Controlling Officers.	1	—	1	—
Assoc. of Scientific Workers.	92	—	92	—
Birmingham Sheet Metal Workers.	12	—	12	—
Civil Service Clerical Association.	43	—	43	—
Civil Service Union.	175	—	175	—
Electrical Power Engineers' Association.	3	—	3	—
Engineer Surveyors' Association	17	—	17	—
Fed. of Trade Unions of Salt Workers etc.	1	—	1	—
General Union of Loom Overlookers.	22	—	22	—
Guild of Insurance Officials.	1	—	1	—
Inland Revenue Staff Federation.	15	—	15	—
Iron & Steel Trades Confederation.	45	—	45	—
London County Council Staff Association.	1	—	1	—
Merchant Navy & Air Line Officers' Assoc.	5	—	5	—
Midland Glass Bevellers' Society.	9	—	9	—
Ministry of Labour Staff Association.	3	—	3	—
Nat. Assoc. Card Blowing & Ring Room Oper.	2	—	2	—
Nat. Assoc. of Theatrical & Kine Employees.	1	—	1	—
Nat. Coal Board Labour Staff Association.	3	—	3	—
Nat. Federation of Insurance Workers.	115	—	115	—
Nat. League of the Blind.	1	—	1	—
Nat. Silk Workers' Association.	2	—	2	--
Nat. Soc. of Metal Mechanics.	20	—	20	—
Nat. Soc. of Op. Printers & Assistants.	13	—	13	—
Nat. Soc. of Pottery Workers.	6	—	6	—
Nat. Union of Agricultural Workers.	4	—	4	—
Nat. Union of Dyers, Bleachers, etc.	53	—	53	—
Nat. Union of Funeral & Cemetery Workers.	1	—	1	—
Nat. Union of Hosiery Workers.	15	—	15	—
Nat. Union of Journalists.	10	—	10	—

271

Unions Added Under Rationalisation	Courses in Force Jan/Dec 1963	Courses in Force Jan/Dec 1962	Increase	Decrease
Nat. Union of Printing, etc. Workers.	128	—	128	—
Nat. Union of Public Employees.	404	—	404	—
Nat. Union of Seamen.	83	—	83	—
Nat. Union of Vehicle Builders.	25	—	25	—
Northern Carpet Trade Union.	12	—	12	—
Nottingham & District Hosiery Finishers.	14	—	14	—
Post Office Engineering Union.	108	—	108	—
Scottish Horse & Motormen.	7	—	7	—
Screw, Nut, Bolt & Rivet Trade Society.	3	—	3	—
Shipconstructors & Shipwrights.	17	—	17	—
Sign and Display Trades Union.	3	—	3	—
Soc. of Goldsmiths, Jewellers, etc.	2	—	2	—
Soc. of Shuttlemakers.	1	—	1	—
Tobacco Workers' Union.	76	—	76	—
Union of Post Office Workers.	606	—	606	—
USDAW.	154	—	154	—
United Patternmakers' Association.	10	—	10	—
United Road Transport Workers.	69	—	69	—
United Soc. of Engravers.	13	—	13	—
Yorkshire Society of Textile Craftsmen.	5	—	5	—
TOTAL NEW UNIONS	2670	—	2670	—

SUMMARY				
Total NCLC Schemes.	18542	17751	791	—
Total New Unions.	2670	—	2670	
Total Postal Courses	21212	17751	3461	—

NUMBER OF POSTAL COURSES ACCORDING TO SUBJECTS —

1962 and 1963

Subject	1963	1962	Increase	Decrease
English (3 Courses).	3312	2574	738	—
Agriculture.	9	8	1	—
Arithmetic & Statistics (2 Courses).	3545	3103	442	—
Automation for Trade Unionists (2 Courses).	150	141	9	—
Beginners' Course.	450	463	—	13
Britain's Tasks Today.	5	10	—	5
Chairmanship.	534	444	90	—

Subject	1963	1962	Increase	Decrease
Challenge of the 'Sixties.	11	34	—	23
Conference & Committee Duties.	95	77	18	—
Co-operative Movement Today.	16	15	1	—
Costing for Trade Unionists (2 Courses).	591	501	90	—
Early History of Man.	146	128	18	—
Economics (3 Courses).	1304	888	416	—
Electioneering.	21	25	—	4
Esperanto (2 Courses).	347	292	55	—
European History to 1914.	82	77	5	—
Europe Since 1914.	44	47	—	3
Finance.	70	69	1	—
Great Powers & World Problems.	11	13	—	2
History of the British Working Class.	58	55	3	—
How Britain is Governed.	44	42	2	—
How Industrial Disputes are Settled.	52	52	—	—
Industrial Injuries Insurance.	188	182	6	—
Industrial Law.	249	253	—	4
Industrial Management for Trade Unionists (2 Courses).	364	365	—	1
Industrial Negotiations.	178	136	42	—
International Developments and our Wages.	1	5	—	4
Labour and the Emergent Countries.	—	1	—	1
Labour and Election Method.	17	9	8	—
Labour and Local Government.	72	61	11	—
Labour Party — Yesterday and Today.	25	18	7	—
Local Government (England & Wales) (2 Courses).	393	245	148	—
Local Government (Scotland).	62	52	10	—
Mathematics for Trade Unionists (2 Courses).	2860	1965	895	—
National Health Service.	88	83	5	—
National Insurance.	142	120	22	—
Nationalisation & Social Control.	25	26	—	1
Parliamentary Candidates' Course.	38	42	—	4
Payment by Results.	83	64	19	—
Pay Packets, Prices and Profits.	20	16	4	—
Pioneers of the Labour Movement.	8	8	—	—
Political Geography.	37	34	3	—
Public Speaking (2 Courses).	829	578	251	—
Questions Affecting Britain's Future.	2	—	2	—
Rise and Growth of the Labour Movement.	14	17	—	3
Safety and Health at Work.	362	431	—	69
Science and Industry.	64	60	4	—
Secretaryship.	663	454	209	—
Shop Stewards & Their Functions.	684	650	34	—
Social History.	59	65	—	6

Socialism.	92	105	—	13
Standard of Living: Cost of Living.	13	7	6	—
Time & Motion Study for Trade Unionists (2 Courses).	666	815	—	149
Towards the Welfare State.	—	2	—.	2
Trade Union Branch Administration.	275	228	47	—
Trade Unions and the Law.	90	84	6	—
Trade Union Movements Abroad.	49	62	—	13
Trade Unionism Today.	107	97	10	—
Western Europe's Struggle for Unity.	67	82	—	15
Workers' Control and Joint Consultation.	43	42	1	—
Work Study for Trade Unionists (2 Courses).	1327	1184	143	—
Young Workers' Course.	59	45	14	—
			3796	
			335	
	21212	17751	3461*	335

*Net increase.

NUMBER OF CLASSES, CLASS STUDENTS, ETC. ACCORDING TO DIVISIONS AND AREAS — 1963

Div./Area	Classes				Students				Day & Week-end Schools				Students				Other lectures				Attendance Other Lectures			
	1962	1963	Inc.	Dec.	1962	1963	Inc.	Dec.	1962	1963	Inc.	Dec.	1962	1963	Inc.	Dec.	1962	1963	Inc.	Dec.	1962	1963	Inc.	Dec.
1 North	46	48	2	—	653	710	57	108	13	11	—	2	307	252	—	55	208	170	—	38	6779	5713	—	1066
1 South	50	46	—	4	945	837	—	108	16	17	1	—	469	398	—	71	227	248	21	—	3743	2717	—	1026
2	33	28	—	5	487	418	—	69	5	4	—	1	67	85	18	—	169	141	—	28	7930	3499	—	4431
3	20	24	4	—	498	495	—	3	19	8	—	11	372	212	—	160	80	52	—	28	2393	1680	—	713
4 East	24	21	—	3	341	278	—	63	9	16	7	—	186	405	219	—	53	33	—	20	1284	802	—	482
4 West	64	62	—	2	1115	1084	—	31	9	20	11	—	202	410	208	—	31	28	—	3	712	558	—	154
5	43	40	—	3	561	585	24	—	18	23	5	—	573	546	—	27	75	104	29	—	2313	3301	988	—
6	44	23	—	21	531	378	—	153	6	8	2	—	226	281	55	—	105	74	—	31	2674	1958	—	716
7 North	66	48	—	18	924	787	—	137	26	31	5	—	712	834	122	—	124	90	—	34	6030	4774	—	1256
7 South	49	50	1	—	957	925	—	32	26	27	1	—	788	870	82	—	171	156	—	15	4454	3785	—	669
8 East	14	19	5	—	192	304	112	—	14	14	—	—	484	414	—	70	125	126	1	—	3180	3142	—	38
8 West	47	36	—	11	629	442	—	187	22	19	—	3	580	526	—	54	87	96	9	—	2368	2080	—	288
9 North	46	48	2	—	766	770	4	—	35	37	2	—	1038	772	—	266	66	57	—	9	1938	1143	—	795
9 South	34	36	2	—	707	719	12	—	15	13	—	2	637	412	—	225	79	75	—	4	2384	1991	—	393
10 East (a)	34	13	—	21	471	140	—	331	10	3	—	7	543	159	—	384	104	81	—	23	2443	1480	—	963
10 West (b)	74	70	—	4	1006	894	—	112	31	24	—	7	1450	1263	—	187	115	93	—	22	2833	2575	—	258
11	52	50	—	2	1082	838	—	244	18	16	—	2	538	515	—	23	43	48	5	—	1260	1363	103	—
12	26	30	4	—	392	428	36	—	6	6	—	—	134	212	78	—	102	89	—	13	1775	1423	—	352
	766	692	—	74	12257	11032	—	1225	298	297	—	1	9306	8566	—	740	1964	1761	—	203	56493	43984	—	12509

(a) This area was without a full-time Organiser from April, 1963 because of TUC objection.

(b) Honorary Organising Tutor assisted during winter sessions.

TOTAL OF EDUCATIONAL WORK DONE IN 1963

Organisation	Class Students	Postal Course Students	Day & W/End School Students	Summer School Students	Branch Lectures No.	Attend.	GRAND TOTAL
AEU	2435	4290	1184	138	382	9653	17700
Amal. Moulders' Union.	—	6	68	—	—	—	74
Amal. Slaters, Tilers, etc.	6	6	16	—	—	—	28
Amal. Soc. of Litho. Printers.	13	35	2	—	1	28	78
Amal. Soc. of Painters.	150	265	115	—	12	244	774
Amal. Soc. of Woodworkers.†	264	41	218	—	36	803	1326
Amal. Union of Asphalt Workers.	2	3	—	—	—	—	5
AUBTW	271	230	154	7	17	430	1092
ASLEF	97	304	54	8	7	169	632
Assoc. Govt. Supervisors & Radio Offs.	—	267	—	—	—	—	267
A. Soc. Moulders & Foundry Workers.	3	3	—	—	—	—	6
Assoc. of Cine, etc. Techs.	9	48	101	—	—	—	158
Assoc. Correctors of the Press.	—	10	—	—	—	—	10
ASSET	89	327	71	—	25	513	1000
British Roll Turners.	1	13	1	—	—	—	15
Card Setting Machine Tenters.	—	—	—	—	—	—	—
Chemical Workers' Union.	1	35	20	—	1	18	74
Cigarette Machine Operators.	—	—	—	—	—	—	—
Clerical & Admin. Workers.	214	1019	266	1	20	369	1869
Cloth Pressers' Society.	—	—	—	—	—	—	—
Comp. Section. (NFBTO).	3	22	3	—	—	—	28
Con. Health Service Employees.	25	374	83	—	1	21	503
Constructional Engineering Union.	14	83	34	2	1	16	149
DATA	109	961	65	3	11	148	1286
ETU	525	1205	459	—	92	1922	4111
Fire Brigades' Union.	25	806	82	—	1	14	927
General Iron Fitters.	—	10	—	—	—	—	10
Heating & Dom. Eng. Union.	1	50	3	—	5	77	131
Hinckley Hosiery Warehousemen.	—	3	—	—	—	—	3
Iron, Steel & Metal Dressers.	7	21	12	—	—	—	40
Laminated & Coil Spring Workers.	—	5	—	—	—	—	5
Leicester, etc., Hosiery Trimmers.	—	5	—	—	—	—	5
Liverpool Vict. Wkrs. Union.	4	17	5	—	2	33	59
London Jewel Case Makers.	—	—	—	—	—	—	—
London Typographical Soc.	87	209	5	—	6	90	391
Managers & Overlookers.	—	47	—	—	—	—	47
Military Musical Inst. Makers.	—	17	—	—	—	—	17
Mono. Casters & Typefounders.	—	10	—	—	—	—	10
Musicians' Union.	9	44	9	—	4	70	132
NAU Life Assurance Workers.	9	10	46	—	1	4	69
N. Assoc. Colliery Overmen.	187	285	225	93	4	115	905
N.A. Op. Plasterers.	10	32	15	—	1	6	63
N.A. Transport Employees.	7	12	6	—	—	—	25
N.S. Brushmakers.	—	3	—	—	—	—	3
N.S. Elecro. & Stereotypers.	4	78	—	—	—	—	82
N.U. Blastfurnacemen.	7	67	8	—	—	—	82
N.U. Boot & Shoe Operatives.*	28	57	31	2	—	—	118
NUFTO	136	154	48	—	7	226	564
N.U. General & Municipal Wkrs.*	258	1171	297	7	4	164	1897
N.U. Gold, Silver etc. Trades.	—	11	—	—	—	—	11
N.U. Lock & Metal Workers.	24	18	24	—	2	66	132
NUM	1484	1249	1235	169	31	845	4982
N.U. Packing Case Makers.	—	13	—	1	—	—	14
N.U. Pearl Agents.	2	15	—	—	—	—	17

† Two districts only in 1962.
* Limited facilities only prior to 1963.

Organisation	Class Students	Postal Course Students	Day & W/End School Students	Summer School Students	Branch Lectures No.	Branch Lectures Attend.	GRAND TOTAL
N.U. Press Telegraphists.	—	31	—	—	—	—	31
NUR	445	843	272	—	38	880	2440
N.U. Scalemakers.	—	40	5	—	2	48	93
N.U. Shale Miners.	—	1	3	—	—	—	4
N.U. Sheet Metal Wkrs. & Coppersmiths.	116	523	38	6	6	228	911
N.U. Tailors & Garment Workers.*	25	56	55	2	—	—	138
N.U. Waterworks Employees.	1	25	5	—	1	10	41
Nelson Weavers.	—	—	33	—	—	—	33
Plumbing Trades Union.	35	210	58	—	10	193	496
Power Loom Carpet Weavers.	—	2	2	—	—	—	4
Rossendale Valley Textile Workers.	—	—	5	—	—	—	5
Scot. Brass Turners.	6	14	46	—	1	40	106
Scot. Carpet Trade Workers.	1	12	9	—	1	16	38
Scot. Lace & Textile Workers.	—	1	2	—	—	—	3
Scot. Operative Glaziers.†	—	4	—	—	—	—	4
Scot. Painters.	15	—	11	—	—	—	26
Scot. Plasterers.	—	19	4	—	1	30	53
Scot. Power Loom Tenters.	—	7	5	—	1	20	32
Scot. Slaters, Tilers, etc.	5	5	1	—	—	—	11
Scot. Transport & Gen. Workers.	3	2	—	—	—	—	5
Scot. Typographical Assoc.	19	60	8	—	2	99	186
Scot. Union of Bakers.	8	28	12	—	—	—	48
Soc. of Litho. Artists.	6	87	8	14	1	22	137
Soc. of Tech. Civil Servants.	9	159	18	2	1	31	219
Springmakers & Toolmakers.	—	2	3	—	—	—	5
Transport & Gen. Workers, Union.*	724	915	415	—	9	234	2288
TSSA*	69	533	102	2	17	327	1033
Typographical Assoc.	39	348	32	—	1	40	459
Union of Jute, Flax & Kindred Textile Ops.	—	2	—	—	—	—	2
Union of Polish Craftsmen.	—	—	—	—	1	45	46
United French Polishers.	—	—	—	—	—	—	—
United Rubber Workers.	3	11	—	—	—	—	14
US Boilermakers.	85	405	50	—	2	48	590
Watermen, Lightermen, etc.	—	10	—	—	2	62	74
Total NCLC Union Schemes	8134	18321	6167	457	771	18417	51496
Tutors.‡	—	—	—	29	—	—	29
Locally Affiliated, Special Schemes, Paying Students, etc.	2025	221	1432	67	946	24667	28412
Total NCLC Schemes	10159	18542	7599	553	1717	43084	79937

Unions Added Under Rationalisation

Organisation	Class Students	Postal Course Students	Day & W/End School Students	Summer School Students	Branch Lectures No.	Branch Lectures Attend.	GRAND TOTAL
Amal. Assoc. Beamers, etc.	—	8	2	—	—	—	10
Amal. Assoc. Oper. Cotton Spinners & Twnrs.	—	1	—	—	—	—	1
Amal. Soc. Blacksmith's, Farriers, etc.	2	—	2	—	1	20	24
Amal. Soc. Leather Workers.	—	1	—	—	—	—	1
Amal. Soc. Oper. Lace Makers, etc.	1	1	—	—	—	—	2
Amal. Soc. Textile Workers.	—	9	—	—	—	—	9
Amal. Soc. Wire Drawers, etc.	1	16	1	—	—	—	18
Amal. Soc. Woodcutting Machinists.	7	62	4	—	—	—	73
Amal. Textile Warehousemen.	—	—	4	—	—	—	4
Amal. Union of Foundry Workers.	30	95	74	—	1	12	211
Carried Forward	41	193	87	—	2	32	353

† New Scheme.
‡ Not including those who gave only one or two lectures.
* Limited facilities only prior to 1963.

Organisation	Class Students	Postal Course Students	Day & W/End School Students	Summer School Students	Branch Lectures No. Attend.	GRAND TOTAL
Amal. Union of Oper. Bakers, etc.	9	30	9	—	—	—	48
Amal. Weavers' Assoc.	—	5	3	—	—	—	8
Assoc. Blacksmiths, Forge, etc.	—	5	—	—	—	—	5
Assoc. Building Technicians.	2	6	—	—	—	—	8
Assoc. P.O. Controlling Officers.	—	1	—	—	—	—	1
Assoc. Scientific Workers.	22	92	13	—	—	—	127
Birmingham Sheet Metal Workers.	—	12	4	—	—	—	16
British Actors' Equity.	2	—	—	—	—	—	2
British Lace Op. Federation.	1	—	—	—	—	—	1
Civil Service Clerical Assoc.	17	43	35	—	—	—	95
Civil Service Union.	1	175	2	—	—	—	178
Electrical Power Engineers' Assoc.	1	3	1	—	—	—	5
Engineer Surveyors' Assoc.	—	17	—	—	—	—	17
Fed. of TU's of Salt Wkrs., etc.	—	1	—	—	—	—	1
General Union of Loom Overlookers.	—	22	—	—	—	—	22
Grimsby Steam etc. Fishing Vessel Eng.	—	—	1	—	—	—	1
Guild of Insurance Officials.	1	1	1	—	—	—	3
Inland Revenue Staff Federation.	1	15	1	—	—	—	17
Iron & Steel Trades Confederation.	56	45	52	—	2	41	194
Leeds & District Warpdressers.	—	—	1	—	—	—	1
London County Council Staff Assoc.	1	1	—	—	—	—	2
Merchant Navy & Air Line Officers' Assoc.	—	5	—	—	—	—	5
Midland Glass Bevellers' Soc.	—	9	—	—	—	—	9
Ministry of Labour Staff Assoc.	5	3	—	—	—	—	8
Nat. Assoc. Card Blowing & Ring Room Ops.	—	2	2	—	—	—	4
Nat. Assoc. Theatrical & Kine Employees.	1	1	2	—	1	7	11
Nat. Coal Board Labour Staff Assoc.	—	3	—	—	—	—	3
Nat. Fed. Insurance Workers.	18	115	14	—	5	80	227
Nat. League of the Blind.	5	1	9	—	—	—	15
Nat. Silk Workers' Assoc.	—	2	—	—	—	—	2
Nat. Soc. Metal Mechanics.	6	20	14	—	2	102	142
Nat. Soc. Operative Printers, etc.	7	13	7	—	3	36	63
Nat. Soc. Pottery Workers.	9	6	2	—	—	—	17
N.U. Agricultural Workers.	21	4	35	—	6	112	172
N.U. Bank Employees.	5	—	2	—	—	—	7
N.U. Co-op. Officials.	5	—	6	—	—	—	11
N.U. Dyers, Bleachers, etc.	3	53	40	—	—	—	96
N.U. Enginemen, Firemen, etc.	17	—	8	—	2	48	73
N.U. Funeral & Cemetery Workers.	—	1	—	—	—	—	1
N.U. Hosiery Workers.	16	15	1	—	—	—	32
N.U. Journalists.	10	10	42	—	7	169	231
N.U. Leather Workers, etc.	2	—	2	—	—	—	4
N.U. Printing, etc. Workers.	16	128	51	—	—	—	195
N.U. Public Employees.	52	404	88	—	2	40	584
N.U. Seamen.	8	83	7	—	1	22	120
N.U. Stove, Grate etc. Workers.	1	—	—	—	—	—	1
N.U. Vehicle Builders.	29	25	58	—	1	16	128
Northern Carpet Trade Union.	—	12	—	—	—	—	12
Nottingham & Dist. Hosiery Finishers.	2	14	—	—	1	19	35
P.O. Engineering Union.	58	108	38	—	4	89	293
Radio Officers' Union.	—	—	9	—	—	—	9
Rossendale Boot & Shoe Ops.	—	—	8	—	—	—	8
Scottish Horse & Motormen.	3	7	7	—	1	10	27
Screw, Nut, Bolt & Rivet Society.	—	3	—	—	—	—	3
Sheffield Amal. Union of File Trades.	—	—	1	—	—	—	1
Sheffield Sawmakers Protection Society.	—	—	1	—	—	—	1
Shipconstructors and Shipwrights	6	17	10	—	—	—	33
Sign & Display Trade Union	—	3	1	—	—	—	4
Soc. of Goldsmiths, Jewellers, etc.	—	2	—	—	—	—	2

278

Organisation	Class Students	Postal Course Students	Day & W/End School Students	Summer School Students	Branch Lectures No.	Attend.	GRAND TOTAL
Soc. of Shuttlemakers.	—	1	—	—	—	—	1
Tobacco Workers' Union.	4	76	5	—	—	—	85
Union of P.O. Workers.	57	606	46	—	1	11	720
USDAW.	338	154	233	—	3	66	791
United Patternmakers' Assoc.	13	10	7	—	—	—	30
United Road Transport Workers.	1	69	—	—	—	—	70
United Soc. of Engravers.	—	13	—	—	—	—	13
Yorkshire Assoc. Power Loom Overlookers.	—	—	1	—	—	—	1
Yorkshire Soc. of Textile Craftsmen.	—	5	—	—	—	—	5
TOTAL NEW UNIONS	873	2670	967	—	44	900	5410

SUMMARY

	Class Students	Postal Course Students	Day & W/End School Students	Summer School Students	Branch Lectures No.	Attend.	GRAND TOTAL
TOTAL NCLC SCHEMES	10159	18542	7599	553	1717	43084	79937
TOTAL NEW UNIONS	873	2670	967	—	44	900	5410
	11032	21212	8566	553	1761	43984	85347

LABOUR COLLEGE MOVEMENT'S PUBLICATIONS

Outlines of the History of the Modern British Working Class Movement by Will W. Craik—*London District Council NUR.*

Easy Outlines of Economics by Noah Ablett—*Plebs League.*

A Short History of the Modern British Working Class Movement by W. W. Craik—*Plebs League.*

A Worker looks at History by Mark Starr—*Plebs League.*

A Worker looks at Economics by Mark Starr—*NCLC Publishing Society.*

What to Read — A Guide for Worker Students—*Plebs League.*

Creative Revolution by Eden and Cedar Paul—*Plebs League.*

Proletcult by Eden and Cedar Paul—*Plebs League.*

An Outline of Psychology by H. Lyster Jameson—*Plebs League.*

An Outline of Psychology completely revised by Eden and Cedar Paul and Edward Conze—*NCLC Publishing Society.*

An Outline of Modern Imperialism by T. Ashcroft and Others—*Plebs League.*

An Outline of Economics by W. McLaine and W. T. Collyer—*NCLC Publishing Society.*

An Outline of European History by Maurice H. Dobb—*Plebs League.*

An Outline of Political Geography by J. F. Horrabin (originally published as An Outline of Economic Georgraphy)—*NCLC Publishing Society.*

An Outline of Finance by Arthur Woodburn, P.C., M.P.—*PCNP NCLC Publishing Society.*

An Outline of Man's History by Patrick Gordon Walker—*NCLC Publishing Society.*

An Outline History of Unemployment by W. T. Collyer—*NCLC Publishing Society.*

A Short History of the British Workers by R. W. Postgate—*Plebs League.*

A Workers History of the Great Strike by R. W. Postgate, Ellen Wilkinson, M.P., J. F. Horrabin—*Plebs League.*

A Pocket History of the British Working Class by R. W. Postgate—*NCLC Publishing Society.*

An Introduction to Dialectical Materialism by Edward Conze—*NCLC Publishing Society.*

Manual of English by George Ogilvy (Edited by Christine Millar)—*NCLC Publishing Society.*

The Trade Unionist's Guide to the Stock Exchange by Frank Summary—*NCLC Publishing Society.*

Why War? A Handbook for those who will take part in the Second World War by Ellen Wilkinson and Edward Conze—*NCLC Publishing Society.*

Marxism and History by John S. Clarke—*NCLC Publishing Society.*

Socialism's New Start: A Secret German Manifesto Preface by H. N. Brailsford—*NCLC Publishing Society.*

How Empires Grow by J. F. Horrabin—*NCLC Publishing Society.*

A Short History of the British Empire by J. F. Horrabin—*NCLC Publishing Society.*

Trade Unionism by Allan Flanders—*NCLC Publishing Society.*

Economic Doctrines of Karl Marx by Karl Kautsky—*NCLC Publishing Society.*

Commercial Crises of the Nineteenth Century by H. M. Hyndman—*NCLC Publishing Society.*

The Life and Teaching of Karl Marx by M. Beer—*NCLC Publishing Society.*

Lies and Hate in Education by Mark Starr—*NCLC Publishing Society.*
Man Makes Himself by Gordon Childe—*NCLC Publishing Society.*
The ABC of Chairmanship by Lord Citrine—*NCLC Publishing Society.*
The Worker and the State by Frank Tillyard CBE—*NCLC Publishing Society.*
A History of British Socialism by Max Beer—*NCLC Publishing Society.*
Thinking by Fred Casey—*Labour Publishing Company.*
The Nature of Morality by Fred Casey—*F. A. Casey.*
Method in thinking by Fred Casey—*South East Lancs. Labour Colleges.*
The Builders History by R. W. Postgate—*Nat. Fed. Building Trades Operatives.*
Trade Unionism: Past and Future by Mark Starr—*Plebs League.*
The Co-operative Movement by J. Hamilton—*Plebs League.*
Fascism. Its History and Significance by L. W.—*Plebs League.*
Plebs Atlas by J. F. Horrabin—*NCLC Publishing Society.*
Students' Outlines on Philosophic Logic, by W. W. Craik.
The Theory of Historical Development and Marxian Economics—*Halifax Branch CLC.*

Vest Pocket Booklets

The Vest Pocket Guide to Nationalisation by Arthur Woodburn M.P.—*NCLC Publishing Society*
The Vest Pocket Chairman by R. Heathwood and G. Horsman—*NCLC Publishing Society*
The Vest Pocket Speaker by J. P. M. Millar—*NCLC Publishing Society*
Trade Union Education—Some Vital Issues by J. P. M. Millar—*NCLC Publishing Society*

Pamphlets

The Burning Question of Education by the Executive Committee of the Plebs League—*Plebs League.*
What is Independent Working Class Education—*Plebs League.*
Education and Progress by Lester F. Ward—*Plebs League.*
Education: End or Means?—*Plebs League.*
Do your own Thinking—*Plebs League.*
What Education means to the Workers—*Plebs League.*
AUBTW Education Fund Manifesto by J. F. Horrabin—*AUBTW.*
Our Next Step — Education by J. F. Horrabin—*AUBTW.*
Building Trade Workers Education Scheme—*AUBTW.*
A Plea for a Labour College for Scotland. The address given at the 1916 Foundation Conference—*SLC.*
More production and More Poverty. The case for the Labour Colleges by J. P. M. Millar. Preface by Robert Smillie. *SLC Edinburgh District. A number of colleges published editions of this pamphlet with details of local work at the back.*
Education and the Industrial Revolution by W. D. Morris—*NCLC Publishing Society.*
Labour and the Educational Problem embodying a memorandum on State Education in Scotland submitted by the NCLC to the Advisory Council on Education in Scotland by J. P. M. Millar and Christine Millar—*NCLC Publishing Society.*
The Rise of Capitalism by Lester Hutchinson—*NCLC Publishing Society.*

281

The **"Trained Mind" Trained for What** by J. P. M. Millar—*NCLC Publishing Society.*

The **Working Class and Education**—*CLC.*

Education for a new Social Order by J. F. Horrabin—*NCLC Publishing Society.*

What is Workers' Education by J. P. M. Millar—*NCLC Publishing Society.*

Ideas and the Shadow of War by Arthur Woodburn—*NCLC.*

Thirty Years of Independent Working Class Education by J. P. M. Millar — *NCLC Publishing Society*

Labour's Educational Needs by Arthur Woodburn—*NCLC.*

Why Trade Union Education? by J. P. M. Millar—*Amalgamated Union of Upholsterers.*

Post War Education — A Labour View by J. P. M. Millar—*NCLC.*

Labour and Education by Arthur Woodburn—*NCLC.*

Education and the Struggle for Power by Arthur Woodburn—*NCLC.*

Education and the World Crisis by W. A. Strawbridge—*NCLC.*

The Trade Union Movement and Post War leisure. A memorandum submitted by the NCLC to the Trade Union Congress General Council—*NCLC.*

George Hicks on the NCLC—*NCLC.*

Is There Need for Independent Working Class Education? by W. A. Strawbridge —*NCLC.*

Trade Unionism and the Menace of Fascism by W. A. Strawbridge—*NCLC.*

Education for Social Change by W. A. Strawbridge — *NCLC.*

After the Storm — the NCLC's Part by George Hicks—*NCLC.*

What's wrong with the Schools? by T. Ashcroft—*NCLC Publishing Society.*

Education and the Working Class by W. F. Hay—*Liverpool and District Council for IWCE.*

Syllabus on Political Economy by Nun Nicholas—*Division 4 NCLC.*

Labour and Leisure by J. P. M. Millar—*NCLC.*

Education towards Revolution by James Younie—*James Younie.*

Bias in the Schools by J. P. M. Millar and Arthur Woodburn—*NCLC Publishing Society.*

Education Nationalism and War by A. Hodgetts—*NCLC.*

Independent Working Class Education by J. Horrabin. A reprint from the Journal of Adult Education.

Independent Working Class Education by Eden and Cedar Paul—*Workers Socialist Fed. London.*

A History of the North Eastern Labour College—*North Eastern Labour College.*

Other Publishers' Books on the Labour College Movement

Working Class Education by J. F. and Winifred Horrabin—*Labour Publishing Co. Ltd.*

The Central Labour College by W. W. Craik 1909-29—*Lawrence and Wishart.*

Workers' Education in England and The United States, by Margaret T. Hogden.—*Kegan Paul, Trench, Trubner & Co. Ltd.*

Epoch in Workers' Education by A. J. Corfield—*WEA.*

NOTE: J. P. M. Millar has a large collection of syllabuses published by Colleges all over the country including a complete collection of the

Edinburgh SLC syllabuses from 1920 to 1925. These usually give details of the classes, the names of the tutors and sometimes of the affiliated local bodies. The collection includes the Huddersfield class of the Central Labour College syllabus of 1917-18, the Wigan, Warrington, etc., classes on Marxian Economics by Nun Nicholas, 1911-12, a syllabus published by the Labour College, London, for the use of NCLC classes on Modern History: Revolutionary Periods, published about 1922, etc.

The Gold Pound and the Paper Pound

In order that readers of the book may be able to evaluate the purchasing power of the £ during the Labour College Movement's history it may be helpful to refer to the answer to a question recently put in the House of Commons. Sidney Bidwell, M.P., a former NCLC Organiser, on 7th November, 1974, asked the Chancellor of the Exchequer to give the value of the £ sterling in relation to the gold £ in August, 1914, and its purchasing power for each five years subsequently. The answer was as follows:

Taking the internal purchasing power of the pound as 100p in 1914, its value in each of the following years is estimated to have been:—

1914	100p
1919	46
1924	57
1929	61
1934	71
1938*	64
1946*	38
1949	32
1954	26
1959	23
1964	20
1969	16
1974 (Sept)	10†

Source: The leaflet on "International Purchasing Power of the Pound" (October 1974) issued by the Central Statistical Office.

Except for 1974 the figures do not refer to specific months in the years shown. Because of continual changes in the pattern of consumers' or household expenditure, estimates of change over long periods in purchasing power can only be regarded as approximate. Over a period as long as 60 years, when the pattern of expenditure has changed very considerably, and when the current pattern includes purchases of many goods and services which were not available earlier, estimates of change should be regarded as only impressionistic.

* Figures for 1939 and 1944 are not available.

†On Sunday, 21st November, 1976, *The Observer* reported that, according to a Parliamentary reply, the 1914 pound was now worth 7p.

Bibliography

A Note on Sources

Sources for the study of the Labour College Movement fall into two main categories: (a) an important collection of original papers assembled over many years by J. P. M. Millar, most of which are now deposited in the National Library of Scotland, and (b) documentary evidence appearing in published works.

The papers deposited in the National Library of Scotland are contained in nearly 200 boxes and volumes. The key collection is contained in 35 boxes and includes: letters and miscellaneous papers relating to the Central Labour College from its inception in 1909 until its closure in 1929; some correspondence, minutes and papers relating to the Plebs League 1919-1927; minutes and correspondence of the Scottish Labour College 1919-1967; general material relating to the NCLC including (a) correspondence with the TUC, the WEA, the Labour Party and various international associations, and (b) documents concerning aspects of working-class and trade union education. The collection further comprises: minutes of the executive committee and the Annual Conference of the NCLC, 1923*-1963 together with quarterly and annual reports; minutes of the Central Labour College house meetings 1910-1915; minutes of the Manchester Plebs League Council 1918-1920; minutes of the Scottish National Committee 1923-1967; minutes of the NCLC Publishing Society some of which are bound in the NCLC minute books; miscellaneous minutes of the NCLC divisions and local Labour Colleges; quarterly and annual reports on the work of the Postal Services Department; correspondence and papers relating to the NCLC divisions. The NCLC minute books contain the Annual Reports.

Other boxes contain press cuttings, press cuttings books and copies of correspondence with the press; collections of lectures and notes for courses; circulars issued by the central office of the NCLC; statistics on classes 1923-1961. The National Library has also bound volumes containing the 76 NCLC Postal Courses in use in 1964. It has also unbound copies of the Courses that had been superseded. In April 1975 large volumes containing NCLC publicity and Postal Course publicity leaflets were also transferred to the National Library as well as bound copies of NCLC

*The first minute book – a small note book – has not been traced but the *Plebs* contains the main points.

general circulars sent to College Secretaries and NCLC Organisers' Circulars sent to organisers.

In the Department of Printed Books of the NLS there are sets of Plebs League and NCLC Publishing Society pamphlets and books and a set of *Plebs*, minus a few copies. The same Department has in two bound volumes a collection of pamphlets entitled NCLC History and Reports starting with The National Council of Labour Colleges History, Report and Directory, 1924, Education for Emancipation (several editions), The War of Ideas (several editions), Education and Power (several editions, Education and Power (several editions) and Trade Union Education Today. These covered the years 1924-1963.

J. P. M. Millar himself continues to retain the following: a comprehensive collection of original pamphlets relating to working-class education dating from the beginning of the present century, including virtually all the pamphlets published by the Plebs League and the NCLC; a complete set of NCLC executive committee minutes; a complete set of Plebs*; miscellaneous papers and correspondence relating to the Ruskin College strike, the Central Labour College, the Plebs League and the NCLC; correspondence between himself and a number of public personalities; a large collection of syllabuses and leaflets prepared by local colleges; a complete collection of Edinburgh Labour College syllabuses 1920-1930 (the National Library has also copies of many of these) and collections of class syllabuses and leaflets covering colleges all over the country; an unpublished manuscript by Charles L. Gibbons entitled 'Recollections of the Movement for Independent Working Class Education 1908-1914.' Not the least important part of Millar's archives are the many photographs of groups of people and individuals connected with the Labour College Movement. The National Library has copies of many of these and original

*Apart from the British Museum, the New York Public Library and the Library of the London School of Economics also possess complete sets of *Plebs* as does the NCLC Publishing Society. Krauss has reprinted the whole of *Plebs* but has not always produced the interesting covers. Copies of the reprints may be obtained from the NCLC Publishing Soc. Ltd. 11 Dartmouth St. London SW1

cartoons by Horrabin and others, plus Horrabin manuscripts. Millar hopes to arrange for many of the Papers still in his own hands, of which the Library has no duplicates, to go to the National Library of Scotland in order that all NCLC archives may be preserved in one place.

Miscellaneous material relating to the Labour College Movement may be found in contemporary newspapers, journals and trade union records and journals — the *Railway Review* (NUR) in particular. References to the NCLC and to the issue of workers' education regularly appeared in *The Daily Herald, Justice, The Socialist* and *Forward;* since the latter two journals were printed for many years in Glasgow they also contain a good deal of information about the Scottish Labour College. The NCLC assiduously tried to ensure that favourable comment on its views and activities appeared in union journals and local Labour party publications.

The best introduction to independent working class education is J. F. and Winifred Horrabin's *Working Class Education* (1924). Margaret Hodgen in *Workers' Education in England and the United States* (1925) dealt extensively and perceptively with the aims and problems of past and present workers' educational programmes. W. W. Craik, *Central Labour College* (1964), provides a wealth of autobiographical recollections about the Ruskin strike and the subsequent tribulations of the Labour College but a few of his interpretations of events suffer from personal bias against the NCLC, partly because he was out of the country during part of the period and partly because he had no access to some of the original records, especially CLC minutes. Some relevant information is contained in F. Moxley's contribution to P. Bagwell, *The Railwaymen* (1963) which is entitled 'Railwaymen and Working Class Education.' There is also some unique information in J. Clunie, *Voice of the Labour Movement* (1958). T. Bell, *John Maclean, a Fighter for Freedom* (1944) describes episodes in the history of the Scottish Labour College as also does Nan Maclean Milton in *John Maclean* (1973). The latter book had the disadvantage of being written without any contact with Millar who had a unique knowledge of the SLC. In *Solo Trumpet* (1953) T. A. Jackson touches on his own experiences as the first full-time lecturer for the North Eastern Labour College. James Griffiths in *Pages from Memory* (1969) recalls some of his experiences as a Central Labour

College student. Other sources worth consulting are Brian Simon, *Education and the Labour Movement 1870-1920*, the *International Review of Social History* (Amsterdam 1969, Vol. 14), *Educating Marxists*, a study of the early days of the Plebs League by Eian R. Frow in *Marxism Today* (October 1968).

While the present work was being prepared J. P. M. Millar gave permission to J. H. Roberts, a post-graduate student, to consult the original material in his possession. Roberts completed an M.Sc. thesis in 1970 entitled 'A study of the Growth of the Labour Colleges with special reference to independent working class education in Scotland' (Edinburgh University Library) which furnishes a detailed and authoritative account of the Labour College movement in Scotland. It should, however, be compared with J. P. M. Millar's comments on the thesis which will go to the National Library, as well as his comments on several other theses.

R. Barker, *Education and Politics 1900-1951; a study of the Labour Party* (1972) throws a flood of light on the attitude of the Labour Party to working class education. A. J. Corfield, *Epoch in Workers' Education* (1969) deals comprehensively with the origins and history of the WETUC and is scrupulously fair in his account of the relations between the WETUC and the Labour Colleges. Finally, Brian Simon, *Education and the Labour Movement 1870-1920* (1965) devotes several chapters to the early history of the independent working class education movement.

Pamphlets

Aschroft, T., *What's wrong with the Schools* (London undated).
AUBTW, *Our Next Step – Education* (London undated).
AUBTW, *Education Fund Manifesto.*
AUBTW, *Education Scheme.*
Coxon, W, *A Short History of the North Eastern Labour College* (Newcastle undated).
Ellis, A., *A Secret History of the NCLC* (Birmingham 1937).
Hay, W. E., *Education and the Working Class* (Liverpool 1920).
Hicks, George, *After the Storm: The NCLC's Part* (Edinburgh undated).
Hicks, George, *George Hicks on the NCLC* (London 1929).
Hodge, P., *Working Class Education* (Fife 1920).
Hodgetts, A., *Education, Nationalism and War* (London undated).

Horrabin, J. F. & W. H., *What Does Education Mean to the Workers?* (Oxford 1917).

Horrabin, J. F., *Education and a New Social Order* (London 1937)

De Leon, D., *Two Pages from Roman History* (New York 1908).

Morris, W. D., *Education and the Industrial Revolution* (Tillicoultry 1937).

Millar, J. P. M. & Christine, *Labour and the Educational Problem* including *Memo on State Education in Scotland* (Alva 1944).

Millar, J. P. M. & Christine, *The Trade Union Movement and Post War Leisure* — an NCLC Memo submitted to the TUC (Perth undated).

Millar, J. P. M., *More Production — More Poverty* (Edinburgh 1921).

Millar, J. P. M., *Labour and Leisure* (Perth 1944).

Millar, J. P. M., *Post War Education* (Tillicoultry 1943).

Millar, J. P. M., *What is Workers Education?* (Tillicoultry 1950).

Millar, J. P. M., *The Trained Mind — Trained for What?* (Edinburgh undated).

Millar, J. P. M., *Millar and the Educational Problem* (Tillicoultry 1951).

Millar, J. P. M., *Thirty Years of Independent Working Class Education* (London undated).

Millar, J. P. M., *Why Trade Union Education?* (London undated).

Millar, J. P. M. & Woodburn, Arthur, *Bias in the Schools* (London undated).

Millar, J. P. M. & Woodburn, Arthur, *Post War Education — a Labour view* (Alva 1943).

Plebs League, *The Burning Question of Education* (Oxford 1908).

Plebs League, *What does Education mean to the Workers?* (1917).

Plebs League, *What is Independent Working Class Education* (undated).

Plebs League, *Education — End or Means?* (undated).

Plebs League, *Do Your Own Thinking* (undated).

Plebs League, *Education in Progress.* Address given by Lester F. Ward, Professor of Sociology, Brown University, R.I., USA. lecture to 1909 Annual Meeting of Plebs League.

Paul, Eden & Cedar, *Independent Working Class Education* (London 1918).

Strawbridge, W. A., *Education and the World Crisis* (London undated).

Strawbridge, W. A., *Education and Social Change* (London undated).

Strawbridge, W. A., *Is there a need for IWCE?* (London 1930).

WEA, *A Review 1946-52* (London undated).

Woodburn, A., *Labour's Educational Needs* (London 1938).

Woodburn, A., *Education and the Struggle for Power* (London 1936).

Younie, J., *Education Towards Revolution* (Lossiemouth undated).

CLC, *The Working Class and Education* (about 1912).

CLC, The Labour College, London — Annual Report 1919.

CLC, The Labour College, London — Leaflet on help for local classes.

CLC, The Labour College, London — Correspondence Course Dept. Syllabus (1919).

     i) The Science of Understanding.
     ii) Industrial History of England.
     iii) Economics.
     iv) English Literature.

CLC, The Labour College, London — Correspondence Course Dept. Syllabus.

     i) English Grammar.
     ii) Science of Understanding.
     iii) Evolution.
     iv) Industrial History of England.
     v) Economics (Marxian).
     vi) English Literature (1919).

CLC Prospectus of the Labour College London, (1919).

CLC, The Labour College London — Curriculum (1921) including sample examination papers for admission.

CLC, Syllabuses for NCLC lecturers.

     i) Revolutionary periods in History.
     ii) The British Labour Movement.

CLC, Table of Lecture Classes at Labour College 1919.

Unpublished Theses and Dissertations

Barclay, J. B., Adult Education in South-East Scotland (Ph.D., Edinburgh, 1960).

Barker, R., The Educational Policies of the Labour Party (Ph.D. London, 1968).

Fienstein, Lloyd (Ph.D. Thesis, New Jersey, USA), on Workers' Education in England.

Frow, Ruth, Independent Working Class Education with particular reference to South Lancashire, 1909-1930 (Manchester University, 1968).

Jepson, N. A., The Origin and Development of the Oxford and Cambridge University Extension Movement between 1873 and 1902 (Ph.D. Leeds, 1955).

Hamilton, Ian, Education for Revolution, the Plebs League and London College Movement 1908-21 (Warwick, 1972).

McCann, W. P., Trade Unionist, Co-operative and Socialist Organisations in relation to Popular Education 1820-1902 (Ph.D., Manchester, 1960).

Macleech, B., Workers' Education in Britain: an Evaluation (undated).

Marwick, A. J. B., The Independent Labour Party (B.Litt., Oxon, 1960).

Pashley, B. W., Role Definition and Fulfilment in English Adult Education (M.A., Liverpool, 1966).

Phelan, T., Some Aspects of Working-Class Education (1830-1930) with particular reference to Scotland (M.Ed., Glasgow 1969).

Roberts, J. H., A Study of the Growth of the Labour Colleges with special reference to Independent Working Class Education in Scotland (M.Sc., Edinburgh 1970).

Shatton, B. M., The Plebs League and the Central Labour College with special reference to the influence on the South Wales Miners Union.

Books

Allaway, A. J., *Adult Education in a Changing Society* (Leicester, 1951).

Arnott, R. P., *The Miners Years of Struggle, a History of the Miners Federation of Great Britain.*

Bagwell, P. S., *The Railwaymen; the History of the National Union of Railwaymen* (London, 1963).

Bagwell, P. S., The South Wales Miners, Britain (London, 1953), 1898-1914 (London, 1967).

Barker, R., *Education and Politics 1900-51* (Oxford, 1972).

Bell, T., *John Maclean: Fighter for Freedom* (Glasgow, 1944).

Bell, T., *Pioneering Days* (London, 1941).

Bevan, Aneurin, *In Place of Fear* (London, 1952).

Blunden, M., *The Countess of Warwick* (London, 1967).

Bonner, A., *British Co-operation* (Manchester, 1961).

Boyd, W., *Education in Ayrshire through Seven Centuries* (London, 1961).

Carr Saunders, A. M., Florence, P.S., and Reese R., *Consumers' Co-operation in Great Britain* (London, 1938).

Checkland, S. G., *The Rise of Industrial Society in England, 1815-85* (London, 1964).

Cole, G. D. H., and Postgate, R., *The Common People, 1746-1946* (London, 1949).

Cole, G. D. H., *A Short History of the British Working Class Movement* (London, 1948).

Cole, Margaret, ed. *Beatrice Webb's Diaries* (London, 1952).

Craik, W. W., *The Central Labour College: 1909-29* (London, 1964).

Craik, W. W., *Bryn Roberts and the National Union of Public Employees* (London, 1955).

Clunie, J., *The Voice of Labour* (Dunfermline, 1958).

Corfield, A. J., *Epoch in Workers' Education* (London, 1969).

Curtis, S. J., *History of Education in Great Britain* (London, 1963).

Dobbs, A. E., *Education and Social Movements 1700-1850* (London, 1919).

Draper, W. H., *University Extension, A Survey of Fifty years: 1873-1923* (Cambridge, 1923).

Ellis, Albert, *A Secret History of the NCLC* (Birmingham, 1937).

Evans, David, *Labour Strife in the South Wales Coalfields* (Cardiff, 1911).

Evans, E. W., *The Miners of South Wales* (Cardiff, 1961).

Flanders, A., *British Trade Unionism* (London, 1948).

Foot, Michael, *Aneurin Bevan* Vol. I (London, 1962).

Furniss, H. Sanderson, *Memories of Sixty Years* (London, 1931).

Gallacher, W., *Revolt on the Clyde* (London, 1936).

Gleason, A., *Workers' Education, American Experiments* (New York, 1921).

Gould, F. J., *Hyndman, Prophet of Socialism* (London, 1928).

Green, E., *Adult Education: Why this Apathy?* (London, 1953).

Griffiths, J., *Pages from Memory* (London, 1969).

Guttsman, W. L., *The British Political Elite* (London, 1963).

Hansome, M., *Workers' Educational Movements: Their Social Significance* New York, 1931).

Harrison, J. F. C., *Learning and Living: 1790-1960* (Toronto, 1961).

Hodgen, Margaret, *Workers' Education in England and the United States* (New York, 1925).

Hodges, F., *My Adventures as a Labour Leader* (London, 1925).

Horner, A., *Incorrigible Rebel* (London, 1960).

Horrabin, J. F. and Winifred, *Working Class Education* (London, 1924).

Jackson, T. A., *Solo Trumpet* (London, 1953).

Joint Committee of University and Working Class Representatives. Report on the relation of the University to the High Education Workpeople, *Oxford and Working Class Education* (Oxford, 1908).

Jones, M. S., *The Charity School Movement in the Eighteenth Century* (Cambridge, 1938).

Kelly, T., *A History of Adult Education in Great Britain* (Liverpool, 1962).

Kendall, W., *The Revolutionary Movement in Britain 1900-21* (London, 1969).

Lawson, J., *A Man's Life* (London, 1932).

Lovell, J., and Roberts, B. C., *A Short History of the TUC* (London, 1968).

Lowe, J., *Adult Education in England and Wales* (London, 1970).

Lowndes, G. A. N., *The Silent Social Revolution* (London, 1937).

Macdonald, Ramsay, *Syndicalism* (London, 1912).

Mackinder, H. J., and Sadler, N. E., *University Extension: Past Present and Future* (London, 1891).

Mackintosh, M., *Education in Scotland* (Glasgow, 1962).

Mansbridge, A., *University Tutorial Classes* (London, 1913).

Mansbridge, A., *An Adventure in Working Class Education* (London, 1920).

Mansbridge, A., *The Trodden Road* (London, 1940).

Mansbridge, A., *The Kingdom of the Mind* (London, 1944).

Marsh, D. C., *The Changing Social Structure of England and Wales 1871-1951* (London, 1958).

Marshall, R. C., *Co-operative Education* (Manchester, 1948).

Martin, L. Currie, *The Adult School Movement, its Origins and Development* (London, 1924).

Middlemass, R. K., *The Clydesiders* (London, 1965).

Ministry of Education, *The Organisation and Finance of Adult Education in England and Wales* — The Ashby Report (HMSO 1954).

Ministry of Reconstruction, Adult Education Committee, *First, Second, Third and Final Reports* (HMSO, 1919 Report).

Ministry of Reconstruction, abridged version entitled *A Design for Democracy*, ed. R. D. Waller (London, 1956).

Murphy, J. F., *New Horizons,* (London, 1941).

Neill, A. S., *Is Scotland Educated?* (London, 1936).

Owen, R., *A New View of Society* (Pelican ed. London, 1970).

Parry, R. St. J. (ed.) *Cambridge Essays in Adult Education* (Cambridge, 1920).

Peers, R., *Adult Education in the East Midlands* (Nottingham, 1920).

Peers, R., *Adult Education in Practice* (London, 1934).

Peers, R., *Adult Education: a Comparative Study* (London, 1958).

Pelling, H., *America and the British Left* — from Bright to Bevan (London, 1956).

Pelling, H., *The British Communist Party: a Historical Profile* (London, 1958).

Pelling, H., *A History of British Trade Unionism* (London, 1963).

Phillips, H. B., 'Charles Beard, Walter Vrooman and the Founding of Ruskin Hall' in *South Atlantic Quarterly* (Spring, 1950).

Picht, W. (trans. Cowell, C.A.), *Toynbee Hall and the Settlement Movement* (London, 1913).

Postgate, R., *A Short History of the British Workers* (London, 1928).

Price, T. W., *The Story of the Workers' Educational Association from 1903 to 1924* (London, 1924).

Pugh, A., *Men of Steel* (London, 1951).

Raybould, S. G., *The WEA – the Next Phase* (London, 1949).

Raybould, S. G., *The English Universities and Adult Education* (London 1951).

Raybould, S. G., ed. *Trends in English Adult Education* (London, 1959).

Roberts, B. C., *Trade Unions in a Free Society* (London, 1959).

Roberts, B. C., *The Trades Union Congress 1868-1921* (London, 1958).

Ruskin College, *The Story of Ruskin*, (Oxford, 1968).

Sadler, M. E., (ed.) *Continuation Schools in England and Elsewhere* (Manchester, 1908).

Shadwell, A., *The Revolutionary Movement in Great Britain* (London, 1921).

Sheffield — St. Philip's Settlement, *The Equipment of Workers* (London, 1919).

Silver, H., *The Concept of Popular Education* (London, 1965).

Silver, Eric, *Victor Feather, TUC* (London, 1973).

Simon, B., *Studies in the History of Education, 1870-1920* (London, 1960).

Simon, B., *Education and the Labour Movement 1870-1922* (London, 1865).

Smith, H. P., *Labour and Learning: Albert Mansbridge, Oxford and the WEA* (Oxford, 1956).

Socialist Secondary Schools — a Manual (Glasgow, 1918).

Starr, M., *Lies and Hate in Education* (London, 1929).

Stocks, M. O., *The WEA: the First Fifty Years* (London, 1955).

Sturt, M., *The Education of the People* (London, 1967).

Styler, W. E., *Who were the Students?* (London, 1950).

Thorne, W., *My Life's Battle* (London, 1925).

Trades Union Congress (Enquiry Committee) *Report* on Educational Facilities for Trade Unionists (London, 1921).

Trenaman, J., Communication and Comprehension (London, 1952).

Turgy, H. J., *An Outline History of Co-operative Education* (Manchester, 1924).

Verner, C. (ed.) *Pole's History of Adult Schools* (Washington, D.C., 1967).

Waller, R. D., *Hand List of Studies in Adult Education* (London,]

Wood, N., *Communism and British Intellectuals* (London, 1959).

WEA, *Educational Year Book*, 1918 (New York).

WEA, *Report on the Purpose and Organisation of the Organisation* (1934).

WEA, *Foundation and Purpose* (1947).

WEA, *The WEA 1946-52 – A Review* (1953).

WEA, *Trade Union Education* (1953).

WEA, *WEA Retrospect* (1953).

WEA, Working Party Report, *Aspects of Adult Education* (1960).

WETUC *Workers' Education and the Trade Union Movement: a Post-War Policy* (1944).

WETUC, *The Workers' Educational Trade Union Committee: Administration, Finance and Structure* (1949).

Yeaxlee, B. A., *Spititual Values in Adult Education* (2 vols. London, 1925).

Articles
Allaway, A. J., 'A Blow for Leicester – and Freedom' in *Adult Education*, Vol. XXXVIII, No. 1, May 1965, pp.40-5.

Bruce, M., 'Oxford and Working-Class Education,' in *Adult Education*, Vol. XXV, No. 4, Spring 1953, pp.27-9.

Bullock, A., 'The Universities and Adult Education,' in *The Summer Highway*, May-September 1952, PP.1-7.

Cole, G. D. H., 'Trade Unionism and Education,' in *The WEA Education Yearbook, 1918*, Part VI, pp. 370-3.

Cole, G. D. H., 'The Tutorial Class in British Working-Class Education' in *International Quarterly of Adult Education*, Vol. 1, No. 3, November, 1932, pp.127-48.

Cole, G. D. H., 'Education for Industrial Democracy,' in *The Summer Highway*, June/September, 1950, pp.3-10.

Cole, G. D. H., 'What Workers' Education Means, in *The Highway*, Vol. 44, October, 1952, pp.2-11.

Cole, G. D. H., 'Workers' Education Jubilee: The WEA's Fifty Years,' in *Journal of Education*, Vol. 85, No. 1006, May 1953, pp.209-10.

Collins, H., 'Working-Class Education and the University Standards,' in *The Highway*, Vol. 44, January, 1953, pp.131-2.

Constable, W. G., 'The Tutorial Class Movement,' in *Cambridge Essays on Adult Education*, ed. R. St. J. Parry, 1920, pp.181-205.

Craik, W. W., 'Working Class Education' in *School Government Chronicle 22*, Feb., 1924.

Dent, W. D., 'The Decay of Interest in University Extension Work,' in *University Extension Bulletin*, No. 18, Summer 1913, pp.11-2.

Dickson, H. C., 'Education with Social Relevance,' in *The Highway*, Vol 50, March 1959, pp.136-7.

Feis, H., 'Economics in the British Workers' Education Association' in *Quarterly Journal of Economics*, 1920.

Floud, Jean, 'The Educational Experience of the Adult Population in England and Wales as at July, 1949,' in *Social Mobility in Britain*, ed. D. V. Glass 1954, pp.98-140.

Frow, Edmond and Ruth, *Educating Marxists — a study of the Early Days of the Plebs League in the North West. Marxism Today*. Oct., 1968.

Greenwood, A., 'Labour and Adult Education,' in *Cambridge Essays on Adult Education*, ed. R. St. J. Parry, 1920, pp.111-32.

Halstead, R., 'An Alliance with Co-operation and Trade Unions; in *University Extension Journal*, Vol. VIII, No. 70, April 1903, pp.100-1.

Harrison, J. F. C., 'The WEA in the Welfare State,' in *Trends in English Adult Education*, ed. S. G. Raybould, 1959, pp.1-29.

Hoggart, R., 'What Shall the WEA Do?,' in *The Highway*, Vol. 44, November, 1952 pp.46-53.

Horwell, G., 'The WEA: Past, Present and Future,' in *The Tutors' Bulletin*, Autumn, 1950, pp.7-11.

Kenny, R., 'Brains Behind the Labour Movement' in *English Review*, March, 1912.

Mack, J. A., 'The Future of Adult Education,' in *Bulletin of the World Association for Adult Education*, 2nd Series, No. XLI. May, 1945, pp.11-4.

Malone, E. W. F., 'The WEA — A New Phase,' in *Adult Education*, Vol. XXXIII, No. 2, July, 1960, pp. 78-82, and No. 3. September, 1960. pp. 116-21.

Mansbridge, A., 'Working Men and Continuation Schools,' in *Continuation Schools in England and Elsewhere*, ed. M. E. Sadler, 1908, pp.369-87.

Masterman, J. H. B., 'University Extension and the Education of Workers,' in *University Extension Bulletin*, No. 17, Lent 1913, pp.6-7.

Millar, J. P. M., 'The WEA Spider and the TUC Fly,' in *Plebs*, Vol. XIV, No. 8, August, 1922, p.25. (many other articles in *Plebs*.)

Millar, J. P. M., 'Forty Years of Independent Working-Class Education,' in *Adult Education*, Vol. XXI, No. 4, June 1949, pp.210-5.

Millar, J. P. M., 'The Struggle for Socialist Education' in *Plebs*, Summer 1969. pp.3-9.

Millar, J. P. M., 'The General Strike and the NCLC' in *Bulletin* No. 2 of the Society for the Study of Labour History (Spring 1970).

Millar, J. P. M., 'The Destruction of the Labour Colleges' in *The Times*, April, 1975.

Millar, J. P. M., 'Why Union Pensioners Do Not Get a Fair Deal,' in *The Times*, September, 1975.

Morgan, E., 'Answering Mr. Campbell,' in *The Highway*, Vol. 43, November, 1951. pp. 45-6.

Nicholson, J. H., 'Why Adult Education?' in *Bulletin of the World Association for Adult Education*, 2nd Series, No. 10. August, 1937. pp. 1-13.

Peers, R., 'The Nottingham Experiment in Adult Education,' in *Bulletin of the World Association for Adult Education*, 2nd Series. No. 11, August, 1935. pp. 1-16.

Phillips, H. B., Charles Beard, Walter Vrooman and the Founding of Ruskin Hall, in *South Atlantic Quarterly*, Spring. 1950.

Pickles, W. 'Trade Unions and the Political Climate,' in *Industrial Relations*, ed. B. C. Roberts, 1962, pp.28-61.

Pickstock, F., 'The WEA for those who need it,' in *The Highway*, Vol. 45, December, 1953, pp. 82-7.

Raybould, S. G., 'Changes in Trade Union Education' in Trends in English Adult Education, ed. S. G. Raybould, 1959, pp.30-51.

Ritchie, W. D., 'What is the NCLC?' in *Scottish Adult Education*, August, 1909.

Saunders, J. W., 'University Extension Renascent,' in *Trends in English Adult Education*, ed. S. G. Raybould, 1959, pp.52-82.

Sedgwick, G. F., 'The Manual Workers' Question,' in *The Highway*, Vol. 43, December, 1951, pp.107-8.

Shaw, R. 'The Movement's Mid-Century Blues,' in *The Highway*, Vol. 44, February, 1953, pp.162-5.

Shaw, R., 'Controversies,' in *Trends in English Adult Education*, ed. S. G. Raybould, 1959, pp.181-221.

Sims, G., 'A Working Men's College' in *International Socialist Review*, April, 1912.

Sims, G., 'Subsidising the College.' in *ibid.*, December, 1909.

Tawney, R. H., 'An Experiment in Democratic Education' in *Political Quarterly*, No. 2, 1914.

Thomas, B. B., 'R. D. Roberts and Adult Education,' in *Harlech Studies*, ed. B. B. Thomas, 1938, pp.1-35.

Thompson, A., 'Is University Extension Suffering from an Excessive Devotion to Amusement?,' in *University Extension Bulletin*, No. 15, Summer, 1912, pp.12-3.

Thompson, A., 'The University Extension Movement,' in *Cambridge Essays on Adult Education*, ed. R. St. J. Parry, 1920, pp.155-80.

Turner, H. A., 'The NCLC, the WEA and the Unions: An Enquiry' in *The Plebs*, December, 1951, January, 1952.

Wootton, B., 'the Need for Differentation,' in *Journal of Adult Education*, Vol. II, September 1927, pp.55-67.

IN MANUSCRIPT

Minutes
Central Labour College*
  Provisional Committee held at the House of Commons 21st July 1909.
  Rough notes of meetings in George Sims' hand 14.9.1909-6.4.1910.
  Executive Committee 11.1.1924, 16.1.1924 and 27.2.1924.
  Board of Governors 27.8.1919 to 17.6.1927.
  House Meetings, 1910-20.
  Students' Debating Society 1909-12.
  Agenda and Resolutions 1910-13, 1919-20.
  London Propagandist Committee, Nov. 1911.
National Council of Labour Colleges:
  **Executive Committee of the Scottish Labour College 1919-1967.
  Edinburgh and District Committee of the Scottish Labour College 1919-43.
  Glasgow and West of Scotland District of the Scottish Labour College 1928-62.
Extracts from NUR minutes 1909-1916 relating to CLC.

Correspondence
NCLC and the TUC
NCLC and the WEA
Scottish Labour College.
Central Labour College.

Miscellaneous
Plebs League 4.2.1925-2.6.1927.
* The CLC minute books have disappeared. In response to enquiries by J. P. M. Millar neither Tom Ashcroft nor George Phippen nor the SWMF nor the NUR could say what happened to them. Ashcroft thought that Jim Reynolds might have kept them. Millar had duplicates of the Minutes for parts of the period. *Plebs* records the main decisions.

** The first NCLC minutes were recorded by George Sims in a small note book. It was not to be found when he disappeared from the Labour College, London. (CLC)

Original documents relating to the Ruskin 'strike' at Ruskin College including a 'Round Robin' signed by all the students who went on strike. (Now in the National Labour Museum, Tower Hamlets, London).
Central Labour College.
NCLC Divisional Papers.
NCLC Local Colleges papers.
Annual Reports of the NCLC incorporated in Executive Committee Minutes.
NUR papers relating to the dissolution of the CLC.

PRIMARY SOURCES

PRINTED
Annual Reports
Board of Education.
Labour Party Conference.
Ministry of Education.
National Council of Labour Colleges. The National Council of Labour College History Report and Directory 1924 and other editions from 1925-1963 with different titles.
Scottish Trades Union Congress.
Trades Union Congress.
WEA (England and Wales) 1903.
WEA Scotland.
WETUC 1924.
WETUC Financial Statements.

Publicity Leaflets
NCLC large bound volumes of copies.
NCLC syllabuses.

Government Publications
Commission of Enquiry into Industrial Unrest (Wales) HMSO 1917.
Committee of Council on Education in Scotland.
Ministry of Reconstruction, adult Education Committee, Final Report, 1919. (HMSO 1919).
Committee on Finance and Industry 1931 (Macmillan Committee). (HMSO 1931)

Miscellaneous
A Plea for a Labour College in Scotland (undated. Printed in

1918 and reprinted by the John Maclean Society with a slightly misleading preface in some respects — see Millar's comments in Nat. Library).

AUBTW, *Education Fund Manifesto (London, 1922).*

Gibbons, Charles L. *Recollections of the Movement for Independent Working Class Education.*

Oxford and Working Class Education

(Being the Report of a Joint Committee of University and Working class representatives on the relation of the University to the Higher Education of Work People.) (Oxford, 1909).

Proposed Prospectus to be submitted to a conference to be held in Glasgow on 16 March 1918.

Prospectus of the Scottish Labour College, 1919-1920.

Prospectus of the Scottish Labour College, Edinburgh 1923-4.

Report of the provisional Committee to the National Conference of the Scottish Labour College, 29 May 1920.

The Burning Question of Education (Oxford, 1909).

SECONDARY SOURCES

Journals and Periodicals

Adult Education.

British Journal of Educational Studies, The.

Communist, The

Education.

Forward.

Highway, The.

International Quarterly of Adult Education, vols. i-ii.

International Review of Social History.

Journal of Adult Education, vols. i-iv cont. as *Adult Education.*

Journal of Education.

Plebs, The 1909-1969.

Scottish Educational Journal, The.

Socialist, The.

Times Educational Supplement, The.

Tutors Bulletin Nos. 1-105.

University Extension Journal, vols. i-v, new series vols. i-ix.

AUBTW of Great Britain and Ireland, *Trade Circular and General Reporter, 1921-5.*

INDEX